Insubordinate Spaces

Barbara Tomlinson and
George Lipsitz

Insubordinate Spaces

IMPROVISATION AND ACCOMPANIMENT FOR SOCIAL JUSTICE

TEMPLE UNIVERSITY PRESS
Philadelphia • *Rome* • *Tokyo*

TEMPLE UNIVERSITY PRESS
Philadelphia, Pennsylvania 19122
tupress.temple.edu

Library of Congress Cataloging-in-Publication Data

Names: Tomlinson, Barbara, 1946- author. | Lipsitz, George, author.
Title: Insubordinate spaces : improvisation and accompaniment for social
   justice / Barbara Tomlinson and George Lipsitz.
Description: Philadelphia : Temple University Press, [2019] | Series:
   Insubordinate spaces | Includes bibliographical references and index. |
   Identifiers: LCCN 2018037467 (print) | LCCN 2018039736 (ebook) |
   ISBN 9781439916995 (E-book) | ISBN 9781439916971 (cloth) |
   ISBN 9781439916988 (pbk.)
Subjects: LCSH: Space—Social aspects | Space—Political aspects. | Social
   justice. | Equality.
Classification: LCC HM654 (ebook) | LCC HM654 .T65 2019 (print) | DDC
   303.3/72—dc23
LC record available at https://lccn.loc.gov/2018037467

CONTENTS

Acknowledgments

Writing this book has in itself been an exercise in improvisation and accompaniment. The evidence, ideas, and arguments it contains emerged organically from conversations and collaborations with the wide range of activists, artists, and academics we have encountered on our journeys. In the midst of a world that seems to be unraveling in many ways, they have shown us how to improvise new ways of knowing and new ways of being that can imbue the world with the potential to create a more decent and dignified existence. In this acknowledgments section, we wish to thank some of them by name, with full awareness that in scholarship and struggles for social justice alike, the whole is greater than the sum of their parts, that the work done by individuals gains its full meaning from the ways in which the pieces fit together. From our point of view, we all do this work together, and everyone contributes and everyone counts. We do wish, however, to make special mention of those whose accompaniment proved crucial to the completion of the book.

Sarah Banet-Weiser and Henry Giroux helped us recognize and reinforce our key arguments through adept editing of the parts of this book that appeared in the *American Quarterly* and the *Review of Education, Pedagogy and Cultural Studies*. The Interdisciplinary Humanities Center at the University of California, Santa Barbara, under the leadership of Susan Derwin, provided us with grant support for this project at a critical time. We came to appreciate improvisation as a broad social practice and a generative source of new knowledge through discussions with scholars and artists affiliated with the International Institute for Critical Studies in Improvisation at the University of Guelph. We received wonderfully instructive and enlightening comments and criticisms on chapters in progress from Jodi Byrd, Deborah McGregor, Ingrid Waldron, Leela Viswanathan, Martha Gonzalez, Walter Johnson, Jodi Rios, Rosa Linda Fregoso, and Deborah Wong. Our understanding and appreciation of art as a complex social practice has been enriched immeasurably through conversations with cultural workers Quetzal Flores, Russell Rodriguez, Micaela Diaz-Sanchez, Ramiro Gomez, Natasha Thomas-Jackson, Tef Poe, Kalamu Ya Salaam, Sunni Patterson, and Rick Lowe. We have learned much about the work we want our work to do from engagement with the social movement activism of the African American Policy Forum, Asian Immigrant Women Advocates, Students at the Center, the Free-Dem Foundations, the Woodstock Institute, and the National Fair Housing Alliance.

We very much appreciate the organizations, institutes, and academic departments who invited us to discuss our work in progress with them. In Europe we presented our work to the Nordic Association for American Studies, the American Studies program at Bayreuth University, Amerika Haus in Munich, the Regensberg European American Forum, the American Studies Program at the University of Manchester, and the Institute for Black Atlantic Research. In the United States we presented this work in progress to the Five Colleges Faculty Seminar, the Department of Music at Brown University, the College of William and Mary American Studies Department, the Clarke Center for Contemporary Issues and the American Studies Department at Dickinson College, the Vanderbilt University American Studies Department, the Countering Colorblindness Across the Disciplines Initiative, the American Studies Department at the University of Wyoming, the Cultural Psychology Research Group at the University of Kansas, the Center for the Study of Race and Ethnicity at Stanford, and the Interdisciplinary Humanities Center at the University of California, Santa Barbara.

We thank our colleagues in the departments of Feminist Studies, Black Studies, and Sociology at UCSB for their accompaniment. We have also drawn particular insight and inspiration from colleagues across the continent and around the world including Kimberlé Crenshaw, Luke Charles Harris, Devon Carbado, Daniel HoSang, Glenn Adams, Dorothy Roberts, Celeste-Marie Bernier, Alan Rice, Doris Sommer, Susan Gillman, Tricia Rose, Robin Kelley, David Kim, Susan Phillips, Julie Sze, Mary Watkins, Edward Casey, Susan McClary, Rob Walser, Nan Enstad, Finn Enke, Joe Austin, and Rachel Buff.

Insubordinate Spaces

1 / INTRODUCTION

Listening to Jerome Smith

In "Theses on the Philosophy of History," philosopher Walter Benjamin analyzes memories that "flash up" in a moment of danger (1968, 255). Our current "moment" of danger has lasted for decades, confronting us with a seemingly endless stream of recurrent crises and chaotic conditions. The society we live in seems to be unraveling at the seams. Paroxysms of hate, hurt, and fear permeate politics and popular culture. The technological advances, economic arrangements, and political adjustments only recently hailed as harbingers of peace and prosperity have instead produced a toxic blend: unending warfare, ecological crisis, economic injustice, and political repression. For millions of people around the globe, life has become haunted by cycles of dispossession, displacement, deportation, and death. *Insubordinate Spaces* emerges from and speaks to this "moment" of danger.

The aims of this book coalesce around one particular memory from the past that flashes up in this moment of danger. More than fifty years ago, in a time of crisis and confusion much like our own, James Baldwin spoke sadly about living in a nation that could neither hide nor excuse its injustices. In the course of being interviewed on public television by social psychologist Kenneth Clark, Baldwin exuded weariness as he described what he discerned to be the absolute refusal by white Americans to recognize the basic humanity of Black people, the seeming impossibility of being able "to communicate to the vast, heedless, unthinking, cruel white majority" that he and other Black people were human and deserved dignity and justice. Baldwin noted that his concern was not just for himself but for the nation as a whole: "I'm terrified at the moral apathy—the death of the heart which is happening in my country." Noting that he was judging white Americans not on what they *said* but on what they *did*, Baldwin concluded, "they have become, in themselves, moral monsters. It's a terrible indictment," he acknowledged, but went on to insist, "I mean every word I say." Shaken and stunned by the gravity of the situation, Baldwin said sadly, "There are days, this is one of them, when you wonder what your role is in this country, and what your future is in it" (American Experience 1963).

Many people today feel as James Baldwin did in 1963—and justifiably so. Ample evidence of the "death of the heart" and "moral apathy" pervades contemporary political and popular culture. Mustering optimism and hope seems almost impossible in lives filled with frustration and fear, in a world replete with corruption and cruelty. In this moment of danger, Baldwin's words flash up to remind us that present-day problems have a long history as products of processes that have been going on for decades and even centuries. Each evasion of moral and political responsibility in a particular moment of danger makes the next one even worse. Because the people of Baldwin's day did not solve their problems, ours are worse; if we fail to address the injustices of our time, the challenges facing future generations will increase.

In 1963, James Baldwin was criticizing the callous indifference to the dignity and humanity of Black people that he viewed as the core of national culture and politics. A half century later, a new round of cruel policies and practices persecutes the poor, foments hatred toward immigrants and members of racial, religious, and sexual minority groups, compromises reproductive rights and due process, and plunders the public sphere for private gain. The ranks of the "moral monsters" that Baldwin described grow larger every day.

Baldwin's comments to Kenneth Clark focused on the nation's general acceptance of the disposability of Black life as a national principle. But they also emerged in response to a particular incident that took place just hours before the televised interview. Earlier that day, Baldwin and Clark had participated in a contentious meeting between Attorney General Robert Kennedy and civil rights activists and advocates held at a New York apartment owned by the Kennedy family. Baldwin had invited a distinguished group of Black and white artists and activists to speak to Kennedy, the nation's highest law enforcement officer, in order to impress upon him the dire need for the government to respond to the reign of terror then being visited daily on civil rights workers. Participants in the discussion included Baldwin; his brother David; performers Lena Horne, Harry Belafonte, and Rip Torn; playwright Lorraine Hansberry; civil rights leaders Edwin Berry, Clarence Benjamin Jones, and June Shagaloff; as well as a young civil rights worker from New Orleans who had been beaten and jailed in Mississippi, Jerome Smith. The meeting went badly—largely because Kennedy failed to listen to Jerome Smith.

Expecting gratitude from the group for his taking the time from his busy schedule to meet with them, Robert Kennedy started by boasting proudly about his record on voting rights: the Department of Justice that he supervised had "three Negro lawyers" and "twenty-nine Negro clerks" and had filed twenty-nine lawsuits on behalf of Black voting rights, winning about half of them (Eucher 2011, 120). Awkwardly, the artists and activists struggled to explain to the attorney general how inadequate they considered these measures to be—when every day Black people were being brutalized, fired from their jobs, and evicted from their homes for attempting to register to vote. They spoke for and from an emerging understanding within the Black freedom movement that merely securing the legal right to vote in the abstract would not necessarily mean that votes could actually be cast or counted, that there would be anyone on the ballot worth voting for, or that municipal and state voting district lines would be drawn in such a way that all citizens would secure genuine representation. Moreover, while Black voting rights comprised the part of the civil rights agenda most valuable to Robert Kennedy and to a Democratic Party that was gradually losing Southern white voters, access to the ballot was not necessarily the prime goal for the masses of Black people facing racist exclusion and oppression in employment, education, and housing. The artists and activists challenged the attorney general to explain why the administration did not intervene in other ways: for example, why it did not bring pressure on corporations in industries like steel that were headquartered in the North to reject segregation in their Southern establishments (Horne and Schickel 1965, 280).

The activists knew that the attorney general's brother, the president, had appointed openly racist judges to federal courts in the southern districts. They wanted to know how Robert Kennedy would defend the actions of officials from the Department of Justice and the FBI who, rather than protecting their rights, frequently attempted to convince demonstrators to disperse. Listening to these concerns, however, angered the attorney general. Being bolder on civil rights, he explained, would alienate Southern segregationists "and we have to be somewhat considerate about how to keep them onboard if the Democratic party is going to prevail in the next elections"

(Belafonte 2011, 267). Kennedy conveyed to the group his belief that while his office had done everything possible to advance civil rights, Black people remained exasperatingly impatient, as evidenced by the very conversation at that meeting. Kennedy advised the group to control those who lacked patience, warning that too many Black people were becoming attracted to extremist Black nationalist groups—an attraction, he warned, that would cause real trouble. Frustrated by the attorney general's calculated political response to demands that had life and death ramifications for Southern Black people like himself, Jerome Smith spoke sharply to Kennedy, exclaiming, "You don't have no idea what real trouble is. . . . Because I'm close to the moment where I'm ready to take up a gun" (Branch 1989, 810).

Jerome Smith spoke out frankly and passionately from personal experience. He had been part of a group of nonviolent demonstrators attacked by a white mob that used brass knuckles, sticks, and fists to pummel their defenseless victims. He had escaped death numerous times by being smuggled out of towns wrapped in a blanket and hidden in a car. Southern sheriffs and police officers had arrested him time and time again on trumped-up charges and racist judges sentenced him to serve time in local jails and at Mississippi's notorious Parchman Prison farm. At the meeting, Smith told Kennedy that the attorney general's complacency and political calculation made him want to vomit. The young activist began to weep as he recounted times when he was being beaten by Southern vigilantes and law enforcement officers, while Department of Justice representatives at the scene did not intervene. They would just "stand around and do nothing more than take notes while we're being beaten" (Jones 2009, 193). Smith stated that these experiences were making him rethink his lifelong commitment to nonviolence. "What you're asking us young black people to do," he told the attorney general, "is pick up guns against people in Asia while you have continued to deny us our rights here" (Belafonte 2011, 267). When Baldwin interjected and asked Smith if he would ever serve in the military to defend the United States, Smith shouted, "Never! Never! Never!" (K. Rogers 1993, 143). This response stunned and angered the attorney general.[1]

Shocked by what he perceived as Smith's ingratitude and lack of patriotism, the attorney general turned to the older members of the delegation for help in quieting Smith. He related to the group his own story of family upward mobility: how his ancestors had been immigrants from Ireland who had experienced discrimination, yet now his brother was the president of the United States. Baldwin responded that *his* family had a longer history in the nation than Kennedy's but had not experienced similar upward mobility.

Upset that the attorney general seemed to expect her to contravene Smith's statement, Lorraine Hansberry said, "You've got a great many very, very accomplished people in this room, Mr. Attorney General. But the only man who should be listened to is that man over there," pointing at the young activist (Schlesinger 2002, 332). Kennedy's response to Jerome Smith caused the entire delegation to realize that the attorney general did not understand the basic realities of the national racial order. Lena Horne later recalled how Jerome Smith's passion required her to respond, to renounce some of her privilege and, to take the side of the masses of Black people struggling for dignity and freedom. She recalled, "You could not encompass his anger, his fury, in a set of statistics, nor could Mr. Belafonte and Dr. Clark and Miss Horne, the fortunate Negroes, who had never been in a Southern jail, keep up the pretense of being the mature, responsible spokesmen for the race anymore. All of the sudden the fancy phrases like 'depressed area' and 'power structure' and all the rest were nothing. It seemed to me that this boy just put it like it was" (Horne and Schickel 1965, 280).

As Clark interviewed him later that day, Baldwin was still visibly shaken from the effects of the meeting with Kennedy. He recounted, "We were talking to a Negro student this afternoon who has been through it all, who's half dead and only about 25. Jerome Smith. That's an awful lot to ask a person to bear" (American Experience 1963). Kennedy's inability to listen to Jerome Smith confirmed Baldwin's worst fears about the moral apathy and death of the heart that he sensed in the nation. The attorney general had been insulted by the way the meeting went and seemed contemptuous of the participants. Robert Kennedy later misrepresented grievously what took place at the meeting, charging that Hansberry and the other artists had vowed they were going to get guns and give them "to people on the street, and they were going to start to kill white people" (Guthman and Shulman 1991, 225). Kennedy called Baldwin "a nut" and ridiculed his homosexuality. The attorney general claimed that NAACP official Clarence Jones only went along with the other Black people at the meeting because he was married to a white woman and probably felt guilty about it (E. Thomas 2002, 224). Ignoring his own hysterical reaction to the meeting, Kennedy later described it as "all emotion and hysteria." He dismissed Smith, Baldwin, Hansberry, and Horne with the claim, "you can't talk to them" (Schlesinger 2002, 334). But while he could not "talk to them," Kennedy could monitor, surveil, and harass them. Four days after the meeting, a memo circulated in FBI headquarters requesting surveillance of Baldwin. At the same time, agents in the New York office of the bureau were told to search their files for information on the activist author, "particularly of a derogatory nature." J. Edgar Hoover eventually added Baldwin's name to the FBI Security Index, a list of people who would be arrested first in the event of a state emergency (Campbell 1999, 11). The FBI eventually assembled nearly two thousand pages of gossip and innuendo in the file the organization maintained on Baldwin. The author was obviously correct in wondering about his role in the nation and his future in it.

More than five decades later, Baldwin's words flash up in this moment of danger because the nation is still not listening to its Jerome Smiths. In the midst of the systemic breakdown of the major structural institutions of the society—the economy, the environment, the educational system—experts and power brokers offer top-down technical and managerial solutions to what at root are political problems. Masses in motion in the streets testify to the inability and unwillingness of the political system to "listen" to demands for dignity and justice. The Jerome Smiths of the present poured into the streets of Ferguson and Baltimore to protest unprosecuted police killings of unarmed Black people. They assembled in public places in response to the Occupy movement's challenge to economic inequality. They stood with the Standing Rock Sioux Tribe against the North Dakota Access Pipeline. They flocked to the largest mass demonstration in U.S. history—the Women's March protesting the Donald Trump administration. These mass demonstrations are the most visible manifestations of something larger, of innumerable grassroots campaigns and mobilizations, of struggles by houseless people resisting the criminalization of their survival strategies; by defenders of the rights of immigrants and religious minorities; by workers in fast-food establishments fighting for a living wage; by advocates for environmental and reproductive justice; and by students, parents, and teachers fighting against high-stakes testing, school closings, and other aspects of the corporate takeover of public education. These mobilizations express the anger and imagination of direct eyewitnesses to war, migration, low-wage labor, hunger, housing insecurity, mass incarceration, reproductive injustice, and environmental degradation. These people and many more today are wondering—as James Baldwin did a half century ago—what their role is in this nation and what their future is in it.

The Nature of Insubordinate Spaces

In this book, we propose the idea that new practices, new politics, and new polities are emerging inside what we call insubordinate spaces. This argument stems from two seemingly contradictory yet mutually constitutive aspects of the current conjuncture. The subordination of democratic opportunities and aspirations has become a primary goal of major social institutions. This subordination is enacted through the privatization of public resources, the militarization of international relations, the commodification of all aspects of human interaction, and the mass criminalization and incarceration of abandoned and despised populations. At the same time, powerful currents of resistance to unlivable destinies are shaping struggles by aggrieved groups determined to forge their own futures. People struggling for self-determination and social justice are envisioning and enacting new identities, identifications, affiliations, and alliances in many different kinds of insubordinate spaces, from sacrifice zones and seemingly abandoned and forgotten places ranging from rural regions organized around the economics of resource extraction and agricultural production to urban underscapes plagued by poverty and predatory policing, unemployment, environmental racism, housing insecurity, and political underrepresentation.

Insubordination in this context is a tool rather than a goal. Defiance, disobedience, and intractability can have transformative and redemptive power when mobilized as weapons against exploitation and hierarchy, when they fuel resistance to unjust and illegitimate authority. Yet insubordination in itself is politically and morally neutral. Like transgression, it can exacerbate problems as well as solve them. An abstract allegiance to insubordination can cause great harm. Unconnected to collective goals of social justice, mutuality, and solidarity, insubordination can degenerate into truculence, selfishness, and exhibitionism, fomenting and reinforcing antisocial attitudes and actions.[2] The insubordinate spaces that we analyze in this book emerge initially from acts of resistance and refusal, from the pledge to be "idle no more" by Indigenous activists in Canada, from the cry of "Ya basta!" (Enough!) by the Ejército Zapatista de Liberación Nacional (EZLN) across the U.S.-Mexico borderlands, and from the insistence that "Black Lives Matter" voiced by mobilized and militant Black youths in the streets of North American cities. Yet while insubordinate to the imperatives of empire and dispossession, to gender violence and generational abandonment, to misogyny and trans- and homophobia, to austerity and the criminalization of poverty, these movements all go beyond simple insubordination to envision and enact new ways of knowing and new ways of being. They seek to turn poison into medicine, to transform humiliation into honor, to counter the dominant ethos of hate, hurt, and fear with restorative collectivity and resilient love. They temper denunciation of the existing order with annunciation of a new world on its way. These movements bring together differently situated people to engage in common projects that imbue the world with the potential of making right things come to pass.

In this book, insubordination is an activity located within concrete spaces and places. The social order is also a spatial order, and the economic, political, and social projects of the neoliberal conjuncture are place-making projects. The spatial and social ecologies of neoliberalism demonstrate that ideas attain their full force and import when they pervade the practices of everyday life where places are structured in dominance. In order for social change to *take place*, it takes *places*. Research in philosophy and human geography teaches that a sense of place serves as a key mechanism for developing understanding, self-reflection, thought, interpretation, and action (Adams, Hoeslscher, and Till 2001; Casey 1993, 1997; Casey and Watkins 2014). Struggles to create insubordinate spaces are not primarily battles over territory or turf; they are, at heart, efforts to develop new ways of knowing and new ways of being. Countering the disasters of neoliberalism, as Henry A. Giroux argues, entails "the challenge of developing a politics and pedagogy that can serve and actualize a democratic notion of the social" (2011). The creation and cultivation of insubordinate spaces can play an important role in that development. Place making is a means of generating new knowledge paradigms that rely on the mutually constitutive links between ideas and actions. As biologists Humberto Maturana and Francisco Varela contend, "every act of knowing brings forth a world" (1992, 26). Yet new worlds also bring forth previously unexplored ways of knowing. "All doing is knowing and all knowing is doing," Maturana and Varela explain (1992, 26).

It is inside "insubordinate" community spaces all across the United States and around the world that new politics and new polities are emerging through reciprocal practices of speaking and listening, asking and answering, teaching and learning. Pauline Lipman emphasizes the key role played by seemingly marginalized spaces in constructing new social imaginaries, pointing specifically to community gardens, urban farming initiatives, arts spaces, and economic cooperatives. These are places where people discover and develop "seeds of a democratic, cooperative way of living together" (2011, 147). They emerge from and speak to the needs of social movements, doing important ideological and activist work inside struggles for rights, recognition, and resources. In their extraordinarily insightful work creating psychological practice crafted to serve the purposes of liberation, Mary Watkins and Helene Shulman provide a comprehensive survey of the many different functions of strategic spaces (2008). They point to the utility and generative capacity of spaces "where people can experiment with stepping outside inherited scripts and unconsciously assumed identifications to consider alternative performances" (2008, 25), spaces where people encounter difference without dominance (2008, 83), where economic, social, and personal realities can be restructured (2008, 234), and where new forms of cultural practice create "local islands of self-reliance and resourcefulness unnoticed by experts and elites who expect to be in charge of any project of improvement" (2008, 222). These spatial projects are also knowledge projects. As Robin Kelley reminds us, "social movements generate new knowledge, new theories, new questions. The most radical ideas often grow out of a concrete intellectual engagement with the problems of aggrieved populations confronting systems of oppression" (2002, 9).

Yet places do not exist in isolation. Seemingly unconnected locales are united by the politics of place. For example, increased consumption of fast foods and instant meals in affluent metropoles entails concomitant growth in the use of disposable plates, cups, and wrappers, accelerating the destruction of old-growth forests in resource peripheries. This resource extraction on the periphery damages the economies and cultures of Indigenous peoples, while producing a massive increase in wastepaper in the metropole, where the high costs of land in affluent neighborhoods pushes garbage incinerators and waste dumps into urban "sacrifice zones" inhabited by impoverished communities of color (Hayter 2003, 710; LaDuke 2015, 115–134; Sze 2007, 117–118). The reordering of rural and urban places by free trade agreements that eliminated price supports in Mexico and devastated small agricultural enterprises in that nation's central and southern regions forced displaced peasants and workers to migrate to urban and border regions in Mexico, and later to the United States. They scrambled in their new locales to secure low-wage work as gardeners, cooks, cleaners, and child care workers. Their undervalued labor then subsidized the high-consumption lifestyles of the wealthy urban professionals who profited as both investors and consumers from the surplus value created by the original free trade agreements (Hondagneu-Sotelo 2001, 7). Cambodians displaced from their homelands by the U.S. military's saturation bombing and by the violence and brutal repression of the Khmer Rouge government become refugees in the United States. They never really found refuge, however, because they were shunted to dwellings in ghettos and barrios where they shared with their Black and Puerto Rican neighbors the unresolved and enduring consequences of slavery and colonialism through what Eric Tang aptly describes as "racialized geographic enclosure, displacement from formal labor markets, unrelenting poverty, and the criminalization of daily life" (2015, 5).

Relations between people of different races are relations between people relegated to specific places. Yet every place is a relational entity; all places are connected to and shaped by other places that they in turn influence. Nancy McLean demonstrates how scholarly theories developed initially at the University of Virginia and the University of Chicago in the 1950s and 1960s—with the intent of thwarting school desegregation, and attendant ascendant patterns of economic and social democratization—were used by the Pinochet dictatorship in Chile in the 1970s and 1980s to make changes in that nation's institutions to provide protection in perpetuity for Chile's propertied classes. Those actions in South America in turn provided the Koch Brothers, the American Legislative Exchange Council, the American Enterprise Institute, the Federalist Society, and the Supreme Court under the direction of Chief Justice John Roberts with a model for replacing the U.S. constitutional system of checks and balances with a system of locks and bolts, making racial capitalism impervious to democratic dissent and popular redress of grievances (McLean 2017, 154–168).

A similar pattern of transnational interaction between the Northern and Southern hemisphere led Father Gregory Boyle to a very different set of practices. Contact with South American peasants provided him with lessons very different from those gleaned by the Koch Brothers and their employees, allies, and functionaries. Boyle grew up in Los Angeles during the 1950s, but it was not until he turned thirty and spent a year with the Christian base communities in Cochabamba, Bolivia—where, he asserts, "the poor in Bolivia evangelized me,"—that he felt a calling to minister to the poor in his native city. He became associate pastor and then pastor of the poorest parish in Los Angeles, the Delores Mission Church, where he worked with young people in gangs, showing them love, and founding Home Boy Industries, which ran a bakery and other businesses providing employment as an alternative to the violence of the streets (Boyle 2010).

Geographer Ruth Wilson Gilmore explains how uneven social and economic conditions across places can produce seemingly unlikely associations, affiliations, and alliances, especially in the light of profit-driven transformations in spaces vital to the maintenance and expansion of racialized capitalism. Gilmore relates how financiers, farm owners, politicians, and developers came to view a wave of prison construction in California's Central Valley as a social and spatial "fix" to the broad array of problems posed by drought, declining land values, job-killing automation, capital flight, and urban insurrections. Yet this put urban dwelling ex-inmates and relatives of prisoners in dialogue with rural immigrant (and often Indigenous) farmworkers and environmental justice advocates who convened the Joining Forces conference in 2001 to oppose construction of a new prison in Delano, California. Gilmore explains how this alliance between people of different races was also a collaboration of people from different but similar and related places. "Their consciousness," Gilmore argues, "is a product of vulnerability in space coupled with unavoidable and constant movement through space (an inversion, if you will, of gated communities and full-service suburban malls, but based in related conditions and logics)" (2008, 43).

Gilmore locates the social ecology of insubordinate activism and affiliation inside what she calls "forgotten" places, spaces where organized abandonment by the state and capital creates disorder and cumulative vulnerabilities. Yet these spaces are not simply sites of deprivation. They are the first places to bear the full brunt of the brutality and belligerence of subordinating institutions. Their marginalization creates new opportunities for unbridled exploitation and profiteering that then serve as models to be spread to the rest of society. For that very reason, however, the resistance and resilience that emerges from these spaces can guide and instruct others. Gilmore insists that "forgotten" places are not outside history but rather reliable registers of the problems of the present and their trajectory in the future (2008, 31). As Jean and John Comaroff argue convincingly, sacrifice zones in Africa, Asia, and Latin America contain "traces of things about to happen" elsewhere. In the United States, the Comaroffs note, the organized abandonment of the Black poor living in New Orleans when Hurricane Katrina struck in 2005 revealed to the world what local residents already knew all too well: "the extreme poverty, abjection, and inequality in their midst, the hidden effects on national infrastructure of the retraction of the resources of state, the absence of a commonweal, the deep fissures of race and class among them, the ruthlessness of police in dealing with the indigent, the callousness of power in the face of human catastrophe" (Comaroff and Comaroff 2012, 17).

Although sacrifice zones may be tactically forgotten by those in power, the people living in them cannot afford to be forgetful. They know that their imperiled present has its roots in the past, in the enduring legacies of Indigenous dispossession, slavery unwilling to die, and imperial warfare. Their histories and memories contain many examples of insubordinate practices emerging within subordinating institutions. The slave cabin in the antebellum South served as a site of seemingly total subordination of people, living without rights or even recognition of their humanity. Slave owners positioned slave quarters within the sight of the main house for easy surveillance. Nighttime curfews confined slaves to their cabins on the plantations while chains, overseers wielding whips, and patrollers with bloodhound dogs prevented escape during the day. Yet enslaved African people in America imbued the cabin with a dual identity. They displayed abolitionist prints on inside walls and hid them in underground vaults when slave owners or overseers stopped by. They sheltered runaways from other plantations inside their cabins and furnished them with provisions for their flights to freedom. They slipped away to nighttime revels and frolics where they gathered in clearings in an African manner, and reclaimed the work body for worship and play on their own terms (S. Camp 2014, 10, 44). A similar inversion took place when federal authorities in the United States established boarding schools for Indigenous youths in order to pull them away from tribal lands, end their use of tribal languages, rupture tribal allegiances, and destroy tribal cultures. Yet these classrooms became insubordinate spaces when instead of embracing white Anglo-Saxon identity and culture, the students used their contact with members of other Indigenous nations and the pervasiveness of English as the lingua franca to forge a militant nationalist pan-Indian identity (Nagel 1997, 115–117). Jeff Corntassel (Cherokee) and Taiaiake Alfred (Kahnawake Mohawk) define Indigeneity itself as a place-based form of insubordination, as "an oppositional place-based existence, along with the consciousness of being in struggle against the dispossessing and demeaning fact of colonization by foreign peoples," as what "fundamentally distinguishes Indigenous peoples from other peoples of the world" (quoted in Byrd 2011, xxix).

The mass mobilizations mounted by the Idle No More and the Black Lives Matter movements and the cultural politics of Chicanx artivistas provide the central insubordinate spaces examined and analyzed in this book. Each of them is extraordinary, but none of them is exceptional. They resonate with the same determination to create new spaces for democratic self-activity that has characterized other acts of insubordinate place-making around the world from the liberation theology of the Ti Legliz, Tet Ansanm, and Lavalas movements in Haiti to the Indigenous women's human rights activism of the Defensoras Comunitarios in Peru, to the environmental justice struggles of the South Bronx Clean Air Coalition in New York (Aristide and Richardson 1995, 192; Fregoso and Bejarano 2010b, 29; Sze 2007, 66). Insubordinate spaces are sites where people who lack material resources display great resourcefulness in deepening their capacity to free themselves and others from subordination, to imagine how things could be otherwise, and to move toward enacting that vision.

Insubordinate spaces are not liberated zones or free spaces. They are not utopian places that offer a blueprint for a perfect world. They remain immersed in the contradictions of the current conjuncture not transcendently independent of them. Yet they are places of possibility, products of acts of accompaniment and improvisation that reject the division of society into a small elite considered to be, and treated as, exceptional—while the great masses of people are treated as what Pascha Bueno-Hansen describes as "usable, abusable, dispensable and disposable" (2010, 293). They turn many of the tools forged to subordinate them into technologies for liberation. For example, the communications and information technologies that make possible the new global economy of flexible accumulation and "just-in-time" production also enable geographically dispersed Indigenous activists in Canada to "meet" online, to connect with environmental and Indigenous rights activists around the globe, and to circulate images and ideas outside the proximate reach of corporate media outlets. Twitter feeds and online streaming permit street demonstrators in Ferguson to move swiftly and strategically through the metropolitan area one step ahead of the police, to receive knowledgeable advice on self-defense against tear gas and pepper spray from experienced activists in Palestine, and to challenge police pronouncements and propaganda. Digital technologies enable Chicanx artivistas to convene online fifteen women from five different countries to write and record songs about motherhood in the age of neoliberal austerity. These acts turn hegemony on its head by using the circuits and networks of domination for oppositional ends.

In fooling the enemy, however, aggrieved groups can sometimes fool themselves. The social media technologies that facilitate grassroots communication are also instruments of surveillance. Prominence online can lead activists to confuse visibility with viability and to mistake fame for freedom. Virtual contacts can give an illusion of intimacy that serves as a poor substitute for actual accompaniment. Creative conjurers can turn poison into medicine, but counterinsurgency can always turn medicine back into poison. Yet, precisely because no single technology or technique will ever suffice, projects in insubordinate spaces become indispensable sites for improvisations that deepen the democratic deliberation and decision-making necessary for the creative thinking and action needed to imagine—and to live—otherwise. Acts of improvisation and accompaniment inside insubordinate spaces are at one and the same time political projects, cultural projects, and knowledge projects. In this context, politics is more than a set of proclamations, policies, and attempts to take power: it is a diffuse, plural, and diverse set of practices that, as Robin Kelley reminds us, comprises "many battles to roll back constraints and exercise some power over, or create some space within, the institutions and social relationships that dominate our lives" (1994, 9–10).

Subordinated people can and do create insubordinate spaces where they can cultivate a collective capacity to discern the "what can be" inside the "what is," where they can hone and refine tools for turning the toxic present into a tonic future, and where they can refuse closure and open up possibility. Insubordinate spaces are places where acts of improvisation and accompaniment fuel the creation of new social relations and new social realities. At a time when corporations, governments, and philanthropic institutions have largely abandoned the masses, the peoples of the world have to find each other. They have to find value in undervalued things, places, and people. They must do so in many different ways in many different kinds of places: for instance, in women's centers and workers' centers, in college classrooms and community-based arts and education projects, in food co-ops, and in fights for fair housing.

This book argues that paying attention to what transpires in insubordinate spaces will make audible what Robert Kennedy could not hear in 1963: what Fred Moten calls "the piercing insistence of the excluded" (2003, 223). It explores the challenges facing people committed to social justice in an era when key social institutions have increasingly been reconfigured to conform to the imperatives of a market society. It explores and analyzes exemplary projects in progress in communities and on campuses responding to current crises. It draws on key concepts from social justice struggles in the global south—such as accompaniment, *konesans*, and *balans*—to advance ideas about reciprocal recognition and cocreation as key components everywhere in the construction of new egalitarian and democratic social relations through art, activism, and academic research and teaching. Inside the very institutions set up to support subordination, people can create insubordinate spaces that draw on nonmarket aspirations, ideas, archives, imaginaries, epistemologies, and ontologies. New forms of interactive and collaborative sociality emerge every day. Opposition to the rule of capital and cultivation of capacities for democratic collective life permeate street demonstrations and social media discussions, story circles and spoken word performances, performance spaces, and popular education programs. Mobilizations across race, place, and class challenge the acceptance of war and torture as ordinary acts and policies. They act on behalf of the unhoused population's right to the city. They identify putatively nonnormative gender and sexual identities as potentially productive of more egalitarian, democratic, decent, and humane social relations. In these insubordinate spaces, people can nurture a collective capacity for democratic deliberation, collective decision-making, public engagement, and accountability that challenges the hegemony of neoliberal institutions and practices.

Plan of Subsequent Chapters

Insubordinate Spaces argues that education, the arts, and activism are not simply incidental endeavors suffering collateral damage from neoliberalism's insistence on the fiscalization of social relations; rather, they are key terrains of political and ideological conflict, sites where neoliberal social relations and priorities are learned and legitimized through a pronounced public pedagogy and a conscious cultural training program. We analyze the tools and actions central to that struggle in the following chapters.

A focus on conceptual tools that help bring to light the significance of insubordinate spaces in these intemperate times begins in Chapter 2 ("Concepts for Insubordinate Spaces in Intemperate Times") with discussions of the metaphor and practice of accompaniment articulated by Archbishop Oscar Romero in El Salvador, of the paired ideals of "*konsesans* and *balans*" that fueled Father Jean-Bertrand Aristide's *lavalas* movement in Haiti, and of the political temporality of Immanuel Wallerstein's concept of the middle run. We then turn to consider three extraordinary insubordinate spaces: (1) the knowledge projects and insubordinate practices of the Idle No More movement launched by Indigenous people in Canada in Chapter 3 ("Idle No More"); (2) the deliberate acts of convening outside commercial culture instigated by *son jarocho* music performance and Fandango celebrations in Mexico and the U.S. Southwest, the performance art of Chingo Bling, and the installation art of Ramiro Gomez in Chapter 4 ("Artivistas"); and (3) the mass protests in Ferguson, Missouri—insubordinate spaces responding to police killings of Black youths in Chapter 5 ("Ferguson"). The challenges to improvisation and accompaniment posed by hegemonic knowledge projects are explained and analyzed in Chapter 6 ("Coloniality and Neoliberalism as Knowledge Projects"). We explore the complications of developing cultures of accompaniment for insubordinate spaces within the subordinating institutions of college and university research and teaching in Chapter 7 ("Accompaniment and the Neoliberal University"). Chapter 8 (Conclusion: "Carry the Struggle, Live the Victory") concludes the book with a discussion of the ways in which activists, artists, and academics have learned to use improvisation and accompaniment to not only carry on the struggle but also to live the victory by creating more decent and democratic social relations, practices, and institutions.

Listening to Learn Today

The power and potential of one insubordinate space was visible during a 2014 visit to classes taught under the aegis of the learning community known as Students at the Center in inner-city high schools in New Orleans. In morning classes at Eleanor McMain High School in the Garden District and at afternoon classes at McDonogh #35 High School, then in the Seventh Ward, instructors Jim Randels and Kalamu ya Salaam deployed an interactive, collaborative, and improvisational pedagogy that requires students to read challenging texts, relate them to their own lives, and read their written work out loud to the entire class as a basis for shared group discussion. Without paper or computers, the students wrote their compositions on and read from their cell phones. In this pedagogy, listening to other students, asking them questions, and offering them comments is as important as a student's own writing. The process blends the personal narratives and perspectives of individuals with the collective wisdom of the group, making the classroom a site of solidarity and mutuality, a place where young people develop their collective capacity for reciprocal respect and recognition and for deliberative talk and democratic decision-making (Lipsitz 2015, 2016).

Halfway through one afternoon session, a tall man who appeared to be in his seventies entered the room and took a seat among the students. He did not seem to be connected to the school, but he was not wearing a visitor's badge either. He seemed completely comfortable, sitting in one of the little classroom chairs despite his height. Without prompting, the stranger started to talk about the importance of what the class was doing, emphasizing how knowledge would enable the students to draw on and advance the fight for freedom in their community. The teacher of the class, Kalamu ya Salaam, wanted the students to know who was speaking to them, so he asked the visitor to identify himself. "They call me Big Duck," the man answered in a deep, booming, and resonant voice. "When I was a little kid," he continued, "I was tall for my age and when the other kids followed me, the people would say, 'There's the big duck and all his little ducks following after him.' And I'm still Big Duck, and that's why I'm here today to see how all my little ducks are doing [pointing to the students]." The visitor related that he had been in jail with Fannie Lou Hamer in Mississippi in the 1960s and that he had come to the class to convey to the young people the need for them to work hard and to continue to carry on the struggle for "our people." Still eager to have the students know the name of the man who was speaking to them, the teacher persisted, trying another tack. "What is your government name?" he inquired. Pretending to take offense, Big Duck answered slowly and pedantically, "I am *governed* by the historical struggles of our people who have named me Big Duck." Unwilling to give up, Salaam tried again. "What is the name on your driver's license?" Big Duck winced; he announced that a driver's license was a document issued by the state that controls and administers the unjust racial order in which they all lived. Joining the laughter of the students, the teacher attempted to get the information one more time. "What did your parents name you?" he asked. "Oh," Big Duck answered calmly, "Jerome Smith."[3]

This visitor to Students at the Center was the very Jerome Smith who had challenged Robert Kennedy fifty-one years earlier, still speaking out, and still not being heard outside of his immediate circles. His unbroken history of struggle included not only jailings, beatings, and arguments with the attorney general but speaking at a memorable reception at Lorraine Hansberry's upstate New York home shortly after the 1963 meeting with Robert Kennedy. At Hansberry's house, Smith solicited donations for the freedom movement, raising a sum that was used for many different purposes. The money raised that day helped with the purchase of the station wagon that civil rights workers James Chaney, Michael Schwerner, and Andrew Goodman were riding in during the summer of 1964, when Neshoba County sheriffs and deputies in concert with local members of the Ku Klux Klan stopped the vehicle and killed its occupants.

During his years as a civil rights activist, Smith noticed how the unifying goal of Black liberation enabled New Orleans residents to overcome neighborhood rivalries and work collaboratively together. He prized the ways in which bold, yet diverse, currents of resistance propelled participation in the movement among activists whose families treasured memories of activities inside insubordinate spaces created by Black nationalist organizations, trade unions, and fraternal orders. Smith had especially high regard for the Mardi Gras Indians, the groups of working class Black people who spend all year designing and sewing elaborate costumes that they wear as they parade through their neighborhoods on only two days—Mardi Gras Day and St. Joseph's Day. Different "tribes" represented different neighborhoods, competing with one another for status and prestige, but they also functioned as fraternal orders providing aid for members in times of need. Smith interpreted the Mardi Gras Indian ritual as an unconscious affirmation of Black power because the Indians' costumes, chants, and dances displayed the excellence, uniqueness, and creativity that racial capitalism suppressed and obscured (Lipsitz 1994, 74). Along with fellow CORE freedom fighter Rudy Lombard, Smith formed the Tambourine and Fan organization, a group dedicated to highlighting the culture and tradition of the Mardi Gras Indians as a point of entry for young people to learn about Black culture (Dent 2018, 187).

Smith recognized that the neighborhood focus of the Indians both enabled and inhibited their work. Neighborhood bonds enhanced social cohesion and augmented support networks based on face-to-face contact. The Indians helped residents feel secure in place and proud of where they lived. Yet that very allegiance to the neighborhood could give rise to competition with people in other sections of the city, to rivalries and resentments that sometimes erupted into violence. Although headquartered in the Seventh Ward neighborhood where Smith grew up, Tambourine and Fan sought to unify the city's Black population: "We had to contend with the extreme neighborhood mentality of New Orleans," he recalls (Dent 2018, 188). Smith remembered how civil rights struggles created an insubordinate space where Black people from different neighborhoods, class statuses, skin colors, and religions could work together. He remembered how his labors as a longshoreman unloading shipments of bananas enabled him to work collaboratively and creatively with Black people from all over the region (Dent 2018, 188). He persuaded the different groups to stage a unified parade on St. Joseph's Day as an act of creative exchange rather than an exercise in competition. The effort was so successful that it was moved to the Sunday after St. Joseph's Day, given the title "Super Sunday," and quickly became a central part of Black participation in carnival season (Medley 2014; Dent 2018, 188).

Smith continues his work with Tambourine and Fan to this day. It serves as an insubordinate space where young people learn to play music, march in parades, and study Black history (K. Rogers 1993, 146, 184). The organization views antiracist politics not only as a matter of removing expressly racist impediments from Black lives, but rather creating new humane and democratic practices and institutions. "Our mission is not civil rights," Jerome Smith explains. "We demand that our humanity be respected" (DeBerry 2014).

The emphasis on the arts and expressive culture in Tambourine and Fan grew organically from Smith's life experiences. Growing up in New Orleans, Smith witnessed his mother develop her talents as a seamstress, photographer, and furniture maker as a way of cultivating her own creativity and dignity while employed as a housekeeper. In his early years in elementary school, Smith stammered so badly whenever he had to talk that he was ashamed to speak in class. A teacher at Craig Elementary School, however, recognized the youth's potential and used music to help Smith overcome this serious speech impediment. The teacher assigned to him the bass drum to play, giving him a word to pronounce each time he beat on the instrument. The sound of the drum protected his words from being heard by others, which built up his confidence so much that Smith eventually accepted a role in a school theater production, delivering his lines flawlessly (Arend 2016). Having made unusual use of a musical instrument, Smith discovered there could be music even when no instruments were present. On the streets of New Orleans he loved the pitch, melody, and diction in the voices of produce vendors calling out to potential customers. Even the ways people said "good morning" or "good evening" seemed to be performances: greetings that served as shows of care and respect. "That's what I teach these youngsters—recognize the humanity of the other," he says, speaking about Tambourine and Fan, adding "That's a healthy thing. It has to do with a decency of spirit and it's reflected in the song of saying 'good morning' and 'good evening'" (Neighborhood Story Project 2014). When parades would pass by his elementary school classroom, Smith remembers sometimes "rolling out" the first floor window to join them. "Black people used the streets and the music they created to express themselves," he recalls. In the face of relentless racial suppression, subordination, and exploitation, expressive culture provided a reason to live. Remembering all the "artists" he encountered growing up, Smith asserts, "They invented something that prevented us from committing suicide" (Arend 2016).

Jerome Smith's introduction of himself as Big Duck in the classroom at McDonogh #35 in 2014 deepened the role of Students at the Center classes as an insubordinate space. As he did in Robert Kennedy's luxurious Central Park apartment and Lorraine Hansberry's elegant home in Croton-on-Hudson, New York, Smith deployed imagination and improvisation to turn an ordinary place into an insubordinate space. In his words to the students that day as well as in his work with Tambourine and Fan, Smith uses interruption, inversion, surprise, and disguise as performance mechanisms that reconfigure social relations. He learned much about this in his civil rights fieldwork in Mississippi. There he discovered that ordinary people possessed extraordinary talents just waiting to be unleashed. In the cotton fields, cabins, and churches of the rural South, Smith saw college-educated volunteers becoming transformed through dialogues with intelligent but unlettered workers. He remembers people who were "drenched in the sophistication of books, learning from people who could not spell their name" about the very books that the educated ones prized the most (K. Rogers 1993, 135).

The insubordinate spaces that Jerome Smith has inhabited and created have provided him with beliefs, values, and a way of life that proceed from principles very different from the market logic of neoliberalism. Insubordinate spaces are innately social, collaborative, and collective. They are places where strangers meet and where unexpected associations, affiliations, and alliances are envisioned and enacted. They are sites where people think in terms of "we" instead of "me." As a civil rights activist, Smith suffered beatings and time in jail. During one four-month incarceration his jailers allowed him only two changes of sheets and pillow cases (Medley 2014). Yet he remembers those days fondly, because the shared work of struggle, in his words, "gave you strength, a sense of not being alone. It gave you a confirmation; it certified the rightness of your purpose. It minimized your fear, helped you to overcome your fear. There was a collective strength, even when you were by yourself" (K. Rogers 1993, 185).

As he learned to be cooperative and contributive rather than competitive, Jerome Smith discovered that extraordinary things can happen inside insubordinate spaces. They can allow people to realize untapped potential within themselves and to meet parts of their persona that they previously did not know were there. In late November 1961, Smith was part of a group of "freedom riders" traveling by bus through Southern states in an attempt to desegregate previously all-white lunch counters at interstate bus stations. When the group entered the bus station in McComb, Mississippi, a group of whites screaming "Kill 'em!" and "Nigger!" attacked the demonstrators with their fists, brass knuckles, and sticks. Escaping outside to the streets, Smith encountered a dirty old truck moving slowly on the street, driven by an elderly Black man transporting grain to feed his pigs. The driver spoke softly to Smith and invited him to "roll over" into the back of the truck. As Smith hid underneath the animal fodder, the man drove him to safety at a backwoods "juke" joint. Smith later learned that the driver who saved him had a reputation in town as an "Uncle Tom," as a cowed and frightened man who seemed invariably obedient and subservient to whites. It was exactly that reputation, however, that led whites to not inspect the truck as he was driving away from the scene of the violence. In that moment, something about the crisis made the truck driver see his life—his role in this country and his place in it—differently and to chart a new course of action. The experience taught Smith not to write off or underestimate anyone. It became clear to him that under the right circumstances, inside insubordinate spaces, everyone can contribute and everyone should count.

In 1963, Robert Kennedy was unable to listen to Jerome Smith. He dismissed the words spoken to him as immature and impertinent. Smith, on the other hand, felt that the problem was not his own behavior but Kennedy's insensitivity to the suffering of others. He thought that the attorney general could not hear what was being said to him because of his "addiction to power." In Smith's opinion, Robert Kennedy had surrendered his humanity in the service of his ambition. Kennedy was told the truth but could not hear it. Armed with the clarity, conviction, and courage forged for him through work with others in the movement, Smith was neither intimidated nor impressed by the occasion of speaking to the attorney general. To him, the meeting was "nothing special," just "an extension of my service," like walking a picket line or going to jail (K. Rogers 1993, 143). His experience in insubordinate spaces made him feel as much at home in a Central Park West apartment as he felt inside a sharecropper's cabin. The attorney general, on the other hand, could not get past the markers of race and class that led him to dismiss what he was being told by Jerome Smith.

The people who wield power in society today have shown themselves to be similarly unable to hear what Jerome Smith—and so many others like him—have said and continue to say. The words, ideas, understandings, and aspirations of people without wealth, power, and influence will not be represented inside the plutocratic political system, disseminated by corporate media conglomerates, or studied in the increasingly fiscalized, virtualized, and vocationalized educational system. Inside insubordinate spaces, however, they have a rich, ongoing, ever-changing, and infinitely generative life.

In 1963, James Baldwin was driven to the brink of despair because he realized that the "unthinking white majority" of his time refused to acknowledge that he was human. He died in 1987, but his words still resonate in the present. They help us understand why in recent years, in the face of wave upon wave of unprosecuted police and vigilante killings, young Black people and their allies staged mass demonstrations insisting that Black lives matter. These seemingly spontaneous and unorganized actions proceeded in large part because for a short time young people turned "Black Twitter" into an insubordinate space of information, education, agitation, organization, and mobilization. The demonstrations built on an infrastructure of mutual recognition and regard cultivated in a broad range of sites including hip-hop shows, political reading groups, spoken word performances, community development organizations, and college classes in Black, feminist, and queer studies.

In an era of concentrated economic, political, military, and police power, searching for insubordinate spaces may seem like a disturbingly inadequate response to a massively large problem. Yet big concentrations of power rest inescapably on small practices, processes, and perceptions widely dispersed throughout society. As Stuart Hall argues, following Antonio Gramsci and Michel Foucault, the state and other sites of centralized power are not "things" to be overthrown, smashed, or seized but rather complex formations spread across diverse arenas that require a wide range of strategies and struggles (Hall 1986, 19). It may seem that insubordinate spaces are too small to be sites for large-scale social change. Yet hegemony is both instituted and contested by seemingly small moves—how people argue, how they treat both allies and enemies, and how they accompany those who are like themselves and those who are not. It is never easy to undo decades and centuries of subordination, but, precisely because subjection has been shaped by a long chain of signs and symbols, aggrieved individuals and groups need to forge an equally long chain of counter symbolization. The future is conditioned by the past. The upward arc of recovery often has to trace in reverse the downward arc of injury. Things that can kill can also cure if deployed in the right doses and combinations.[4]

2 / Concepts for Insubordinate Spaces
in Intemperate Times

Inside spaces structured in dominance, in a world suffused with avarice, anger, inequality, and injustice, it is not easy to live honorably and ethically, to sustain the hope of building affirmative and dignified relations with others, and to reckon honestly with the ways in which the global economy unevenly links together the fates of very differently situated people. Inside insubordinate spaces, however, people struggling for social justice have created a tool kit of concepts and practices useful for trying to turn the imperiled present into a fulfilled future. This book surveys the inventory of tools that have been forged for emancipatory purposes from acts of accompaniment and improvisation carried out within the temporality of the middle run and informed by the concepts of *konesans* and *balans*.

Accompaniment

Accompaniment is a disposition, a sensibility, and a pattern of behavior. It is a commitment based on a cultivated capacity for making connections with others, identifying with them, and helping them. Three different formulations of accompaniment inform the deployment of the concept in this book: (1) the articulation and implementation of liberation theology as accompaniment conceived and advanced by Archbishop Oscar Romero in El Salvador in the 1970s, (2) the ways in which accompaniment functions as a practice in music making, and (3) the metaphor of accompaniment as the movement of a community of travelers walking down a road together. Within each of these variants of accompaniment, individuals from different backgrounds with different experiences, perspectives, and interests recognize and reinforce each other's work and worth by joining together. Accompaniment recognizes the inescapably and quintessentially *social* nature of living in the world. It focuses on making connections with others, finding common ground, and uniting around the concerns, interests, and ideas of the people with the greatest need for profound social changes. As liberation psychologist Mary Watkins explains eloquently and insightfully, accompaniment entails looking *at* rather than looking *away*, listening rather than speaking prematurely, and encouraging and respecting the leadership of others rather than always presuming that role for the self (2019).

A practice and a process well worth emulating is the idea and ideal of accompaniment that Archbishop Oscar Romero articulated in the midst of the life and death revolutionary struggle for dignity and democracy in El Salvador in the 1970s.[1] Romero lived in a nation controlled completely by its wealthiest families. For most of his life, his work as a priest pleased the rich. He was nearly sixty years old when he started to break away from their influence and to engage extensively with the poor. At the very moment when he was on the brink of ascending to the top levels of the church hierarchy, he instead moved closer to the people as they grappled with the problems that pervaded their everyday existence. He started to converse with peasants and radical priests as they conducted what they described as "national reality" classes in the fragile and fugitive insubordinate spaces of Bible study groups inside Christian base communities. By listening to others, Romero learned formulations and frameworks that enabled him to see his identity and life mission in new ways. He came to believe that the social ills plaguing El Salvador required ordinary people to take action (Vigil 2000, 213). He perceived that neither salvation nor social justice could be secured primarily by individuals and that meaningful living and effective social change could come only from "the strength of a people who together clamor for their just rights" (Vigil 2000, 248–249).

Romero analyzed class divisions as sins that separated the rich from the poor, alienating them from each other and therefore from God. In a series of Pastoral Letters and conference presentations in 1977 and 1978 he articulated the necessity of responding "to the unjust distribution of the wealth that God has created for all" (Lynd 2012, 110). Romero argued that the long history of the Catholic Church's condemnation of "atheistic Marxism" now calls for "in equal measure the condemnation of the capitalist system" (Lynd

2012, 110). He was influenced by conversations about the Latin American Catholic Church in the 1960s and 1970s that coalesced around the idea of the preferential option for the poor formulated by Peruvian cleric Gustavo Gutiérrez. In English, "option" connotes a voluntary and perhaps casual choice, but in Spanish *la opción* signifies not so much a choice as a commitment. Gutiérrez argued that Christianity requires opposition to systems of deprivation as well as affirmative acts of solidarity alongside those who suffer from poverty. "The whole climate of the Gospel," Gutiérrez contends, "is a continual demand for the right of the poor to make themselves heard, to be considered preferentially by society, a demand to subordinate economic needs to those of the deprived" (Gutiérrez 1988, 69).

Yet Romero recognized that differently situated people see the world differently. The rich cannot possibly really know what it is like to be poor, to be hungry, or to be houseless, no matter how much sympathy or empathy they feel. The poor, on the other hand, can never fully understand, trust, or forgive people whose class privileges and power guarantee them a roof over their heads and meat and bread on their tables. Middle-class and wealthy people are generally unaware of the class condescension they exude when they view the poor merely as objects of pity and recipients of charity. From Romero's perspective, even advocates for the poor from the Catholic Church and oppositional political parties tended to treat poor people instrumentally, as a polity to be converted rather than respected, as people in need of education, uplift, and inspiration rather than as people with knowledge who need to be listened to and accompanied.

Yet despite the deep chasms between classes, the destinies of the rich and the poor remain intertwined. Romero believed that people from diverse backgrounds could come together in shared work, uniting around the needs and interests of the most oppressed. He identified the preferential option for the poor as the key nexus of action, as a way of placing first the needs of people whose concerns might otherwise be addressed last. This did not mean uncritically supporting anything poor people wanted or refraining from criticizing their failings and misdeeds. Instead, it meant making the needs of the most powerless and most oppressed—the people most likely to be left out—into *everyone's* first priority. It entailed asking questions before acting, taking inventory of multiple forms of social exclusion, and learning how to be people who do not succumb to the dominant norms of an acquisitive, aggressive, and antagonistic world.

Romero adopted "accompaniment" as the operative metaphor for his beliefs and actions. The term's Latin roots combine "being together" (com) with "breaking bread" (panis), connoting physical proximity, shared suste-nance, and reciprocity. Romero viewed accompaniment as a meeting among persons with different experiences who possess different areas of expertise yet chart a common course together. Most important, from his perspective, the economically comfortable had to listen to the abused and mistreated poor, and to learn from them, to be cocreators of a process that transformed poor people into "the masters of, and the protagonists in, their own struggle and liberation, thereby unmasking the root of false paternalism, including ecclesiastical paternalism" (Lynd 2012, 121).

Romero's rebellion made him unpopular with the church hierarchy and government officials. Yet the people loved him. Despite rebukes and threats from the powerful, he stood firmly alongside the oppressed peasants of his nation. He told his followers that the national guard was likely to do bad things, but the peasants were not likely to do bad things. Therefore, if the guard attacked the peasants, he wanted his followers to see it as an attack on themselves. "You should be there next to the campesinos," he counseled. "Accompany them. Take the same risks they do" (Vigil 2000, 248).

Archbishop Romero practiced what he preached. On March 23, 1980, he delivered a sermon that urged soldiers in the Salvadoran army to disobey their officers and to follow a higher law by refusing to terrorize the peas-ants. He was assassinated in church the next day while celebrating mass. Romero's murder deepened the commitments of his followers who had learned from him that although accompaniment entailed mortal risks, it also brought unprecedented joy and fulfillment. By forging unity around the needs of the most oppressed, accompaniment allowed Romero and his followers not only to battle against exploitation and hierarchy but also to create new social relationships that *enacted* the utopian hopes that religion and radical politics alike had previously largely only *envisioned*. Action led to new ideas, analyses, and interpretations. "I thought I knew the Gospel," Romero explained, speaking of his former life of prestige and comfort, but because of his contact with struggles by large groups of people, he felt that he was "learning to read it another way" (Vigil 2000, 272).

Oscar Romero's concept of accompaniment emerged in the midst of a revolution, in a context where traditional avenues for redressing grievances had been foreclosed. Yet accompaniment as a practice also has a long and di-verse history of existence in the quotidian practices of societies where social polarization is less extreme. It appears in the second kind of accompaniment central to the ideas and arguments in this book: the world of music mak-ing. Accompaniment shapes the theory and practice of playing together.

Musical accompaniment requires attention, communication, and cooperation. It starts with careful listening, empathy, and identification. It involves augmenting, accenting, and countering one musical voice with others. The music industry and its fans generally pay attention to individual virtuosos and ignore accompaniment. Yet musicians who play together know that every player has important work to do—that when music sounds good, it is because many people are doing their jobs well.[2] In an ensemble, each musician augments, accents, and counters the others. Harmonic and rhythmic accompaniments enhance melodic lines, but they also produce dialogues between melodies and countermelodies. A musician playing block chords augments the primary melody through a succession of sounds that move in the same direction as the rhythm. Sometimes accompaniment means saying less so that others can be heard. A drummer can play sparely and simply to make the bass lines more audible, while compositions played in stop time include breaks that make room for soloists.

Especially in jazz music, accompaniment cannot be achieved by following a formula or obeying fixed rules. It demands alertness and imagination and requires improvisation. Accompaniment can also be a challenging knowledge project, a path toward a new way of thinking. For example, when Herbie Hancock played piano in a group led by trumpeter Miles Davis, he got some advice that he did not immediately understand (Spitzer 2008). Accustomed to getting instruction on which chord changes to make or what rhythms to play in, Hancock was baffled when Davis told him he played too many "butter" notes. It was not at all clear, at least at first, what butter notes might be. The pianist had never heard the term. Possibly no one but Davis had ever uttered it. As he thought about it, however, Hancock concluded that butter was smooth and satisfying, so butter notes must be the obvious and easy notes in any given situation. What might be a butter note at one time would not be a butter note at another. As leader of the group, Davis could have stopped the band when Hancock played a note that he thought was not right. But he wanted to equip Hancock with a tool for deep listening, quick assessment, and rapid adjustment. To gain that tool, Hancock had to be able to see it for himself, to have presence of mind and be fully "in the moment" every time he played. He had to think about how his playing augmented or undermined the other musicians. Learning about butter notes was more a matter of developing a new disposition about music than mastering any particular technique.

To accompany other players entails more than simply adding new sounds to the mix. Accompaniment as a musical practice entails a personal and ultimately political commitment to be a contributor rather than a competitor and to think beyond individual virtuosity and visibility. Jazz and blues bass player Bob Stroger places accompaniment at the center of his art, explaining:

> My job is to try to make the music sound good. Not to get over the top of 'em, but play so they can play on top of me. I try to stay out of everybody's way and give 'em a nice smooth line that they can play on. My style is to accompany people. I listen. I know what sounds good with a person. . . . It all depends on the artist that I'm working with. If he likes to play swing stuff, then I put a little more swing into it. If a guy likes to play off a bump all night, then I'll bump all night. (Moon 2001, 33)

Stroger warns young players about the dangers of thinking of a performance as an opportunity to display their own individual skills.

> If a guy that's really good wants to show off his skills, he'll end up playing lots of junk and it will end up being lots of noise, you know. Lots of the younger guys out there are doing that now. They're trying to show how good they are with their particular instrument and not playing with the artist that they're playing with. I call a good musician somebody who plays good with the artists that you're playing with. Play what he's playing. Don't try to get up and play your skills, 'cause people ain't coming to hear you. They're coming to hear the artist. The first thing they're going to say is that you can't play with the artist. They're not gonna say that the artist can't play with you, 'cause they're not comin' to see you. If he plays bad, you play and try to make it sound good. (Moon 2001, 33)

Good playing does not mean overplaying.

While it might seem like dull and routine work, accompaniment can play a crucial role in enabling others to shine. Rhythm and blues drummer Jockey Etienne explains how the ordinary task of playing on the beat contributes greatly to the virtuosity of others. "You on tempo," he says. "You stay on it. I don't care what they do up there. When they come back, you have to have room to come back. We call that 'stay in the pocket.' You have to hold that bottom down. You got to have the foundation" (Bock 2011, 33). Good accompaniment entails careful listening and creative improvisation.

It means adjusting to mistakes and helping others sound better. In blues and jazz music built around creative chord changes, inevitably someone in the group may fail to make the right change. Yet rather than blaming or shaming the other player, a good accompanist will come to the rescue. "If he made a bad change," Stroger advises, "you make it with him. Ain't no such thing as no bad change if you make it together" (Moon 2001, 33).

A third formulation of accompaniment—that of travelers walking down a road together—captures some aspects of the term that are missing from accompaniment as liberation theology and accompaniment as musical practice. A group of people moving down a road together have to develop collective watchfulness, attentiveness, and solidarity. It does not matter who walks in front or who walks in back at any particular time; the group moves along with awareness of all of its members. There are no set roles or rules. Conversations start and stop. Different combinations of participants coalesce and disperse. The collective rhythms of the group decide the pace of the journey. There is a tacit commitment to proceed collectively, but at any moment individual participants may lag behind, stop to rest, or forge ahead.

Physician, anthropologist, and human rights activist Paul Farmer deploys this sense of accompaniment as a shared journey as the key metaphor guiding the ethics and procedures of his work. "To accompany someone," he argues, "is to go somewhere with him or her, to break bread together, to be present on a journey with a beginning and an end" (Farmer 2013, 234). Farmer developed his understanding of accompaniment as a Harvard University professor engaged in efforts to provide medical care for residents of rural villages in Haiti. He conceives of accompaniment as an informal and open-ended improvised process that brings differently situated people together for particular purposes. The *accompagnateur* or companion makes a pledge to those accompanied: "'I'll go with you and support you on your journey wherever it leads. I'll share your fate for a while.' And by a 'while,' I don't mean a little while. Accompaniment is much more often about sticking with a task until it's deemed completed—not by the accompagnateur, but by the person or persons being accompanied" (Farmer 2013, 234). Farmer's formulation of accompaniment productively focuses on a definition of expertise as more supportive than supervisory, yet it remains primarily concerned with coaxing experts to behave in more ethical ways in an unequal world, rather than valuing the vast knowledge of the poor and affirming their right to determine their own destiny.

When people accompany each other in liberation theology, in music, or when walking down a road together, everyone contributes and everyone counts. Accompaniment is not generally a valued practice in the activities of a competitive neoliberal society. In a world of market times and market places, people are encouraged to think of themselves as entrepreneurs of their own identities, careers, and public images. The dominant reward structures cultivate antagonism and aggression among individuals. Workers compete with each other for management's favor; students learn to desire higher grades than their classmates; scholars compete with colleagues for prestige and reward; poor people are pitted against each other as they scramble for scarce resources and symbolic emblems of prestige. Yet in the survival strategies of the poor, in shop floor collaborations among workers, and in the practices of teaching and learning, what matters most is how the pieces fit together, and what people can create collectively. Accompaniment can thus be the basis of a powerful counterculture inside communities, work sites, and schools. It can help us discover parts of ourselves that we did not know were there by elevating the moral over the material. In a society that constantly urges people *to have more*, the real task, as Archbishop Romero insisted, is to learn *how to be more* (Vigil 2000).

Individuals primed to aspire to be recognized as soloists do not automatically know how to accompany others. People cannot learn accompaniment simply by studying, imagining, or asserting it. They have to inhabit it and practice it, to risk and encounter and overcome failure through both embodied learning experiences and practical action in concrete insubordinate spaces. Ideas and identities do not emerge out of thin air. As Antonio Gramsci asserts, "Ideas and opinions are not spontaneously 'born' in each individual brain" (Gramsci 1989, 192); they emanate from practical experience in the world. Acts of accompaniment and improvisation can set in motion processes that produce new practices and as a result, new kinds of people, new social relationships, and new social imaginaries.

Without minimizing the enormous difference in contexts between the wealthy and the poor regions of the world, between the global north and the global south, between those of us who enjoy the benefits of social inclusion and those who suffer from the relentless cruelties of exclusion, accompaniment carried out in the right ways can function productively and honorably as a guiding principle in the global north just as it did in guiding El Salvador's "national reality" classes.[3] Accompaniment can help transcend the pervasive segregation of society. It offers an opportunity to build on both the dynamics of difference and the solidarities of sameness. It can help people work together respectfully as equals. Accompaniment does *not* erase differences or suppress disagreements in the name of an artificial and premature unity. In accompaniment there are times when it will be wise to work together and times when it will be necessary to remain apart. Yet accompaniment allows disagreements to be seen as evidence of problems yet to be solved, discussions yet to be conducted, and understandings yet to be developed.[4]

The principles of accompaniment appear prominently in the practices of what are known as the new social movements. The old social movements cohered around openly articulated ideologies, clearly defined organizational structures, decidedly hierarchical chains of command, and mutually agreed upon common identities. For example, left and labor radicals assumed that the opposition between labor and capital functioned as the core contradiction in society and therefore unifying the people of the world as workers was the key to transformative social change. Social movements emanating from this tradition generated political sects and parties competing with others for members and mastery of the movement. They fought to place themselves in power with the intention of eventually using the powers of the state to serve the masses. They generally elevated only men to leadership positions, and they distrusted democracy as essentially a delusion, as a luxury that popular movements could not afford because it delayed decision-making, diverted attention away from struggling against enemies, and diluted militancy. These movements presented their programs as the products of modern rational thought and management and as ways to expand the economy and make it more efficient (Wallerstein 1995, 214–215).

Guided by acts of accompaniment, the new social movements proceed from different premises. They are loosely assembled coalescences of decentralized and dispersed power. They do not generally seek to run society immediately but rather to build a new social vision organically from ways of struggling to survive within it with dignity, decency, and hope. Emerging in an era of chronic economic crisis, they take labor's side against capital but view that struggle as merely one of many contradictions in society, not as the key axis for emancipatory change. Surrounded by ecological disasters on all sides, they generally do not believe that unlimited economic expansion or scientific innovation will make things better. They tend to view radical participatory democracy as a profoundly revolutionary and anticapitalist ideal. Their acts of accompaniment treat the different perspectives emanating from experiences of gender, race, and sexuality as sources of strength rather than as impediments to unity. They see opposition to racism, sexism, and homophobia as important by themselves but also as necessary components of struggles against predatory capitalism and imperialism. They promote unity but eschew uniformity. They reject the idea that a shared identity is necessary for shared identification. They encourage ideological disagreement and diversity and promote pluriversality rather than universality. Their aims echo the imperative articulated in the Fourth Declaration from the Lacandón Jungle by the EZLN in Mexico—to seek a world in which there is room for many worlds.[5]

Social moments grounded in accompaniment often start with a scream of personal pain or a shout of social solidarity in the street. These movements emerge as coalitions brought together through articulations of both refusal and affirmation. From the slogan "Ya Basta!" (Enough! or Stop!) that propels the organizing by the EZLN in Mexico, to the deployment of "Idle No More" as both the name and the pledge of a campaign by Indigenous activists in Canada, to the insistence that Black Lives Matter in mobilizations against police and vigilante killings of Black individuals, the new social movements see passivity as a problem and action as an antidote. They seek to accompany one another in breaking with previous patterns of subordination. They refuse to audition for inclusion, to plead their fitness for freedom, or to perform normativity for the approval of their oppressors. They seek respect rather than respectability. In the protests against the killing of Michael Brown in Ferguson, for example, young people who had been demonized for being queer or trans, criminalized for being Black and poor, and marginalized by physical isolation and second-class education marched in solidarity with one another and with very differently situated allies despite all of their differences. On the very streets where they were stopped, searched, and cited, and in the towns where they were charged, convicted, fined, and jailed, the shunned, the segregated, and the silenced joined together to chant "Whose streets? Our streets!" They brought together people with many different social identities who were comfortable following the leadership of Black queer women who presented themselves unapologetically, wearing their everyday clothes and using their everyday speech to affirm that their lives matter. A sign in one of their demonstrations read "Black and Gay and Here to Stay." When reporters asked demonstrators for their names, many responded "I am Mike Brown," expressing solidarity with the slain teenager demeaned by the police and dismissed by the press as a thug whose death was not worth grieving.[6]

Acts of accompaniment can generate creative alternatives to the limitations of the current historical conjuncture. They can help author and authorize a new social warrant grounded in preferential options for the least powerful, in a politics of respect, friendliness, and humility. A social warrant is a widely shared consensus about what is desired and what is feared, what is permitted and what is forbidden, who is included and who is excluded, what has been done and what should be done. A social warrant is rarely written down or openly announced. It comprises a collective common sense that guides attitudes, aspirations, and actions. A social warrant functions as a de facto social charter that contains foundational principles about obligations, rights, and responsibilities. Accompaniment can be an important crucible of a new social warrant because it recognizes that solidarity is not simply found, but rather needs to be forged. It is poetic and pragmatic, diagnostic and therapeutic. It does not see itself as creating "the" revolution but rather moves in the direction of thinkers such as the EZLN's Subcommandante Marcos, seeking experiences of sharing that might ultimately make a revolution possible.

Accompaniment in insubordinate spaces can help transcend the pervasive segregation of society. It offers an opportunity to look for people who are looking for us and to build new affinities, affiliations, and alliances. In the spirit of Archbishop Romero, accompaniment entails giving first priority to the needs of the people most likely to be disregarded, demeaned, and dismissed. Romero began his embrace of accompaniment by attempting to help the poor, but listening to them and learning from them gave him a different vision. Instead of one person helping someone less fortunate, accompaniment envisions a relationship between equals exploring the way forward together (Lynd 2012, 4).

Accompaniment can be extraordinarily difficult in a society that promotes relentless competition and incessant forms of denial of the inequality it produces. The most powerful people and institutions in this society stoke antagonisms based on exaggerated fears of difference that result in moral panics about immigrants and religious, racial, and sexual minorities. Under these conditions, most people have precious little experience working together, especially across classes, races, languages, and nationalities. Attempting accompaniment will produce mistakes, mistrust, and misunderstandings. Frustration and disillusionment can follow when people discover that they do not yet possess the skills, dispositions, and persistence needed to work effectively across the borders and boundaries that fragment society into warring camps. Yet by asking and answering questions important to the increasing numbers of deportable, displaceable, and disposable people in the world, by listening to them, working with them, and seeing our fate as inextricably bound up with them, people all around the world today are forging new social relations and new social realities that offer a promise of a better future.

Accompaniment here functions as a strategic concept, much in the way that the concept of dignity does for the EZLN (and its followers in Mexico and around the world). As Manuel Callahan explains, strategic concepts are categories of analysis that acknowledge and celebrate oppositions. They create spaces for deliberation and the development of strategies for contesting existing injustices. They fuse reflection and action to unite theory and practice. They claim spaces for the production of new ways of knowing and new ways of being. A strategic concept like accompaniment is coproduced both by the conjuncture in which it appears and the people who envision and enact it (Callahan 2016, 260).

The social divisions that Archbishop Romero sought to redress through accompaniment were not merely matters of economic inequality. People from different walks of life have different skills, different speech patterns, and different problem-solving strategies. These impediments to understanding and cooperation can become strengths for social movements because they require reckoning with who people actually are, not who activists wish them to be. Working together entails a sometimes painfully slow process of learning from each other, of working hard to forge mutually beneficial relations and relationships. The thoughts, ideas, histories, archives, and imaginaries of aggrieved people are excised from education, popular culture, and political discourse almost as relentlessly and effectively as are the oppressed people themselves. Envisioning the work that needs to be done in the world through the lens of accompaniment, organizing it around the preferential option for the poor, the shunned, and the silenced, and establishing insubordinate spaces where it can take place have the potential to produce new knowledge forged from seemingly unlikely alliances, associations, affiliations, conversations, and coalitions.

Improvisation

Spaces designed for subordination are structured in dominance. They are almost always well equipped and well funded. Their routines are carefully choreographed to promote stability and predictability. Armies, police forces, courts, jails, advertising campaigns, entertainment venues, and corporate and government bureaucracies revolve around rules, regulations, and routines. They appear to be permanent and monumental. Insubordinate spaces, however, are ephemeral and fugitive. They are forged in furtive ways on the fly and revolve around the unexpected and the unpredictable. Inside them, people cultivate collective capacities for cocreation.

As a term of art describing a form of expressive culture in the Western tradition, "improvisation" denotes a spontaneous unplanned performance without a script. In the popular imagination, it is often conceived of as an art based on the unleashing of private and personal impulses and desires, as an expression of self that is indifferent to any social conventions or obligations. Inside insubordinate spaces, however, improvisation is a quintessentially social activity: a practice that requires working in concert with others through careful listening, responding, and collaborating. As has been demonstrated over and over again in the work of the International Institute for Critical Studies in Improvisation (IICSI) headquartered at the University of Guelph in Ontario, improvisation entails *responding to what came before* and *anticipating responses that will follow.*[7] The word "response" has etymological roots in the word "responsibility." It connotes being morally and socially accountable. In order to respond, one needs to hear, to see, to acknowledge someone else empathetically and then to contribute something new that invites others to respond in turn (Fischlin, Heble, and Lipsitz 2013, 239). The improvisers, investigators, and community artists associated with the IICSI have discovered that improvisation can take place in unexpected places: in hospital operating rooms when surgical teams find that an operation does not proceed exactly as the medical textbooks predict, in airplane cockpits where pilots have to adjust to unexpected conditions, in courtrooms where judge's rulings and witness testimony require a change in course, in political campaigns and social movement mobilizations when unexpected developments require changes in tactics and strategies, and in classrooms when the order and logic of lesson plans clashes with the plural, diverse, fragmented, and ungainly dimensions of students' lives and levels of classroom engagement (Heble 2017).

As a pedagogical, epistemological, and political practice inside insubordinate spaces, improvisation opens doors to a way of life grounded in the promotion of possibility. It is a device for turning passive victims of circumstance into active agents of emancipation and a form of alchemy that transforms poison into medicine and humiliation into honor. Imaginative and innovative artists and educators Lisa Hirmer and Elizabeth Jackson view the active process of improvisation as a mechanism for revealing barriers and interrupting habits, a form of heightened consciousness that combats the human tendency to become trapped inside routine and convention. Improvisation creates new options by revealing possibilities that already exist but have gone unrecognized (Hirmer and Jackson 2016).

Improvisation can make people alert, active, and empathetic. It assumes that ensembles can do more together than their members can do alone. It encourages participants to discern difficulties quickly and shift course creatively. It challenges people to bring out the best in each other. Perhaps most important, it proceeds from the premise that human will and human work can transform the world. Musician and arts administrator Nicole Mitchell explains in response to a poem written about her by Kalamu ya Salaam that improvisers "take blankness or nothingness and create a combination of what's familiar and what's unknown, or what's never existed before, with creativity." Mitchell sees this process as especially important for members of oppressed and aggrieved social groups whose suffering makes them always susceptible to existential despair. She argues that as a practice, improvisation "allows you not to be focused on the smallness of who you are and your reality, but to actually experience the greatness of possibility and surprise and spontaneity" (quoted in Fischlin, Heble, and Lipsitz 2013, 37).

Malcolm X identified improvisation as a political practice that prepares people to imagine and enact new social relations and new social realities. Speaking at the Audubon Ballroom in Harlem at the founding meeting of the Organization of Afro-American Unity on June 28, 1963, he drew a distinction between musicians who play notes as they are written on the score and those who improvise. The musician who reads music can play well, Minister Malcolm conceded, but only what has been played before. The musician who improvises, on the other hand, plays something never before heard, something created anew in that moment. Drawing a parallel between musical and political creativity, Malcolm proposed that the organization being founded that day should improvise and come up with a "philosophy nobody has heard of yet" and "invent a society, a social system, an economic system, a political system, that is different from anything else that exists or has ever existed anywhere on this earth" (Malcolm X 1992, 63–64, quoted in Guralnick 2005, 537). New conditions require new solutions. Improvisation entails a shared process of agency and accountability through which those solutions can be discovered.

The Middle Run

Accompaniment and improvisation appear in this book as tactics for what Immanuel Wallerstein describes as the temporality of the middle run. Creating insubordinate spaces does not necessarily win immediate improvements in living conditions, nor does it provide a blueprint for a perfect future society. It entails the application of middle-range theory to a middle-range temporality. Wallerstein's notion of "middle-run" temporality (2008) along with Stuart Hall's discussion of "middle-level" theory (1986) points the way toward a framework for considering how struggles for insubordinate spaces can produce new possibilities in these intemperate times. Gramsci's concept of hegemony is also helpful in understanding how practices of cultural persuasion lie at the heart of what Henry Giroux calls "neoliberalism as a public pedagogy" (2005) and how the pedagogies that create the neoliberal subject can be analyzed, explained, and countered.

Wallerstein argues that many disputes about political principles and policies are often actually evidence of differences about which temporality is the most important strategically. He explains that most people's attention necessarily focuses on the short run ("what most people think of as life" [2008, 51]), which always requires compromise. In the short run, people fighting for social justice always have to choose the lesser of competing evils. The various arguments raised about the short run thus tend to focus on what constitutes the appropriate compromise.[8] Strategies and moves for the short run can be effective in some ways, especially by interrupting projects of domination. During this decade mass mobilizations and mass demonstrations have given voice to broad popular support for public education in Puerto Rico (Sassen 2010) and for collective bargaining rights for workers in Wisconsin (Davey and Greenhouse 2011). Focused community campaigns have struggled to make equitable high-quality public education available to all in Chicago (Lipman 2011) and to fight against the privatization of public education in Los Angeles (Lippe-Klein and Hendy 2011). Occupy and #BlackLivesMatter have brought affinity politics and direct action protests out into the streets of scores of cities. Yet for Wallerstein, short-run projects, while necessary, are never sufficient because ultimately they can do very little to reverse the overall alignments of power. Arguments about short-term tactics and goals will all be about what compromises must be made.

Frustrations with the co-optation involved in short-term struggles make a long-term perspective appealing. Long-term efforts address a more distant temporality. Activists, artists, and academics focused on the long run can present powerful and important critiques of the origins and evolution of racialized capitalism, of neoliberal proclivities for both exploiting and occluding social identities of race, sex, and gender, and of neoliberalism's perverse propensity for channeling desires for freedom into practices that promote violence, exploitation, and oppression (Goldberg 2009; Reddy 2011; Valdes and Cho 2011). These long-term analyses do important and necessary work.

Some of these projects attempt to sketch out a utopian blueprint for a distant future where the plurality of identities that now define us might interact more justly, humanely, and creatively. In the long run, a changed world system will emerge eventually from the current systemic crises. But Wallerstein argues that the outcome of these crises is probably impervious to our debates about the nature of utopic futures, and "is not in any fashion inevitable" (2008, 61).[9] Unfortunately, the long term, where the most meaningful changes are likely to be made, lies beyond our grasp at the present. The pieces needed for long-term change are not yet in place. We are not yet the people we will need to be to build a genuinely democratic and egalitarian society. Moreover, emphasis on grand theory can direct attention away from the immanent contradictions of contemporary society out of which new ways of knowing and being might arise. It can deny agency to the oppressed and promote an instrumentalism that tends to view people as abstractions, as tools for realizing theoretical goals rather than valuing theory as a way to meet the desires and interests of people. As Doris Sommer and Pauline Strong astutely point out, we have much to learn from Friedrich Schiller, who wrote his *Letters on the Aesthetic Education of Man* in 1794 during the French Revolution because he believed an emancipatory educational practice was needed "to slow theorists down, because theory had run amuck by becoming impatient with the syncopated rhythm of human progress" (Sommer and Strong 2016, 67).

Wallerstein argues that short- and long-term projects need to be supplemented by work in the middle term; that is, by patient and practical political and pedagogical work in the mid-range temporality of the next ten to twenty years. According to Wallerstein, the potentially "unsavory" compromises necessary for the short run are inappropriate for the middle run. Since the construction of a "more democratic and more egalitarian world-system" is not yet possible in the middle run, our actions must point resolutely in that direction (2008, 61). According to Wallerstein:

> It is the middle run where the significant action concerning a left agenda is located . . . The middle run involves a combination of continuous preparatory work (what is called political education) and constant pressures on the powerful (what is called the construction of movements) with a deep patience about seeing the fruition of all this work. Gramsci's famous slogan, "pessimism of the intellect, optimism of the will" is exactly right. For the optimism pushes us to engage in what the pessimism tells us often seems to be and sometimes really is a Sisyphean task. (2008, 53–54)

The rewards of work in the middle run may not be immediate nor the outcome guaranteed. But without our work in the middle run, Wallerstein argues, the new world system may well be worse: "What we can do is to *make possible* the multiple political activities that will end up *tilting the balance against* a richer, better organized, and far less virtuous group—those who wish to maintain or even reinforce another variant of the hierarchical, polarizing systems we have had heretofore" (2008, 61, emphasis added).

People seeking alternatives to disciplinary subordination can use the middle-range temporality of the next two decades to develop practices, processes, and institutions promoting popular ability to participate in processes of democratic deliberation, mutual recognition, and collective accountability. Teachers and students can counter the classroom and public pedagogies of neoliberal racial capitalism by cultivating new methods of inquiry and new social relations of knowledge. Insubordinate spaces in the classroom can be crucibles for radically revising existing understandings of teaching and learning, of reading and writing, and of citizenship and social membership. At the same time, equity-oriented, collaborative community-based research where scholars do not simply study *about* community groups but instead study *with* them can help develop democratic knowledge projects that are useful to people in struggle, while offering scholars access to previously occluded archives, imaginaries, epistemologies, and ontologies. Thinking in terms of the middle run allows us to teach ourselves and others to exploit the fissures and fractures available to us. Wallerstein reminds us that the outcome of the struggle has not been foreclosed, but there is still much to do. Stuart Hall argues that for people in power, "hegemonizing is hard work" (1988, quoted in Lipsitz 2001, 272). Yet dehegemonizing is hard work, too.

Emphasizing middle-level temporality connects fruitfully with thinking in terms of middle-level theory. In his analysis of Gramsci's relevance for the study of race and ethnicity, Hall explains the value of middle-level abstraction in "complexifying existing theories and problems" by connecting large concepts to specific situations (1986, 5). Gramsci's immersion in the everyday struggles of the working class in Italy during and after World War I led him to adapt Marxist grand theory to "another more concrete, 'lower' level of operation" (Hall 1986, 7). Moving to the middle level enabled Gramsci to appreciate the segmented and fragmented nature of the working class and the composite qualities of individuals. He came to see power as dispersed across the entire social field and embedded in the quotidian activities of life. He rejected the short-term view of revolution as a single event through which the state should be smashed or seized as well as the long-term evolutionary view of revolution as the inevitable outcome of the crises built into capitalism. Instead, Gramsci came to argue for a middle-range, protracted "war of position" to be waged across many different sites. Activism plays a central role in Gramsci's analysis because people are subordinated not just by the physical force of the state and the philosophical core of reigning ideas and identities but also by the organic presence of those ideas in their everyday lives. Gramsci argues that the plurality of selves inside any given identity is a collective rather than an individual phenomenon and that aggrieved and insurgent subjects are not *found* but rather *forged* through concrete contestations against the institutions of civil society and the state. Rather than focusing on ideal and abstract schematic formulations about what identities should be, middle-level theorizing attends to concrete struggles over what identities are now and what they are capable of becoming.

The Way You Do the Things You Do: *Konesans* and *Balans*

Even the most well-intentioned actions of accompaniment will fail if they do not include preparation for complex and contradictory realities and if they do not infuse ideas and activism with ethical judgment and wisdom. Good intentions do not guarantee good results. Being against bad things does not make people good. Opposing the social relations of this society does not automatically qualify someone to establish a new society. In life, the right thing can look like the wrong thing and the wrong thing can look like the right thing. What seems like righteousness can merely be self-righteousness in disguise. Seeming victories can really be defeats; defeats can set the stage for future successes.

For those reasons, accompaniment needs to be suffused with *konesans* and *balans*.[10] The brilliant and generative work of Haitian studies scholars Patrick Bellegarde-Smith and Claudine Michel explains that *konesans* and *balans* are important ways of knowing and being (2013). In the ways of knowing attached to the practices of vodou and their influence on the democratic Lavalas movement in Haiti in the late 1980s and early 1990s, *konesans* expresses the understanding that knowledge is more than a matter of mastering skills, facts, and theories. It connotes degrees of discernment, empathy, and judgment that lead to genuine wisdom, qualities gained with age and shaped from respect for people who have walked the path before. Mastery of *konesans* requires that people not only place proximate events in a broader perspective as a historian might do but also acknowledge *the pull of the past on the present*, recognizing the lifetime of indebtedness that individuals have to the suffering, struggle, and sacrifice of ancestors and elders. The worlds in which we work were here before we showed up at the scene, and they will be here after we leave it. Ancestral experiences and epistemologies from the past can be part of the present. People cannot "will" themselves to be outside of history, to disavow its negative or positive impacts, or to escape the responsibilities it requires. By itself, however, *konesans* is not enough; it needs to be infused with the quality of *balans*.

Balans holds that everyone has a part of the truth, that people's weaknesses come from many of the same sources as their strengths, and that the truth and the lie—or the right thing and the wrong thing—are often not mutually incommensurable opposites but instead different poles of a dialogically and dialectically connected unity. The moral judgment cultivated by the concept of *balans* cannot be reduced to a set of rules to follow. Moral excellence comes from *reconciling* opposites rather than *choosing* between them. It emerges from appreciating differences and embracing contradictions. *Balans* demands knowing and honoring history but not being bound by its limitations; being open to new things but not contemptuous of the past; listening to the arguments of enemies and recognizing why they seem plausible to their exponents without surrendering the necessity to struggle to make right things come to pass. Just as with *konesans*, where wisdom amounts to more than accumulating facts, through *balans* morality consists of more than simply avoiding evil. *Konesans* and *balans* require discernment, deliberation, and constant decision-making. Like the physicians of antiquity who recognized that the same things that cause diseases can be used to cure them, thinkers deploying *konesans* and *balans* understand that things that can kill can also cure; poisons can be medicines when they are used in the right ways.

When analyzed through the lens of *balans*, the polar opposites of domination and resistance, optimism and pessimism, contemplation and action become dialogic and dialectically related aspects of the same reality. Paula Ioanide (2011) argues for a kind of politics capable of recognizing these relationships by using a metaphor of two mirrors to describe the work that responsible political engagement requires.[11] The first mirror held up to society reflects all the injustice, inequality, brutality, exploitation, and dehumanization in the world. This mirror shows people what the dominant culture rarely admits: that the advantages, wealth, and opportunities of the comfortable classes are stained with blood and originate in oppression.

Many people shown that mirror will feel compelled to look away in shame and guilt: some because they identify with the oppressor, and others because they fear being identified with the oppressed and being forced to share their suffering. People repulsed by the hurts and horrors of history may seek self-respect by declaring their opposition, yet they can become so fixated on resisting the images in that mirror that they unconsciously echo and imitate them. They can become obsessed with power and behave just like their enemies in the process of attempting to combat them. Still others will be paralyzed by fear and overwhelmed by their own inadequacy to comprehend fully much less contest effectively the injustices they now see in the world.

Yet Ioanide says that there is another mirror that we can hold up that reflects a parallel reality. Just when everyone starts feeling like the system is too big and too powerful to overcome, just when people start thinking "what's the point of resisting anyway—things are never going to change?" the second mirror appears on the scene to reflect the long legacies of struggle against oppression, of irrepressible attempts at autonomy, self-determination, interdependency, and freedom dreaming. Through this mirror, we see that cultural and political expressions produced in the spaces occupied by aggrieved communities are often vibrant and generative places where models of being and thinking crucial to the survival and dignity of all are nurtured and sustained. Ioanide's second mirror resembles what EZLN activists call the mirror of dignity. In this mirror, people see themselves as equals and they become rebels if they are not treated as such (Marcos 2005, 150). Creating insubordinate spaces demands that we use both mirrors: the one that shows the hard facts and occluded realities that the dominant culture covers up, and also the one that shows that people long for freedom and desire democracy. The second mirror helps us see what Ernst Bloch termed the "Not-Yet-Conscious," the emancipatory and utopian hopes that lie embedded inside even the most reactionary elements of hegemonic culture (Bloch 1995, especially 114–177).

Many people committed to social justice will be eager to hold up that first mirror but have no interest in the second. They are ready to scorn tradition but reluctant to embrace the traditions of the scorned.[12] They are fearful of what Seth Moglen calls "the torment of hope" (2007, especially 175–218). They are eager to "not get fooled again," so they propel themselves through life by feeding off the fuel of radical negativity. They feel what Raymond Williams discerned in the 1920s work of Berthold Brecht: "a raw chaotic resentment, a hurt so deep it requires new hurting, a sense of outrage which demands that people be outraged" (1999, 100). It is understandable that people feel this way. This disposition emanates from a courageous willingness to stare into the abyss, from a refusal to believe lies, and from well-warranted suspicions that things will not get better. It resonates with Walter Benjamin's claim that "there is no document of civilization which is not at the same time a document of barbarism," and his observation in the wake of the rise of fascism that the "tradition of the oppressed teaches us that the 'state of emergency' in which we live is not the exception but the rule" (1968, 256, 257).

Radical negativity takes courage. It can fuel a strong sense of commitment. Left to itself, however, it expresses what Ernst Bloch calls "half-enlightenment." It recognizes the need to denounce and destroy, but it ignores the responsibility to construct and create. It overestimates the pervasiveness of alienation, anger, and anomie. It runs the risk of turning despair into an aesthetic pleasure—into the only affect by which the self is legible. It cultivates a combination of outrage and pessimism that is of little utility to suffering people whose survival struggles do not afford them the luxury of resignation (Sommer 2014, 93). It can, in fact, create a contempt for aggrieved people and their communities that precludes the possibility of learning with them and from them.

Michel Foucault explains how the radical negativity that enables honest acknowledgment of all that is wrong with the world need not lead to political paralysis. "My point is not that everything is bad," he argues, "but that everything is dangerous, which is not exactly the same as bad." The ubiquity of danger, from this perspective, means that people always have meaningful work to do. Rejecting an either/or binary choice between resigned apathy and naive activism, Foucault instead calls for "a hyper and pessimistic activism" that requires recognition each and every day of what at that moment is the main danger (Foucault 1984, 231–232).

Holding up Ioanide's second mirror is vital for infusing life with *konesans* and *balans*. This mirror reveals tools for transformation. It displays the wide array of actions, analyses, and ideas that enable people to exist and resist under conditions they do not control. It reminds us that while power and privilege often seem impregnable, they can collapse in the face of bold contestation and the cumulative consequences of their internal contradictions. Yet looking *only* into this second mirror has its own problems. It can produce unrealistic expectations and unproductive actions, induce unwarranted optimism about the ease with which meaningful change can be made, and lead artists, activists, and academics to incite struggles before they can actually be won, leaving participants depressed, defeated, and deprived of self-respect. The optimism inspired by the second mirror can make people oblivious to the full damage done by hierarchy and exploitation and the many steps needed to try to undo it. Accompaniment requires looking into both mirrors adequately and appropriately. What they reveal needs to be assessed in the spirit of *konesans* and *balans* with an equal blend of "pessimism of the intellect and optimism of the will."[13]

Standing at the Crossroads

In this book, we identify and analyze a wide range of projects of accompaniment and improvisation at scenes of argument. Grasping their full significance requires recognition of the specific historical, social, and economic crises that they emerge from and speak to. The systemic breakdown of major social structures and institutions compels people around the world to resist the unlivable destinies to which they have been consigned. The neoliberal conjuncture of the present that we discuss in later chapters is a crossroads where collisions constantly occur. It is at a crossroads, however, where it is possible to look productively in more than one direction, to make moral and political decisions that lead to new destinations.

Without a strong conscious counterculture to combat them, fear and hate will remain at the center of the ways in which people experience the world. The emotional charge of fear inhibits the imagination of alternatives. It functions to justify the most vile and violent feelings and actions. It leads people to cultivate degrees of contempt, callousness, and cruelty that make hierarchy and exploitation seem natural, necessary, and inevitable. Yet fear can also be a source of knowledge and an impetus for action. Accompaniment can be an antidote to fear and a crucible for the emergence of people capable of creating a different kind of world.

Archbishop Romero developed his ideas about accompaniment in the midst of a violent revolutionary situation that led him to profound political, personal, and pedagogical transformations made possible by working alongside peasants. For most of his life he had been a conservative cleric who defended the privileges of the wealthy and feared social upheaval. Yet he changed dramatically when he decided that his ministry compelled him to accompany the poor as they walked through life. By traveling the road with them, he came to see things differently. Peasants shared their experiences with Romero and asked him to stand up for them. His willingness to listen led to a great change. "I've often been accused of consulting with too many people," he said. "But that's the nicest thing anyone could accuse me of, and I don't intend to mend my ways" (Vigil 2000, 3). Listening to the peasants enabled Romero to see things differently. Accompanying them in their struggles transformed him completely. He explained to his friend Father César Jerez that it was as if a piece of charcoal had been lit inside him. Charcoal can be difficult to light. It can fail to catch fire several times before it ignites. Even when lit, it is not always evident that it still burns. Yet once it has been kindled, "you don't have to blow on it much to get it to flame up again," Romero observed (Vigil 2000, 159). Thinking only about the short run can produce what is known in El Salvador as *llamarada de petate*, a flash in the pan, a fire that appears dramatically but quickly burns out. Thinking about the middle run requires a fire that smolders, that might have fewer flames and less intense heat, yet is made to last.

There are many things we cannot do, cannot change, and cannot influence. The years ahead will be difficult. Yet indignities, injustices, and indecent social conditions of our time will not change without a fight. The practices of accompaniment and improvisation informed by *konesans* and *balans* inside the temporality of the middle run can make a difference. Nobody can do everything, but everybody can do something. Our work can be like igniting a piece of charcoal. It will be a slow, painstaking, difficult, and often frustrating endeavor. But once the charcoal is lit, it will last for a long time, burn hot, spread warmth, shed light, and flare up powerfully at the slightest breeze.

3 / IDLE NO MORE

During the winter of 2012–2013, Indigenous people and their supporters across Canada and around the world launched a series of nonviolent, peaceful, yet sometimes deliberately obstructive direct action protests that coalesced around the slogan "Idle No More."[1] Sparked by opposition to legislation proposed by the federal government that would weaken environmental protections and accelerate resource extraction, a mass movement by Indigenous people and their allies grew into a wide-ranging critique of coloniality and its destructive intellectual, economic, environmental, and social effects. As a movement for Indigenous survivance and sovereignty, as well as for social and environmental justice, Idle No More called for systemic changes in relations between different groups of people as well as changes in relations between humans and the environment.

Both a specific social movement with concrete short-run goals and a manifestation of a broader decolonial awakening focused on building collective democratic capacity for the middle run, Idle No More mobilized Indigenous, Métis, and Inuit people from rural reserves and urban enclaves to march on city streets and provincial highways, to stage round dances inside shopping malls, to establish an encampment on Parliament Hill, to block automobile traffic on urban bridges and rail shipments on rural train tracks, to conduct teach-ins, to form study groups, and to revive traditional languages and cultural practices (Wotherspoon and Hansen 2013, 23). On one single day alone in December 2012, the movement engaged in seventy-nine different actions across Canada (Wood 2015, 619). In forty below zero weather in Denendeh in the Northwest Territories, drummers and dancers joyfully congregated on the road to block traffic on the Deh Cho Bridge (Allooloo 2014, 194). Attawapiskat First Nation Chief Theresa Spence occupied a tipi on Victoria Island near Parliament Hill in Ottawa where she confined her food intake to one cup of fish broth in the morning and one cup at night to protest the government's indifference to the poverty and hunger its policies produced on her nation's land.[2] By putting her life on the line for the cause, Chief Spence dramatized the urgency of being idle no more. Her protest deployed symbolic and semiotic elements in a dramatic way, distilling and crystallizing a collective understanding of a larger reality. As attorney and Mi'kmaw citizen Pamela Palmater observed at one point during the six weeks that Chief Spence ingested only small quantities of water, lemon, and fish broth, "For every day that Spence does not eat, she is slowly dying, and that is exactly what is happening to First Nations, who have lifespans up to 20 years shorter than average Canadians" (Palmater 2014, 40). In a deft recognition of the appropriate symbols deployed by Chief Spence's fast, Mississauga Nishnaabeg writer Leanne Betasamosake Simpson noted, "Chief Spence is eating fish broth because metaphorically, colonialism has kept Indigenous Peoples on a fish broth diet for generations upon generations" (L. Simpson 2014, 155). That diet has been shaped by dispossession and deprivation, but it also evidences the resourcefulness of Indigenous improvisation. As Anishinaabe legal scholar Deborah McGregor points out, fish broth comprises more than a base substance ingested out of necessity. It provides an economical, efficient, and enjoyable source of calcium in communities that historically did not drink milk.[3] Fish broth thus functioned as a multiaccented sign in Indigenous life, as a symbol of both cruel deprivation and creative improvisation.

Idle No More started with a single teach-in organized in Saskatoon, Saskatchewan, by three Indigenous women—Sylvia McAdam Saysewahum (Nehiyaw), Jess Gordon (Pasqua), and Nina Wilson (Nakota and Nehiyaw)—along with a nonnative antiracist activist ally, Sheelah McLean. Their act of accompaniment sought to mobilize opposition to Bill C-45, introduced in the federal Parliament by the ruling Conservative Party. A 457-page revision of existing laws, the bill was designed to reduce environmental protections for rivers and lakes and to make it easier for corporations to extract resources from First Nation reserve lands (Coulthard 2014, 160). In practice, even the already existing environmental laws weakened

FIGURE 3.1. Demonstration in support of Idle No More in Toronto, Ontario, January 11, 2013. (*Victor Biro / Alamy Stock Photo*)

by C-45 did very little to serve the interests of Indigenous peoples (John 2015, 41). However, the new legislation, titled the Jobs and Growth Act, was a decided insult. It was formulated without even consulting with First Nations, much less securing their consent. It altered some sixty-four different regulations and laws in a comprehensive assault on environmental protection (Graveline 2012, 293). The proposed new laws would increase resource extraction throughout Canada by removing environmental protections from waterways and allowing greater leasing of land on reserves and unceded Indigenous territory by oil, gas, and mining corporations (John 2015, 413; Kino-nda-niimi Collective 2014b, 21). Bill C-45 reduced the number of protected lakes, rivers, and ocean waters in Canada from 2.6 million to a mere 87 (LaDuke 2014, 143). The policies promoted by the legislation threatened both the natural environment and the sovereignty and survival of First Nations.

Insubordinate Spaces and Accompaniment

Assembling together in a loose coalition featuring decentralized and decidedly nonhierarchical leadership, what began as a mobilization *against* legislation proposed in Parliament soon became a broader movement *for* the dignity, survivance, and self-determination of Indigenous, Métis, and Inuit peoples. It evolved eventually into a fundamental challenge to colonial institutions and knowledge systems. Unlike social movements led by a single charismatic leader or those organized around the disciplined ideology and agreed upon demands of a core vanguard group, Idle No More emerged organically and unevenly from many different acts of improvisation and accompaniment. Palmater noted the novelty of a political movement that was "not led by any elected politician, national chief or paid executive director" (Coulthard 2014, 162). Simpson identified the "bottom up" nature of the movement as its greatest strength because it drew on the collective energy, imagination, and insights of "hundreds of eloquent spokespeople, seasoned organizers, writers, thinkers and artists acting on their ideas in any way and every way possible" (Coulthard 2014, 162).

Social media served as an important insubordinate site for Idle No More. Announcements on Facebook and Twitter invited people to participate in flash mobs at strategic sites. Online videos conveyed the words and ideas of previously unknown activists to a mass audience. Live streaming and video footage of demonstrations became models for subsequent protests. Online postings created a kind of continuous town meeting in virtual space among participants who might have never been able to meet in person. Off-line, a plethora of face-to-face deliberations, public teach-ins, and private study groups generated and circulated ideas, evidence, and arguments that gradually gained traction among movement participants. The spectacles staged in insubordinate spaces by the movement sought distributive justice in the form of concrete reforms, but they also pursued procedural justice by envisioning and enacting new kinds of social relations. Anishinaabe activist Lori Mainville emphasized the radical nature of the protest movement, pointing to its "relational reciprocity of speaking, listening, and witnessing as a group" (2014, 345).

Social movement mobilizations often offer opportunities for improvisation by people dissatisfied with the status quo and eager for change. Idle No More activist Jenna Wirch was one of those people. A young social service worker for the Aboriginal Youth Opportunities engagement and empowerment project in Winnipeg, Wirch started attending Idle No More protests but generally just listened to speeches by others. One day she grabbed a megaphone and, as she recalls, "just started yelling off facts about Bill C-45, water, and what we were resisting." Her boldness energized the crowd, and soon she spoke up at other rallies. Wirch became known as The Megaphone Girl. Her example provoked other young people to step up and speak out.

"I think me doing that, standing up, really helped other young people," she asserts. "I think it was like, it's okay, there's a young Aboriginal woman, and she isn't afraid to speak up! If that person can do it then why can't I?" (Wirch 2014, 170). Live streaming and videos spread Wirch's message all around the world, enabling others, especially young Indigenous women, to emulate her.

The new forms of political accompaniment that emerged through struggle drew upon old lessons learned from traditional Indigenous land-based activism derived from political sovereignty. Indigenous youths confronted by a school curriculum that marginalized and demeaned them, by a political system that suppressed them, and by a culture industry that acknowledged their existence only through caricatures, turned to traditional Indigenous singing and dancing as exhilarating forms of collective action and as activities where lessons passed down through history could be learned, lessons very different from the ones taught by the social pedagogies of the state and the corporate media. These young people viewed themselves as both contemporary and traditional at the same time.[4] They were hungry for new ways of thinking and new ways of being inside insubordinate spaces but also eager to reconnect with ancestral wisdom. "What Idle No More . . . reveals," Tracy Friedel observed, "is a thirst among Indigenous youths for a place-based pedagogy premised on learning from the land, in the manner of one's Ancestors, as facilitated by Elders and community knowledge holders" (Friedel 2015, 880). That thirst, and the exhilaration in sating it, permeates Jenna Wirch's description of her trajectory as an activist. Crediting rituals and ceremonies with giving her a foundation for her new understanding of the work she needs to do in the world, she confides, "The teachings that come with the drum really opened my eyes to what was really going on around me. . . . When singing those songs," she explains, "you are healing and praying to the ancestors for happiness and good health. Since I've come to know that my life has become better. Not better financially, but my self-identity as a person has been better than any other time in my life" (Wirch 2014, 169).

The improvised insubordinate spaces created by Idle No More exemplified the ideals of accompaniment. They drew differentially situated people together to work for common goals. The participants in Idle No More came from different nations. They spoke different languages, lived on different kinds of territory, and practiced different spiritualties. They included in their numbers the young and the old, the affluent and the indigent, the abled and the disabled. Some came from reserves while others lived in cities. When they joined together in demonstrations, marches, and nonviolent direct action blockades on roads and railroad tracks, however, their differences suddenly seemed small compared to the similarities that bonded them. They assembled and congregated not as members of a single sectarian organization adhering to a single ideology but through a common commitment to action, to be Idle No More.

The energy and imagination of the movement attracted allies, advocates, and accompaniers from settler society. Canadians of many different identities found common cause in Idle No More as followers, supporters, and participants in a movement guided by Indigenous ideas and aspirations. An impressive group of distinguished artists, writers, musicians, dancers, and filmmakers issued a strong statement of solidarity with Idle No More (Canadian Artists Statement 2014, 278–285). More than two thousand university professors from diverse institutions and disciplines signed an open letter to Canadian prime minister Stephen Harper and governor general David Johnston (Kino-nda-niimi Collective 2014b, 394). They called on the government to respond to Chief Theresa Spence's hunger strike, to meet with her in person, and to devise a comprehensive plan of work to address the needs of Aboriginal communities (Academics in Solidarity 2014, 230–233). The Canadian Union of Postal Workers issued a statement honoring Chief Spence, condemning the Canadian state's policies as abusive and indefensible. The union pledged to defend the sovereignty and inherent right of First Nations peoples to resources and lands (Canadian Union of Postal Workers 2014, 225–226). Idle No More garnered public statements of support from the National Farmers Union, Greenpeace, and the Canadian Nurses Association (Kino-nda-niimi Collective 2014b, 402). Three physical geographers published an article in a professional journal announcing their intention to be "Idle No More" about their discipline's evasion of the ways in which the physical places they study were culturally produced by colonialism. They proposed that future research on the physical geography of Indigenous landscapes be conducted in dialogue with Indigenous peoples and with respect for their ways of knowing, especially in respect to "the ethical and/or relational sensitivities they have towards non-human subjects and how we, as (still largely non-Indigenous researchers), can accommodate them" (Kershaw, Castleden, and Laroque 2014, 395).

Well-intentioned acts of accompaniment can easily go awry. Centuries of colonial practice do not provide good preparation for decolonial actions. Some of the support secured by Idle No More from settler allies failed to come to grips with the importance of treaty rights and sovereignty, focusing instead exclusively on single-axis elements of the movement such as its anticorporate, feminist, or environmental dimensions. The inclusionary emphasis of past and present antiracist civil rights struggles led some supporters to frame their activity largely as extending full rights to other Canadians rather than honoring the nation-to-nation relations and affirmative declarations of autonomy and sovereignty by First Nations. Settler ignorance about the diversity of Indigenous peoples sometimes led to describing them as a monolithic group (Gilio-Whitaker 2015, 868). Moreover, some commitments proved to be ephemeral. Some allies galvanized by the excitement of round dances and demonstrations disappeared from the scene once the movement faced the even more daunting challenge of applying its new understandings to solving the everyday life problems of Indigenous peoples.

Yet the uneven and ungainly practices of accompaniment had a profound influence on settler society. The movement offered some settler Canadians opportunities to augment their already existing goals of defending the environment, protesting rapacious capitalism, opposing sexism and assaults against women, and, as well, attempting to cleanse the national conscience by acknowledging and atoning for mistreatment of First Nations. The processes of struggle brought forth new knowledge. For example, challenges to the racist assumptions at the core of federal Indian policy provoked some European, Asian, and Latin American immigrants to Canada (and their descendants) to develop a deeper understanding of the ways in which the justifications for Indigenous dispossession had laid the foundation for Canada's subsequent racialized treatment of immigrants and refugees. Some members of aggrieved groups discerned distinct families of resemblance between their histories and those of Indigenous groups. Writer, poet, and Stó:lō Nation member Lee Maracle noted the ways in which Idle No More crystallized and deepened long-standing affinities and alliances between Indigenous people and Palestinian Canadians. The Idle No More movement made the links between the two peoples clearer because of their similar yet not identical experiences with colonization, exploitation, and displacement.

The global reach and scope of environmentally damaging resource extraction activities, and the solidarity expressed with the movement by environmentalist and Indigenous activists around the world, enabled Idle No More to seek international as well as national solutions to the problems it identified. A call for an International Day of Action in January 2013 produced 265 simultaneous rallies around the world. By the end of that month, supporters of the movement had organized demonstrations, rallies, and round dances in Australia, Bulgaria, Chile, Finland, France, Germany,

India, Mexico, New Zealand, Sri Lanka, Sweden, the United Kingdom, and the United States (Gilio-Whitaker 2015, 868; Kino-nda-niimi Collective 2014b, 395, 403). Idle No More activists called for all the people of the Earth to face up to environmental devastation, to the material and social costs of unbridled materialism, and to the need to establish new relationships with other humans. The upheaval underscored the degree to which the alienation of humans from what settler society calls "nature" also entails people's alienation from one another. Beyond its immediate goals and demands, however, Idle No More also appealed to non-Indigenous sympathizers because its values stood in sharp contrast to the values, priorities, and reigning ideas of racialized neoliberal capitalism. The tactics and strategies deployed by the movement created a participatory public life much richer than that allowed in the realms of corporate-dominated electoral politics. The solidarity, mutuality, and equality experienced in mass mobilizations contrasted sharply with the competitive individualism promoted by neoliberal institutions.

Improvisation and Accompaniment

The importance of improvisation and accompaniment within Idle No More manifested itself most powerfully through the movement's tactical deployment of the round dance as an insubordinate space. Staged in shopping malls and on city streets, the round dance became an improvised form of performative and prefigurative accompaniment. It enacted in real space and time the solidarity that the movement's politics envisioned. In round dances, circles of demonstrators with linked hands move their feet and bodies in rhythm together in a clockwise shuffle, raising one pair of clasped hands and then the other. Linked hands symbolize and dramatize a linked fate. Within the round dance circle, no one person counts more or less than any other. Round dances made the movement and its demands visible in a way that was not obstructive or destructive. For the dancers from Indigenous communities, the ceremony possessed especially important significance. According to Cree traditions, for example, the round dance is understood as a gift given long ago by a deceased mother's spirit to her grieving daughter. As a ritual practice, it summons the ancestors to accompany the living in ceremonies of initiation, mourning, and celebration (Friedel 2015, 884). Cree elder John Cuthand explains, "When this circle is made we the Ancestors will be dancing with you and we will be as one" (884). In this way, the round dance creates an insubordinate space that transcends the temporality of the present—that proclaims unbreakable bonds among the past, present, and future.

For Idle No More participants, the round dance epitomized the kind of transformative experience that makes social movement activity memorable and meaningful. Tanya Kappo of the Sturgeon Lake Cree Nation recalls, "I remember going to the round dance at the West Edmonton Mall—it was massive—the amount of people who showed up to drum, the people that came to sing and dance or just be there was incredible. The power and energy that was there, it was like we were glowing, our people were glowing. For the first time, I saw a genuine sense of love for each other and for ourselves. Even if it was only momentary it was powerful enough to awaken in them what needed to be woken up—a remembering of who we were, who we are" (2014, 70). Kappo's exhilaration at being part of a people who were "glowing," underscores the role of joy and happiness in social movement work. Formed out of necessity in response to brutally cruel and oppressive conditions, Idle No More requires somber and serious reckoning with hurts of history that cannot be wished away. Yet focusing only on injuries and injustices runs the risk of reducing Indigenous existence solely to a reactive defense against white supremacy. As Oneida writer Roberta Hill declares in one of her most compelling poems, aggrieved people need to insist that the phobic fantasies of their enemies do not define their own identities (Whiteman 1996, 89–91). Joy and happiness can be weapons in the struggle, aids to healing that strengthen self-respect, self-reliance, and resilience (Wirch 2014, 171).

Idle No More performed many different kinds of accompaniment, but the flash mob and the round dance took on especially important significance. Flash mobs relied on an advanced capacity for improvisation, on a collective commitment to be ready to assemble at a common spot on short notice, and to work with others on arrival. The sudden appearance in public of masses of people committed to Indigenous issues, responding to Indigenous leadership, and honoring Indigenous framings of the enduring presence of coloniality transformed ordinary places of everyday life into insubordinate spaces. They made visible the ongoing occupation by settler society on unceded Indigenous lands, the routine abrogation and violation of treaty provisions, and the stark disparity between the riches that flow to oil, gas, and mining firms and the exploitation of the people on whose lands resource extraction takes place.

Idle No More highlighted the material ramifications of coloniality with strategic brilliance by staging improvised round dances at large shopping malls at the height of the Christmas buying season. A demonstration in a public plaza or government building can attract police surveillance and supervision. Participants might be stopped and turned away. Parked cars can be ticketed and their owners can be checked for outstanding warrants. Demonstrators might be dispersed by tear gas and police violence. Mobilizations inside a shopping mall, however, create a different dynamic. Malls are easily accessible, have adequate parking spaces, and police officers and security guards cannot easily distinguish demonstrators from the shoppers whose presence is vital for the profits made inside the stores. Like the sit-down strikers in U.S. factories during the 1930s, demonstrators inside a mall gain a certain measure of protection against violent repression because of their proximity to valuable retail property that would be damaged during a physical attack. Shopping malls also possessed significance as symbols of the materialism and acquisitiveness responsible for Indigenous dispossession. "The shopping malls built on stolen lands have been the epitome of consumerism, of capitalism, and of keeping up with what society deems necessary in obtaining," contends Nina Wilson of the Crooked Lake Agency, Kahkewistahaw First Nation in Southeastern Saskatchewan. Round dances at the malls, she adds, reveal an oppositional consciousness rooted in viewing shopping centers as "part of the game, a manufactured colonial culture that keeps people tied to predatory consumerism, and the illusion of debt" (Wilson 2014, 107–108). Round dances turned shopping malls into venues where Indigenous people could be seen and heard in new ways. Kappo remembers that "the non-Native people at the mall that day, people who were just doing their Christmas shopping, there was nothing they could do. They had no choice but to stop and wonder, and to see us, really see us. And it was amazing" (2014, 70–71).

The dimensions and acoustics of malls make them awkward and inefficient locations for speeches and rallies, but the round dance offers an ingenious alternative. Once inside the mall, the demonstrators join hands, forming enormous circles that span the entire expanse of the atrium, perched on each of the three balconies that tower over the courtyards below. Drummers and singers occupy the open area on the ground floor. As they beat out rhythms and sing songs, the Idle No More activists and allies on the floors above dance in a clockwise direction, shuffling to the left, moving their linked hands, one up and one down. Stunned shoppers stop to watch the spectacle as small banners proclaim the ceremony as part of the Idle No More campaign (Friedel 2015, 884). The round dance brings attention and visibility to a cause that settler society generally values little inside a location that the acquisitive and materialist settler society values very much.

The insubordinate spaces improvised by Idle No More devoted strong attention to how knowledge is produced. The beliefs deployed to justify and excuse Indigenous dispossession do not originate in innocent misunderstandings by isolated uneducated individuals; they are instead the product of narrative fictions needed by settler society to escape accountability for its unjust actions. These fictions create deeply entrenched ways of knowing. They permeate the things that ordinary people think, feel, and believe. Portrayals of Indigenous laziness, corruption, and dependency dominate the discourses of political and popular culture in Canada and all around the world. In order to *make a place* for new social relations and new social structures, Idle No More activists had *to displace* reigning notions of Indigenous inadequacy and incompetence. These ideas circulate on the surface in political discourse and popular culture, but they have deep roots in the ways of knowing ensconced in disciplinary learning and the law. Colonial knowledge makes Indigenous dispossession and deprivation appear to take on an overdetermined inevitability that becomes activated in public policy. As a result, part of the project of Idle No More entailed the invention of oppositional epistemologies and ontologies.

Scholar and Temagami First Nation citizen Dale Turner, analyzing a 2013 poll of Canadian public opinion, found that three-fifths of those polled contended that most of the problems that Indigenous peoples face are their own fault. Two-thirds of respondents stated that "Aboriginal" people get too much financial support from the government (Turner 2014, 120–121). These opinions are not based on either firsthand observation or research. They are not accurate descriptions of Indigenous life and society, nor are they knowledgeable about how much material wealth governments have taken from Indigenous people and how little they provide for them. These opinions are simply more evidence of Indigenous dispossession as a never ended and continually renewed colonial project. In the short run, settler society seeks to void Indigenous titles to the land and promote unlimited resource extraction on it. In the long run, the acquisitive individualism at the heart of the colonial project requires the destruction of all alternative ways of knowing and being. Indigenous beliefs and practices based on the collective and communal coexistence of humans with each other, and with the natural world, challenge the seeming inevitability of settler society's acquisitive individualism. Land-based activism derived from sovereignty proceeds from very different assumptions than the settler system of governance that confines politics to matters of state-supervised personal citizenship.

The impact and appeal of Idle No More stemmed in no small measure from offering to Indigenous people and their allies an opportunity to experience life in ways that were diametrically opposed to the ruling ideas of settler society. The movement sought recognition and resources for Indigenous people, to be sure, but it also affirmed a different view of life in the world rooted in Indigenous practices, a view that Friedel describes deftly as "the notion that the right way to walk involves maintaining good relations among people, between people and the land, and between people and those institutions inherently bestowed with governing powers" (Friedel 2015, 885).

Idle No More discovered that *restoring* Indigenous sovereignty required *restorying* Canada—developing new narratives about the nation's past and present in order to make new social relations plausible and possible. Sheelah McLean explains that "decolonization is a process that requires not only a restorying of our shared history, but a reimagining of our relationships with each other based on respectful solidarity" (2014, 95). Popular education often stood at the center of the restorying project. Métis intellectual and activist Chelsea Vowell asserts that people cannot look to politicians to fix Canada's relationship with its Indigenous peoples—if a better world is to emerge it has to be created by "regular people, dealing with one another as human beings" (2014, 131). As part of that project, Vowell posted online a list of stereotypes and falsehoods about Indigenous people that setter Canadians needed to stop believing. Her post provided concise yet convincing refutations of the myths that Indigenous people get free education and houses, do not work or pay taxes, and face poverty because of internal tribal corruption rather than external exploitation (2014, 131–133).

In a similar vein, journalist and solidarity activist Dru Oja Jay pointed out that the myth of Indigenous dependency stood in stark contrast to the many ways in which settler society profits from exploitation of lands that it has no right to control. Corporations dependent on resource extraction from—and transportation across—Indigenous land in the oil, forestry, mining, and hydroelectric power industries reap revenues and send rich returns to investors, but they offer only minimal compensation to Indigenous peoples. For example, commercial interests extract more than $100 million per year in revenues from the territory of the Algonquins of Barriere Lake, even though no treaty has ever been signed giving up Indigenous rights to the land. Similarly, the Lubicon Cree, who have never signed a treaty or surrendered title to their land, have seen more than $14 billion worth of oil and gas removed from their territory. Many of the Indigenous residents on these lands live in poverty and experience disproportionate disability and premature death because of pervasive pollution and sporadic explosions and spills.

In launching her fast on Victoria Island, Attawapiskat chief Theresa Spence attempted to call attention to the chronic housing crisis facing her people. The community she represents has experienced sewage backups in their homes because of repeated flooding. In an area where subzero temperatures are common, one study found that 85 percent of Attawapiskat housing units were "unfit for human habitation" (A. Simpson 2016, 5). Attawapiskat poverty and deprivation contrast sharply with the wealth extracted from the nearby $1 billion open pit mine that the De Beers Corporation operates. The Impact Benefits Agreement with the Attawapiskat community that allowed the De Beers facility to open was supposed to produce better housing, health care, services, jobs, and recreational facilities. It has not. The mine generated $448.8 million in gross revenues between 2009 and 2011 while the Attawapiskat received only about $2 million per year in revenue (A. Simpson 2016, 5). Significant royalties collected from that mine go to the provincial government but not to the First Nations. Estimates of royalties to be paid to all government bodies in expectation of extraction of oil from tar sands in the western regions of Canada reach as high as $1.2 trillion while returns to First Nations are predicted to never rise above bare subsistence levels (Jay 2014, 109–111).

Just as struggle requires new knowledge, knowledge projects emerge from struggle. Masses in motion interrupt business as usual. Demonstrations and blockades threaten the terms of order. These actions imbue familiar spaces with new insubordinate meanings. Like most social movements, Idle No More combines creative conflict with a knowledge project designed to bring forth a different world. The importance of knowledge within the movement's politics was illustrated brilliantly by a clever play on words that provided the title for an Idle No More forum held in Vancouver: "Idle? Know More! Take Action" (John 2015, 49; Kino-nda-niimi Collective 2014b, 405). Like other social movements, Idle No More fights for rights, resources, and recognition, but it also takes aim at what Stokely Carmichael described as "the dictatorship of definition, interpretation and consciousness" (Carmichael 1966, 639). Imagining a new world is a prerequisite for attaining it. Existing ways of being are always bolstered by existing ways of knowing. Idle No More recognized the degree to which collective subordination stems from acceptance of the doctrine of discovery with its legal fiction that holds that European settlers came to an empty land in Canada. The movement called on the Canadian government to repudiate and abandon these ideas (Amanda Morris 2014, 242).

FIGURE 3.2. Demonstration in support of Idle No More in London, Ontario, January 10, 2013. (*Mark Spowart / Alamy Stock Photo*)

Accompaniment in a Woman-Centered Movement

Like many of the most creative and effective contemporary projects of accompaniment, improvisation, and insubordinate place making, Idle No More draws particular power and insight from the prominence of women in defining, planning, and implementing its goals and tactics. Started by four women activists in Saskatoon, the movement quickly became a vehicle for unleashing the pent-up energy, imagination, insight, and activism of a wide range of Indigenous daughters, sisters, mothers, and grandmothers (John 2015, 38). In their activism, women addressed the concerns they shared with men but also highlighted how they experienced gender specific threats, insults, and injuries. Women's Memorial Marches and a call for an official inquiry into Murdered and Missing Indigenous Women, for example, directed attention toward the nearly one thousand Indigenous women missing and murdered in Canada at the time. Focusing public attention on "missing" Indigenous women—those who had been abducted and killed—led to discussions of other absences, particularly the ways in which women are often "missing" from family, community, and civic life because of the effects of federal policies that separate them from meaningful relationships to the land and from meaningful participation in debates about Indigenous futures (John 2015, 46). The seemingly sudden visibility of women in public life inside Idle No More actions brought to the fore the stark—but previously largely unremarked—absence of women from leadership positions in both Indigenous and settler communities. Sarah Hunt (Kwagiulth) argues that the dehumanization that all Indigenous people experience "is felt most acutely in the bodies of Indigenous girls, women, two-spirit, and transgender people" because of sexual violence against them (2014, 191). Canadian Council of Child Youth Advocates president Mary Ellen Turpel-Lafond of the Muskeg Lake Cree Nation notes how women are left on their own to raise and care for children in ways that harm their participation in the labor force, higher education, and civic life. Women living on reserves often find it difficult to secure child support payments or to assert their matrimonial property rights (Turpel-Lafond 2014, 338–339).

Anthropologist and Chickasaw Nation citizen Shannon Speed notes that "while violence is not a new aspect of indigenous women's experience, it has increased dramatically for them (as it has for many) in the current moment" (2016, 281). In the present historical conjuncture, mass displacement and dispossession, the replacement of the welfare state with the carceral state, the glorification of military and interpersonal violence, and a privatized, personalized culture devoid of collective recognition and responsibility fuels what Alicia Schmidt Camacho aptly describes as the depiction of the racialized and marginalized poor as "alternatively superfluous and a danger to the state," in the process justifying the state's indifference to crimes against women and legitimizing its own tactics of social control (2010, 280). Yet what is novel and inexplicable for some communities of women has a long and well understood history among others. Many Indigenous women activists and scholars possess a *konesans*—a wisdom based on experience—that connects the problems of the present to ongoing practices from the past. They analyze violence against women as something more than the aberrant acts of deviant individuals but rather as part of what Rita Segato in another context describes as "a deep symbolic structure that organizes our acts and fantasies and makes them intelligible" (2010, 74). For women participating in Idle No More activism, that symbolic structure stems from the ways in which hatred and contempt for Indigenous women has been an inextricable part of colonial land dispossession and denial of sovereignty (Coulthard 2014, 157). Mohawk scholar Audra Simpson notes how the enduring presence of these historical practices is openly reflected in public discourses. She provides the example of Canadian prime minister Stephen Harper's claim in 2014 that the phenomenon of missing and murdered Indigenous women had no sociological causes or consequences and that it merely represented the aberrant criminal behavior of individual men. Simpson argues that from Harper's perspective, the shared identity of the victims had no significance, and the abductions and murders had "no context, no structure animating it, no materiality," representing only unconnected individual illegal acts (A. Simpson 2016, 2).

Even when advancing what might be thought of as issues of importance mainly to women, Idle No More activists employed an intersectional approach. They identified hatred and violence directed against Indigenous women as manifestations of misogyny but at the same time as technologies of racist rule. They argued that the binary oppositions at the core of all racist projects constitute crucibles in which cruelty against women is created and developed. They received new lessons on these dynamics from their oppressors' responses to Idle No More. When Chief Spence staged her fast as a way of making her case for the urgent need for new policies, Leanne Betasamosake Simpson (Mississauga Nishnaabeg) entered the scene of argument by posting two sentences supporting Chief Spence on Twitter. Within minutes, online trolls deluged Simpson with sexist comments about Spence's body. Some suggested sarcastically that the hunger strike would be a good way for her to lose weight. Others pictured her as lazy and looking for handouts. One response referred to the Chief as a c—. Simpson recognized that receiving these hateful comments presented an opportunity to teach her readers about the entwined pathologies of sexism and white supremacy produced by the four-hundred-year history of gendered colonial violence. The vulgarity directed at Chief Spence took place, at least in part, Simpson argued, "because it is acceptable to treat Indigenous women this way" (L. Simpson 2014, 156). Anishinaabe/Chicana scholar and activist Dory Nason argues that the efflorescence of misogynist attacks on the movement demonstrates the threat posed to coloniality by the ways in which Indigenous women's love had inspired a whole people to demand justice, challenge environmental destruction, and place the concerns of women and children at the forefront of public consciousness. Repressing that threat, she contended, required the defenders of coloniality to resort to sexist stereotypes and slurs in hopes of depicting Indigenous women's power to love and inspire as something shameful and deviant (Nason 2014, 187–188). Audra Simpson (Mohawk) also connects the online vituperation directed against Chief Spence to the deployment of gender violence historically as a mechanism for suppressing the Indigenous ways of knowing and being that threaten the hegemony of settler values and beliefs. The ruling logic of settler colonialism, she argues, requires the elimination and obliteration of

Indigenous women. Just as a series of laws regulating marriage compelled Indigenous women who married non-Indigenous men to surrender their legal rights as "Indians," settler online posters, kidnappers, and killers seek to obliterate the general threat of otherness posed by Indigenous women's bodily presence and the traditions of matrilineal power that placed Chief Spence in her position of leadership. Simpson argues that in settler societies, the body of an Indigenous woman is seen as dangerous because it signifies "the dangerous possibility of reproducing Indian life and most dangerously, other political orders" (A. Simpson 2016, 5).

The centrality of women to the struggle for Indigenous survival and sovereignty imbued Idle No More with an intersectional quality. It embodied in action ideas that had been theorized for decades by Indigenous feminists and practiced by environmental activists (John 2015, 39). Veteran environmental organizer Clayton Thomas-Muller of the Mathias Colomb Cree Nation explains how environmentalism and feminism had long been fused together in Indigenous communities. Reminiscing about his years working for the Indigenous Environmental Network, he explains, "Our grassroots movement for energy and climate justice was being led by our Native women and, as such, our movement was just as much about fighting patriarchy and asserting as a core of our struggle the sacred feminine creative principle" (Thomas-Muller 2014, 367). The movement critiqued racism and sexism not as separate practices, but as interlocking, interdependent, and mutually constitutive. The protests, demands, and recommendations emerging in the movement positioned gendered attacks on Indigenous women as a core component of anti-Indian racism, while at the same time recognizing the gendered hierarchies of sexism as part and parcel of the binary thinking responsible for racialization.

Accompaniment as a Youth Project

The politics of Idle No More provoked the emergence and flowering of new personalities. Indigenous young people flocked to the movement. Accompaniment online and on picket lines and in round dances fueled the development of a collective consciousness that filled young people with confidence and courage. "We're all going to feed off one another," proclaimed Jenna Wirch, the Megaphone Girl, who further asserted, "If we have the proper teachings, young Native people are going to go places" (2014, 171). Her enthusiasm exemplifies Gramsci's observation that a social movement making a mark on history "cannot but stir up from deep within itself personalities who would not previously have found sufficient strength to express themselves fully in a particular direction" (1985, 98).

Youth activists in Idle No More made extensive use of social media outlets and practices. The Twitter hashtag #IdleNoMore proved especially effective and important in spreading information and coordinating strategy locally and nationally. The dispersed nature of the Indigenous population at a time when more than half of it lives in urban centers, the need to formulate tactical moves and coordinate implementation of them quickly, and the already existing widespread use of Twitter by young people made that medium especially useful to the struggle (Graveline 2012, 293). For Indigenous young people who almost never saw their concerns, lives, or phenotypes represented in mainstream commercial media, Twitter seemed like a welcoming insubordinate space. It offered them opportunities to speak up and speak out. As Kappo explains, "So social media has provided a forum for us. It's like this constant community meeting and you can go and hang out there anytime, a regular space to visit. And especially now that our people live in so many different locations, social media has also become the place to share thoughts on anything and everything" (2014, 68). By late December 2012, more than twenty thousand tweets per day utilized the #IdleNoMore hashtag (Kino-nda-niimi Collective 2014b, 395, 403). The Idle No More Facebook page claimed 48,000 members and had secured 116,000 "likes." Movement organizers estimated that some four hundred regional alliances had coalesced around Idle No More (Kino-nda-niimi Collective 2014b, 409). An especially intelligent, eloquent, and compelling speech by precocious eleven-year-old Ta'Kaiya Blaney of then Sliammon First Nation (now called the Tla'amin First Nation) at an Idle No More Rally in British Columbia alerted viewers around the world to the extraordinary insight, energy, and confidence surging forth from young people.[5]

Turning Hegemony on Its Head

Idle No More turned hegemony on its head. It deployed the beads, feathers, and drums used to make a spectacle out of Indigenous difference in thousands of Hollywood films, television programs, and advertising images to stage a visual performance on behalf of Indigenous sovereignty and survivance. The prominence of Indigenous women at the forefront of a political movement turned the colonized, eroticized, and fetishized Indigenous female body into a repository of knowledge and an apparatus of political and social struggle. Inserting Indigenous bodies into contemporary politics disrupted the settler story about Indians as disappeared parts of the past, while round dances at shopping malls and protests against resource extraction cast light on how settler society's past and present wealth stems from exploitation of both humans and nature. Perhaps most important, the sudden appearance in public of masses of Indigenous people dramatized the hidden dispossessions and displacements central to settler success and prosperity.

In Canada, as in all settler colonial countries, dispossession, displacement, and dispersal physically forced Indigenous communities to the periphery of settler society. Yet capitalist enterprise invariably brought development to these very sites that Indigenous people inhabited—some twenty-six hundred reserves and additional unceded lands rich with oil, gas, and precious metals. Idle No More's natural constituency also lived near exurban developments and military training grounds, along oceans and inland waters, and on territory traversed by shipments of raw materials needed by industry. In cities they inhabited neighborhoods targeted for gentrification and new development (Pasternak 2014, 43).

For thirteen days in 2013, members of the Aamjiwnaang First Nation Band blocked the Canadian National Railway tracks that traverse their reserve. Their ancestral land stood between the oil and gas supplies in the hinterlands of Ontario and the western provinces and Canada's "Chemical Valley," a major industrial concentration in and around Sarnia, Ontario. Every day an average of 450 freight cars carrying nitric acid, butane, ammonium nitrate, ethylene, polyethylene, methanol, propane, and butane pass through the reserve. The Idle No More blockaders contended that the placement of the tracks violated treaty rights. They complained that the chemicals carried by the trains endangered the health and safety of the Band. Moreover, they argued that the presence of the tracks on their reserve was merely one symptom of a larger damaging and dangerous extractivist ideology. It quickly became evident that without the raw materials that came from and were transported across Indigenous lands, Canada's industry could not function. Complaints by petrochemical companies and the likelihood of shortages of fuel for heating homes in eastern Canada impelled an Ontario Superior Court judge to issue an injunction against the protest and to charge the person the judge believed (wrongly) to be the instigator and leader of the action to be personally responsible for compensating the rail line and its customers for the economic damage attributed to the blockade. This draconian response by a judge—a man with preexisting attachments and allegiances to business—illustrated the meanness, mendacity, and corruption of the state and the corporations it protects. At the same time, it offered a direct inversion of the stories about

Indigenous dependency and settler self-sufficiency by revealing the degree to which the Canadian economy depends on the exploitation of Indigenous lands and the suppression of Indigenous rights (Scott 2013, 425–426).

The Middle Run

Like most insurgent movements, Idle No More seeks to author and authorize new ways of knowing and new ways of being. Bill C-45 was offensive enough on its own to attract opposition, but it became the flash point for a broader movement because it perfectly encapsulated so much of what is wrong with settler society: its avarice, arrogance, and abdication of accountability; its contempt for democratic deliberation and decision-making; and its materialist and instrumental view of the human and natural worlds. In the short run, Idle No More sought to stop ill-advised legislation, but for the middle run it aimed to deepen popular capacity for self-determination. As Glen Sean Coulthard (Yellowknives Dene) explains, the dominant society exerts its power not only through repression and violence "but rather from its ability to produce *forms of life* that make settler-colonialism's constitutive hierarchies seem natural" (2014, 152). Idle No More worked to make the familiar strange, to create a new collective common sense about the purpose of life, and to raise questions about what is permitted and what is prohibited, about what is plausible and what is impossible.

In the short run, Idle No More might be seen as a failure. It did not stop Bill C-45, which remains in effect at the time of this writing. Yet Idle No More has been a splendid success in deepening the capacity for democratic self-activity in the middle run. "We're in this for the long haul," explains Palmater. "It was never meant to be a flashy one month, then go away. This is something that's years in the making. . . . You'll see it take different forms at different times, but it's not going away anytime soon" (Coulthard 2014, 165). Idle No More deepens desires for democracy and cultivates capacities for struggle. It has not yet succeeded in restoring Indigenous sovereignty but it has restoried individual and collective understandings in ways that promote decolonial knowledge projects. If a decolonial future is to emerge, Idle No More will be one of the forces that will bring it about.

Konesans

The forms that Idle No More takes in the future will likely manifest elements of both *konesans* and *balans*. As noted in Chapter 2, in Haitian vodou cosmology, *konesans* signifies the wisdom that comes from respect for the experiences of the past and from recognition of its enduring presence and relevance in the present. Before Idle No More emerged on the scene, Indigenous activists and intellectuals had long recognized the value of traditional concepts, ideals, and practices and the necessity for continuing them in the present. Even before the Idle No More movement erupted, Leanne Betasamosake Simpson (Mississauga Nishnaabeg) called for a politics of decolonization that "requires us to reclaim the very best practices of our traditional cultures, knowledge systems and lifeways in the dynamic, fluid, compassionate, respectful context within which they were originally generated" (L. Simpson 2011, 18). In a manifestation of that reclaiming, grandmother Josephine Mandamin led other Anishinaabe women in staging the Mother Earth Water Walks starting in 2003. Part of a broader Indigenous commitment to "walking the land" as a way of learning, the water walkers committed themselves to hiking around the entire perimeter of one of the five Great Lakes every spring for five years. Dismayed by the cumulative and ever-increasing pollution levels in the lakes, they perceived the destruction of the environment as evidence of how human action disrupts the ability of the waters to give and support life, as an injustice that requires renewed commitment to balance and reciprocity. McGregor explains that the water walkers reconnected with and reaffirmed their collective commitment to traditional Anishinaabekwe responsibilities to care for the water and maintain harmony and reciprocity among all beings. Walking around the lakes involved retracing the steps of the ancestors in order to achieve the ideal of *Mnaamododzawin*, which means a state of total well-being based on respectful and reciprocal relations with all of creation. The physical journey around the lakes involved hardships that offered lessons in overcoming challenges, while enabling participants to feel that the ancestors are present. Like the Cree round dance, the Anishinaabek water walk connects the past to the present and future. As McGregor argues

> *Water transcends time and space.* In some respects, the waters we interact with in the present are the same waters our ancestors experienced, and the same ones that may be experienced by future generations in turn, should we take care of the waters sufficiently to insure their (and our) future viability. This understanding holds us, as the current generation, highly accountable, and obliges us to ensure that our grandchildren, great grandchildren, and so on, can engage with the waters as we have. (2013, 72, italics in original)

Idle No More's activists and theorists consistently invoked and honored ancestral practices and wisdom. The Aamjiwnaang First Nation Band blockade of the Canadian National Railway tracks appeared to the Canadian state as a lawless disruption of a just social order. Yet as Coulthard points out, from the Indigenous perspective the blockade was an assertion of traditional law and an affirmation of an enduring responsibility "to uphold the relations of reciprocity that shape our engagement with the human and the nonhuman world—the land" (2014, 170).

The presence of *konesans* helps explain the pervasive presence of Indigenous women in the front lines of Idle No More protests, stemming from a perception that fused traditional roles with insurgent activity. Fyre Jean Graveline (Métis/Cree) explains, "As Aboriginal women, we have a spiritual duty and a daily lived responsibility to care for and nurture the waters, the womb of our Earth Mother. These responsibilities are linked to our roles as life-givers and caretakers of the generations to come" (2012, 296). Yet in different ways, Kim Anderson (Cree), Nason, and Leanne Betasamosake Simpson all caution that an uncritical embrace of traditional gender roles threatens to reinforce an obsolete and destructive masculine understanding of the struggle, an understanding that disrespects and squanders the experiences and insights of Indigenous women and people with LGBTQ identities (K. Anderson 2000; Nason 2013; L. Simpson 2012). Taiaiake Alfred (Mohawk) points out that traditions are not static—they are constantly contested and reinterpreted. In those reinterpretations *konesans* can be like a knife that can cut both ways (Alfred 2009). Held by the handle it is a constructive tool, but held by the blade it is an instrument for self-injury. For that reason, *konesans* needs to be tempered with *balans*.

Balans

With respect to gender, K. Anderson, Alfred, Nason, and Leanne Betasamosake Simpson display an embracing of tradition while challenging and transforming it—a tension that exemplifies the blending of *konesans* with *balans*. The concept of *balans* entails reconciling opposites rather than choosing between them, adopting a *both/and* rather than an *either/or* approach to dilemmas, and finding "balance," as its name denotes. *Balans* honors the history embedded in *konesans*, but refuses to be confined to it. It is a praxis of discernment, judgment, and action.

Like all social movements, Idle No More contains its own contradictions. As discussed in Chapter 2, Wallerstein argues that in the short run all political action entails compromises with the existing order and making decisions about which evils are the least harmful. Attempting to work within the Canadian legal system runs the risk of legitimizing its unjust assumptions and presumptions, but refusing to work within the system leaves anti-Indigenous policies in place. The surface acknowledgment of multiculturalism in Canadian law offers official recognition of putative protection for Indigenous difference yet positions aggrieved populations as supplicants begging for the implementation of state-sponsored rights rather than as self-active authors of more just social systems and forms of governance (Speed 2016, 283; Coulthard 2014, 179). Disrupting business as usual by blocking rail lines provokes repression by the state, but nondisruptive peaceful protests can leave the movement with little actual leverage capable of securing meaningful concessions. Using Facebook and Twitter as key sites of communication and mobilization connects a geographically dispersed polity but exposes the participants to state surveillance and retaliation. Moreover, visibility on social media does not necessarily entail viability as an effective force for change. Traveling to demonstrations by automobile or to conferences on planes builds regional, national, and international solidarity but contributes to the greenhouse gas emissions that threaten the planet. A decentered loosely organized movement encourages mass participation and resists bureaucratic co-optation. But, when the government offers modest concessions, it negotiates with the traditional leadership structures sanctioned by the state, like the Assembly of First Nations. Divisions within First Nations and between Indigenous people and their allies that seem minor at the peak of activism persist once demonstrations end, and it is not clear how the collective learning that took place can be sustained and institutionalized in the days and years to come.

The contradictions facing Idle No More have given rise to creative critical deployments of *konesans* and *balans*. For example, participants in an Indigenous summit meeting on traditional knowledge convened by Idle No More concluded that discerning significant differences between settler and Indigenous ways of knowing makes it possible to fuse them together in a way that might augment the breadth and depth of each (Graveline 2012, 297). David Suzuki, one of Canada's best-known scientists and environmentalists, offered an example of the value of this kind of cocreation through the lessons he learned working with the Haida First Nation that led him to think about the environment in new ways. "As I contemplated these lessons," Suzuki explains, "I realized we had framed the environmental problem incorrectly. We *are* the environment. There is no separation;

there is no environment 'out there' that we have to regulate our interaction with. . . . We are the earth, and so whatever we do to it, we do directly to ourselves" (Graveline 2012, 296). Bringing into accompaniment these seemingly incommensurable knowledge traditions as equally useful exemplified the sense of *balans*—the unity of opposites—that pervaded the pedagogy and politics of the movement. In similar fashion, Idle No More insisted on visibility, inclusion, and fair treatment within Canadian politics but also—and at the same time—collective autonomy and sovereignty as nations in control of territories (John 2015).

In a generative engagement with the ideas of Frantz Fanon, Coulthard argues that internalized forms of self-recognition imposed on oppressed populations by the totalizing power of colonialism need to be taken seriously, but they do not prevent the reclaiming and revitalizing of social and cultural traditions for purposes of collective empowerment (Coulthard 2014, 153). He calls for rejection of the colonial politics of recognition yet acknowledges the necessity of continuing engagement with the state. Coulthard's solution to this dilemma calls for balance, for "critical self-reflection, skepticism, and caution" in dealings with the state, but at the same time for "a resurgent politics of recognition that seeks to practice decolonial, gender-emancipatory, and economically non-exploitative alternative structures of law and sovereign authority grounded on a critical refashioning of the best of Indigenous legal and political traditions" (2014, 179).

Aileen Moreton-Robinson (Goenpul, Quandamooka) presents an exemplary formulation of the *both/and* approach to struggles in insubordinate spaces. She argues, "Our capacity for self-definition lies within a counter-discourse informed by our sovereignty and ontologies, but the discursive nature of racialized discourse means we never are beyond it, even when we are resisting it: our lives are forged through struggle" (2015, 192).

The Metaphor of Two Mirrors

The mobilizations by Idle No More hold up two mirrors that reflect the contradictory dimensions of the present historical conjuncture. One mirror reveals how the pervasive presence of depredation and plunder in the present stems from the unresolved contradictions of the past: from historical and ongoing Indigenous dispossession, conquest, slavery, misogyny, homophobia, and class rule. The other mirror reveals the irrepressible power of masses in motion, the energy and imagination of collectivities forged to refuse an unlivable destiny. Although grounded in the particular and specific circumstances of Indigeneity in Canada, Idle No More has significance for all the people of the planet.

Neocolonial systems of knowledge production portray Indigenous dispossession as a completed historical event, a finite and finished set of practices. Yet all around the world, and especially in settler colonial countries such as the United States, Canada, Australia, and New Zealand, Indigenous dispossession remains a continuing and continuously augmented set of practices that shape the contours of law, learning, land use, possession, property, and personhood. What Moreton-Robinson has aptly named "the white possessive" injures the Indigenous, but it also shapes the settler. The white possessive provides an ideological foundation for a patriarchal, acquisitive, exploitive, and exclusionary society. In order for Indigenous dispossession, slavery, immigrant restriction, and labor exploitation to take place, humans and the land they lived on had to be seen instrumentally. Retaining and augmenting the unjust enrichments of the past requires legal and political systems that value white property more than collective humanity. Colonial knowledge and neocolonial practice have no room for seeing human relations with nature and with other humans as systems of reciprocal relations and obligations. They insist on ownership, exclusion, domination, and control. Moreover, as Coulthard observes, "Settler-colonial formations are *territorially acquisitive in perpetuity*" (2014, 152). Conquest continues today in the form of the seizure of sacred Navajo land in Arizona for use as a ski resort and the pollution of Ojibwe land by zinc mining firms in Michigan. It makes its presence felt in the escalation of resource extraction and pipeline construction on unceded Indigenous land in Canada, and through the brutal suppression of the Standing Rock Sioux trying to protect Lakota land and water in North Dakota (Gilio-Whitaker 2015, 872; LaDuke 2014, 147). The assumptions of Indigenous dispossession and coloniality unwilling to die are felt harshly and directly by First Nations around the globe, but they harm everyone.

A colonial matrix of power and knowledge occupies a pervasive and perverse presence in modern life. Coloniality subjects people to indecent, undignified, undemocratic, and unlivable circumstances. It does not, however, succeed in producing completely compliant subjects. The ruinous consequences of coloniality provoke its subordinated subjects to fight back—to envision and enact decolonial practices and processes. Decolonial projects emerge inside insubordinate spaces where new forms of accompaniment generate new ideas, identities, and identifications. Inside these insubordinate places, people forge the tools of struggle. Practices of agitation, educa-

FIGURE 3.3. Amanda Polchies brandishes an eagle feather as she faces heavily armed Royal Canadian Mounted Police officers about to attack a Mi'kmaq protest demonstration against fracking in Rexton, New Brunswick, October 17, 2013. The 2017 film *Water Warriors: Nothing Can Live Without Water* directed by Michael Premo documents this struggle. Although not a part of the Idle No More movement, the struggle in Rexton expressed powerfully the spirit of Indigenous people and their determination to protect water and land. (*Photo by Ossie Michelin. Reprinted with permission of Aboriginal Peoples Television Network.*)

tion, and organization lead to mobilization, litigation, and legislation. These spaces nurture and sustain practices that have practical utility as means to the end of decolonization. Yet they also function as ends in themselves, as places where celebration and congregation deepen the capacity for people to engage in democratic deliberation and decision-making, to resist disciplinary classification, and to find something left to love in themselves and others in a world that often makes people unlovable. Insubordinate spaces function as sites of struggle, but they are also locales where people get to experience now a taste of the future victory they seek, to carry on the fight but also to live the victory (Patterson 2016).

An expressly political mobilization fueled by powerful cultural currents, Idle No More reveals how improvisation and accompaniment inside insubordinate spaces can contest coloniality. As both a political mobilization and a knowledge project, Idle No More exposes and challenges the hegemony of coloniality's possessive individualism, materialism, instrumental view of humans and nature, equations linking race to place and property, state-centered citizenship, gendered hierarchies, and reigning epistemologies and ontologies. Defending sovereignty and fighting for survival required the movement to establish a collective identity, present transitional demands, develop tactics capable of creating transformative experiences, contest the contradictions of their opponents, and overcome the legal and epistemological legacies of colonial knowledge. Fueled by outrage over proposed laws that threatened Indigenous survivance and sovereignty, Idle No More emanated from the grievances of Indigenous people. Yet the mobilization set in motion a series of events and experiences that led its participants to demand more than better treatment of Indigenous people within Canadian society and the enforcement of treaties that guaranteed their rights to self-determination. It also identified and opposed the "extractionist" ideology that destroys water, air, and land to produce profits for chemical and mining companies. It found ways to create new convivial and collective relationships that challenged the core premises of neoliberal individualism.

Idle No More emerged from many acts of improvisation and accompaniment at the scene of argument. Its insubordinate political agenda relied on and expanded a range of insubordinate spaces. A similar pattern defines the acts of improvisation and accompaniment discussed in the next chapter: the son jarocho Fandango movement, the hip-hop performance art of Chingo Bling, and the installation art of Ramiro Gomez.

4 / ARTIVISTAS

At this dangerous moment in the history of the United States, when vicious and vile attacks on people of Mexican and Central and South American origin have become normalized and legitimized at the highest levels of government, both the immigrant and the native born Latinx find themselves defamed and demonized by what anthropologist Leo Chavez calls the "Latino Threat Narrative." This shared social fiction presents white identity as a beset, besieged, and beleaguered entity, threatened by Latinx people and their allegedly excessive childbirths, welfare dependency, criminality, refusal to learn English, insistence on remaining socially isolated, and alleged desire to seize the southwestern United States and return the territory to Mexico (L. Chavez 2013). Leo Chavez shows that all of these charges are demonstrably false, but even when exposed as factually baseless they persist because they justify and excuse the racial discrimination and exploitation that secures the unfair gains and unjust enrichments that flow from treating a whole people as unwelcome and unwanted.

A seemingly endless stream of accusations and aspersions deployed to defame and demonize Mexican people and Mexican culture excuses and justifies new regimes of labor exploitation and rights violations. Immigrants displaced from their countries of origin because of the disastrous consequences of neoliberal structural adjustment policies are routinely depicted as threats to the existing political and moral order, as people who deserve suspicion and require surveillance, supervision, and suppression. Agribusiness executives deliberately conspire with government officials to set immigration quotas far below the number of workers who are needed and who are likely to migrate. This creates an artificial illegality, a status that employers rely on to promote a docile and tractable workforce unable to bargain fairly and freely over wages and working conditions, a workforce that will be unlikely to file grievances against bosses who violate minimum wage and workplace health and safety laws. The existence of undocumented workers is then used to taint with the stigma of illegality the entire Latinx community, including citizens and documented immigrants.

Yet subordination does not automatically produce silence or compliance. Demeaned and demonized inside other people's stories about the Latino threat, Latinx people tell stories of their own. They organize and mobilize politically to address and redress the injuries of low wages and unsafe working conditions, housing insecurity, environmental racism, racialized police profiling, and vigilante violence. These mobilizations, along with the abuses and injuries that make them necessary, make their presence felt in new forms of expressive culture: in new songs and stories, in novel forms of dress and dance, and in vibrant paintings and posters. At a moment of crisis when conventional ways of speaking, singing, painting and performing suddenly seem inadequate, the witnesses to mass migration, low-wage labor, dispossession, and displacement blend traditional vernacular forms of expression with innovative improvisations. They craft narratives about themselves as active and self-affirming, as people who deserve respect and dignity, as members of society who are entitled to decent lives and democratic futures.

In response to the Latino Threat Narrative, a wide array of immigrant and Chicanx musicians, dancers, and performance and visual artists deploy improvisation and accompaniment to craft forms of expressive culture that function as vehicles for collective validation, political education, and mobilization. Making creative use of the seemingly limited tools at their disposal in the few insubordinate spaces open to them, artivistas (art activists) draw on their own versions of *konesans* and *balans* to mirror both the positive and the negative parts of the present and to contribute to building a collective capacity for democratic deliberation and decision-making appropriate for the temporality of the middle run. Their politically conscious art adopts and adapts traditional art forms to both register and resist current challenges, while foreseeing and forging a fulfilled future. In Fandango convenings organized by son jarocho musicians, in the comedic hip-hop performances of Chingo Bling, and in the visual art installations of Ramiro Gomez, new ideas and new identities emerge and flourish along with new politics and new polities.

Fandango as a Register of a World in Turmoil

In a brilliant book that emerged out of his principled accompaniment with huapango arribeño musicians as both a musician and scholar, Alex Chávez argues that the symbolic borders of national belonging in the United States are both configured and reconfigured on the terrains of expressive culture (A. Chávez 2017, 4). His research delineates the ways in which huapango arribeño gatherings enact powerful reconfigurations of inclusion and belonging through the compositions and performances of migrants to the United States from the upland regions of north central Mexico. These culture creators use singing, dancing, and the playing of instruments to create spaces of mutual accountability and respect sensitive to the experience of crossing borders. Inhabiting and claiming these spaces does not depend on juridical citizenship or social acceptance by elites in either Mexico or the United States, but rather speaks to the needs of people who are constantly in transit, crossing and recrossing national borders and social boundaries. The word "huapango," of Nahuatl origin, means "atop of the wood" referring to the floors on which the dances take place. But Chávez demonstrates that huapango is a place to stand in another sense, a space where migrants who live— "surrounded by the structures they build but alienated by the economies they sustain, ostracized by the larger society they make possible"—affirm their right to exist, to voice their presence, and to congregate and move freely (A. Chávez 2017, 15). In the face of the consequences of neoliberal dispossession and displacement as well as exclusionary and cruel anti-immigrant policies and discourses, huapango arribeño practices bind "lives and geographies across the dense, lingering, and knotted . . . dimensions of the Mexican migrant experience" (A. Chávez 2017, 20). They register, represent, and resist the displacements of the neoliberal era.

Like the huapango arribeño, another musical practice, the son jarocho Fandango, which originated among Afro-Mexican people in the state of Veracruz on Mexico's Atlantic coast, also places emphasis on what takes place on top of the wood, in this case, the rhythms tapped out by the soles on the shoes of dancers who perform on the top of a small wooden box known as la tarima. In standing on the tarima, the dancers take a stand in favor of the creativity, beauty, and dignity of people that the dominant society shuns, segregates, and silences. The Fandango reconfigures the symbolic borders of the United States and Mexico and their ecologies of inclusion and exclusion in ways that are both similar to and different from huapango arribeño. Yet both forms register the dramatic transformations of our time by bringing insubordinate spaces and insubordinate practices into being through accompaniment and improvisation. They are performances by and for collectivities exposed to intergenerational experiences of dispossession, disinheritance, and displacement. They utilize the physical presence and full participation of similarly situated people in performance to process shared social experiences and memories. People lacking in material resources and political power can find that they share access to performance archives and repertoires rich with possibility.

While the Fandango is a cultural practice that originated in Mexico, its current popularity in the Unites States stems not so much from immigrants who brought the form with them as from its adoption by Chicanx art activists as a creative way of expressing both affinity with and estrangement from both U.S. and Mexican cultures. Over the past two decades, throughout the southwestern and Pacific coast regions of the United States, novice and expert musicians have come together regularly to accompany each other in Fandango gatherings held at community centers, schools, houses of worship, and a myriad of other private and public spaces. The Fandango exudes the ethos of what participants describe as *convivencia*, which they define as deliberate acts of convivial congregation outside of commercial culture. Constructed through both literal and figurative improvisation and accompaniment, the Fandango promotes and relies on careful listening, willing engagement, and open minded appreciation of difference.

Fandango and Convivencia

The Fandango revolves around the genre of music known as son jarocho, a complex hybrid blend forged over centuries out of an array of Spanish, Indigenous, and African musical figures and devices. The best-known example of son jarocho in the United States is the traditional wedding song "La Bamba," which was recorded by Ritchie Valens in 1958 and remade by Los Lobos in 1987. Son jarocho music has often been minimalized and marginalized historically in canonical formulations of Mexican culture, in part because it originated in one of the most African-influenced regions of Mexico. That nation's academic institutions and government agencies have given it short shrift, but son jarocho has survived and thrived inside the ceremonial and festive life of the people. It has provided a focal point for honoring patron saints, marking births, observing baptisms, conducting weddings, and holding funerals. In the last quarter of the twentieth century, the emergence of *El Movimiento Jaranero* in Veracruz revived and redeployed son jarocho music and the attendant practice of the Fandango in new ways by fashioning contemporary improvisations of the traditional form. Chicanx musicians from the United States discovered the Fandango revival during the 1990s and 2000s. They eagerly re-created a version of it for themselves and their communities north of the border. They were motivated by the ways in which mass migration, anti-immigrant actions, and revanchist racism gave new meaning to Mexican and Mexican American identities, making it more important than ever to affirm allegiance to their own identity under attack. Yet their experiences as members of an aggrieved racialized group in the United States–often living and working with or near African Americans—made them sensitive to the Mexican government's systematic suppression of the Afro-diasporic dimensions of that nation's past as well as to the ways that Black and brown people in the United States are so often pitted against each other. Moreover, the Fandangueros were influenced by the mobilizations of the Zapatista movement in the 1990s, which promoted new forms of popular participatory democracy rather than simply making demands to the Mexican state for recognition and redress of grievances. In the United States, Fandango became a way to imagine a Mexican American identity that opposed anti-Black racism on both sides of the border, that brought to the surface a long history of affiliation and alliance between equally but not identically oppressed groups.

The Fandango is a festive and fun-filled event, but it serves deadly serious purposes. The sounds of Mexican instruments, the lyrics of songs sung in Spanish, and the coordinated movement of bodies in motion provide a physical, affective, and even sensual expression of linked fates and common concerns. The Fandango becomes a symbol of the possibilities of accompaniment. It brings together people with ties to different regions in Mexico, Spanish-dominant and English-dominant speakers, citizens and noncitizens, Catholics and Protestants, people whose roots are Iberian and people whose roots are Indigenous. It provides a convivial alternative to the radical divisiveness that pervades the lives of racialized workers and immigrants who in everyday life find themselves pitted against each other constantly in competition for jobs, housing, romantic partners, and prestige.

Collective and collaborative songwriting workshops that sometimes precede Fandango performances display an advanced capacity for improvisation and accompaniment. In these events, experienced and accomplished musicians and composers ask participants to suggest a word or phrase or series of key terms to begin the process. They select a rhythm and the outlines of a melody that fits the spoken utterances. Then the entire group joins in. Everyone works together to craft lyrics, melodies, and rhythms flowing from the random point of origin. Improvising and composing together promotes an ethic of cocreation that permeates the music, singing, and dancing that follows when the actual Fandango begins. Fandango gatherings bring together singers, dancers, and musicians with a wide range of ages, experiences, genders, and levels of skill. At the Fandango, no one is simply a spectator. Everyone is expected to play and dance (González 2009; Rodriguez 2009; Zavella 2011). There is no "audience," only participants with many different levels of ability and interest. The blurring of lines in Fandango between spectators and performers, between experts and novices, and between habitual and first-time attendees, means that everyone at the event plays an active role in creating memories that shape the entire group's cultural practice and social identity (Rodriguez 2009, 352). Moments of shared joy and laughter, demonstrations of expert bodily movement and musicianship, and pride in collective songwriting function as ends in themselves, but they also provide powerful alternatives to the humiliating subordinations inscribed in the cultural demonization, poverty, and precarious citizenship status that people of Mexican origin routinely face in the United States. The Fandango encourages participants to think of "we" instead of "me" and to savor their collective creativity and ingenuity as a group. It works to turn negative ascription into positive affirmation.

The Fandango movement calls out to people suffering from the ruinous consequences of neoliberal dispossession to improvise and accompany one another at the scene of argument. It is a participatory cultural project and an antiracist political project, but also in many ways a knowledge project. It mines an often neglected archive for sources of resilience and resistance. Its affirmations and inventions take on special importance in light of the official discourses and classroom pedagogies that seek to outlaw the Spanish language, criminalize Latinx culture, and obliterate oppositional subjectivities.

Chingo Bling

Like the practices attendant to huapango arribeño and son jarocho Fandango, the performance art of Pedro Herrera—the entertainer who calls himself Chingo Bling—also reconfigures the symbolic borders of the nation. He performs comedic rap songs that feature Spanish, English, and Spanglish lyrics.[1] Chingo Bling's songs, videos, stage shows, and public appearances function as a sustained and linked performance piece that revolves around his character's embrace and mastery of hip-hop, punctuated with references to the Mexican American immigrant culture and experience. "Bling" is hip-hop slang for luxury objects displayed ostentatiously, usually some kind of jewelry or clothing. "Chingo" is a Spanish slang term associated literally with sexual intercourse but colloquially signals "a whole lot of something." The rhymes in Herrera's songs enact a creative collision of cultures and languages, while the allusions to sex and jewelry seem to replicate conventional hip-hop clichés. Yet the music, lyrics, and videos that Chingo Bling presents deploy these references playfully to make serious points about anti-immigrant discourse and to rally opposition against it. Blending the codes of two kindred and allied, yet separate and distinct racialized groups, Chingo Bling presents a Mexican American adaptation of Black culture, deploying the rich antisubordination grammar and vocabulary of hip-hop for the cause of immigrant dignity and rights.

In his music video "Walk Like Cleto," Chingo Bling first appears driving a bright red Monte Carlo automobile with steer horns on the hood. He pulls up to the curb at a dark and seemingly deserted street corner. When his contact arrives, Bling pops open the trunk to reveal packages wrapped in tin foil. They appear to contain cocaine or heroin. But when the buyer steps forward to sample the supply, the packages contain only tamales adorned with Chingo Bling's logo (Edge 2011). The vignette is emblematic of the rapper's core message. "Don't pay attention to the stereotypes," he advises. "Our real hustle is selling tamales, our white powder is masa [the corn used to make tortillas]. I just try to represent that" (Edge 2011). In his creations, Mexican immigrants defamed in political and popular culture as drug smugglers and criminals become redeemed as hard-working and law-abiding laborers who get meager rewards for jobs that collectively contribute a great deal to the economy and social fabric of the United States. Chingo Bling's videos emphasize that immigrants do necessary and valuable work and that their poorly paid labor makes possible the high-consumption lifestyles enjoyed by the people who profit from the exploitation of their labor yet consistently condemn them as parasites.

Chingo Bling's 2007 song "Like This and Like That" satirizes and ridicules the moral panic that associates the smuggling of undocumented workers into the United States with the smuggling of drugs. In this song and its accompanying video, Chingo Bling plays with the materialism and macho posturing of hip-hop—boldly rhyming "the hood got my back," with "paper stacks" [accumulating paper money] and "slangin' *masa* [the corn used to make tortillas] like crack [cocaine]." The lyrics of the song mischievously present tortillas and tamales rather than drugs as the lucrative commodity being smuggled across the border. They underscore that rather than making fortunes as drug kingpins, most immigrants earn very little as low-wage workers. Like the poor and working-class Black audiences who may fantasize about the lives of opulent luxury presented to them in hip-hop songs and videos, immigrants may dream of being looked at admiringly while holding large wads of cash, wearing ostentatious gold jewelry, and getting chauffeured around in limousines. Their actual life experiences, however, generally revolve around trying *not* to be seen by immigration control agents, spending long hours doing hard work for low wages, and crowding into old cars and trucks kept in working condition only through their own effort and ingenuity.

The video for "Like This and Like That" presents a sequence of visual scenes and images that underscore the challenge of the song's lyrics to tropes of immigrant criminality. The first scene depicts three male immigrants scrambling furtively though the brush as they attempt to sneak across what a subtitle declares to be the U.S.-Mexico border. The camera eye is framed though the cross hairs of a rifle sight, signaling that the men are the objects of surveillance and suppression. A quick cut shifts to an image of the front grill of a tricked out red Chevrolet Monte Carlo adorned with steer horns that have the name Chingo Bling emblazoned on them in bright red letters. The next shot depicts Chingo himself leaning against the vehicle wearing elaborate ostrich skin boots, an enormous black Stetson hat, mirror sunglasses, and a T-shirt that proclaims "They Can't Deport Us All." At the center of the shirt is a parody of the now famous yellow traffic sign—first used on Southern California highways—depicting a father, mother, and child crossing the road to warn motorists to be aware of immigrants darting across the freeways. The version of the image on Chingo Bling's shirt, however, depicts the silhouettes of a man, a woman, and a chicken crossing the road—an homage to Chingo's pet rooster Cleto, and a symbol of the rural roots of many of those who cross the border.

The narrative then shifts to a small shabbily furnished apartment where the three men are sleeping on makeshift bedding. They wake up early and get ready for the workday. One wears a work shirt with the name "Pedro," written in script above the breast pocket. Pedro is Chingo Bling's birth name and also the name of his father, who might have worn a similar shirt in his work as a laborer in a Houston auto body shop. As the soundtrack continues to feature Chingo's hypnotically rhythmic and repetitious rhyming of the words "like this and like that" with the phrases "masa and crack," "paper stacks," and "the hood got my back," the video depicts Pedro and the other two workers standing in a shopping mall parking lot hoping to get work as day laborers. A white man in a flower print shirt hires them and drives them to a house where they do arduous labor raking the lawn and tending to the grounds in the hot summer sun. When the men are returned to the mall, their employer shortchanges their pay, but they are powerless to complain.

A panorama of distinctly *Tejano* and *Mexicano* images appears in "Like This and Like That." They include the Houston skyline, steer horns on the Monte Carlo car, posters portraying the deceased and deeply loved *Tejana* singer Selena, women playing *lotería*, low riders with spinning tire rims, cock fights, crucifixes on the inside walls of apartments, street murals, an immigration lawyer flashing his business card, a coin laundromat, oil paintings of Mexican movie stars, compact discs for sale at a swap meet, a telegraph office where remittances can be sent to relatives in Mexico, and the ominous and pervasive presence of border control and immigration agents looking to deport people. The images and music of the video contain layers of ironic contradiction. Lyrics and images that appear to celebrate the riches gained ruthlessly through drug dealing, in actuality describe the economic marginality that comes from arduous but poorly paid labor. Yet the defiant confidence of Chingo Bling's rapping and the exuberant festivity of people of many different races dancing in the video holding signs that read "They Can't Deport Us All," position Mexican immigrants and their children not as unwanted aliens but instead as redemptive insiders. The fantasy advanced in the video is that mastery of the popular culture codes of their adopted homeland will enable Chicanx people to attract members of other groups to the side of immigrants, to party with them, and to demonstrate together to protest injustice. Depictions of the dire threat of deportation and the stigma of illegality that permeate immigrant life contrast sharply with the song's celebratory festivity.

The video connects the labors it depicts directly to the immigration debate. After the second verse, image after image shows Latinx, Black people, and Asian Americans holding signs and wearing shirts that say "They Can't Deport Us All" in English and *"No nos pueden deportar todos"* in Spanish. Some stand alone, others in pairs, still others in larger groups. People in the crowds wave the flags of Mexico, El Salvador, and the United States. They sway rhythmically to the beat of the song. Perhaps most important, through

FIGURE 4.1. Chingo Bling at Atlanta Hip Hop Summit, September 16, 2006. (*Photo by Monica Morgan / Wireimage / Getty Images*)

their dancing, dress, and demeanor the participants in the video celebrate the diversity and beauty of the multinational, multilingual, and multiracial world that they inhabit. The song uses the *hypervisibility* of the "illegal" immigrant as a trope in U.S. culture and politics to call attention to the *hyperinvisibility* of the hard work, determination, and dignity of low-wage workers performing humble tasks—landscaping grounds, cleaning apartments, houses, and pools, caring for children and the elderly, picking crops, and cooking and serving meals.[2]

Chingo Bling continues his act offscreen and offstage. In promoting the album *They Can't Deport Us All*, which contains the song "Like This and Like That," he proclaimed: "Chingo Bling made his fortune smuggling tamales, one dozen at a time. He built his empire on masa, pork shoulder, salt and cumin. . . . I don't have a conscience. . . . Old ladies, little kids, pregnant women—I don't care who I sell to" (Lomax 2003). Unlike rappers who travel in tricked out Aerostar vans, Chingo Bling tours in a tamale truck which he describes as a new kind of promotional vehicle. When he decorated the truck with the title of his album, "They Can't Deport Us All," it was repeatedly defaced, once even riddled with bullets, and eventually stolen. Herrera rented space on a billboard to place his picture and the words "They Can't Deport Us All" in full view of commuters on one of Houston's busiest freeways. In response, right-wing radio talk show hosts and an array of journalists and politicians protested vigorously against what they perceived to be a celebration of illegality. Herrera's attorney responded shrewdly that the billboard was not making a political statement but merely advertising a commercial product—the name of Chingo's album. Bowing to the majesty of the market in a neoliberal world, the protestors generally withdrew their opposition. By way of explanation, Chingo announced that if Mexicans looked like Canadians there would be no moral panic about them. Stressing all the vital and necessary work that undocumented immigrants perform, he charges that Mexicans are scapegoated as criminals but in reality are just hard-working people finding ways to make their daily bread, or, as he puts it more precisely, their daily tortillas (Guera 2007; Lomax 2007).

Ramiro Gomez

The symbolic borders of the nation are reconfigured in novel ways in the interruptions intrinsic to the installation art of Ramiro Gomez.[3] Gomez developed the idea of an art that could document the lives and honor the dignity of displaced low wage workers during the course of his own labors as a nanny tending to the children of affluent white families in the Hollywood Hills and Beverly Hills. There he encountered a seemingly endless array of Latinx gardeners, housekeepers, pool cleaners, valets, and construction workers. They reminded him of his mother who is a school janitor, of his father who is a truck driver for Costco, and of the many other members of his family who labor at low-wage jobs. From Gomez's perspective, the homes and grounds in these wealthy areas look beautiful because of the barely compensated labor of immigrants. Yet because of their national origins, citizenship status, and language, these workers are despised rather than appreciated. Gomez attempts to honor them with his art. He uses spray paint on cardboard to create lifelike images of low-wage laborers. He attaches these paintings to bushes, walls, trees, and bus stops. When coming across his art, it is not always easy to know whether one has encountered an image of a worker or an actual worker, a doubt that underscores how the labor of low-wage workers is always visible while the humanity of the workers themselves remains hidden, sometimes by choice to evade disciplinary surveillance.

Gomez's mother, Maria Elena, and his father, Ramiro Sr., first came to the United States without papers. They consistently encouraged their three children to express themselves. Ramiro's artistic skill attracted the attention of Mrs. Owen, his Anglo first grade teacher, who set up opportunities for Gomez to draw and develop his talents. He loved to play soccer, a game he learned by improvising, kicking around a two-liter soda bottle in his backyard because his family could not afford a ball. He used a sagging clothesline for the goal (Weschler 2016, 11). Gomez planned on a career as a professional athlete until a diagnosis of hemophilia led him to focus his attention on art. Yet soccer provided valuable training for his creative work. Soccer players have to see patterns and seize opportunities. There is a flow to a soccer game that Gomez found similar to what happens in drawing and painting (Lipsitz 2012). He attended the California Institute of the Arts in Valencia for a short time, but financial exigency and dissatisfaction with the school led him to drop out and secure employment as a nanny for wealthy families. Surrounded by other Latinx service workers whose undercompensated and largely unappreciated hard work brought great value to the families that employed them, Gomez found himself creating works of art that questioned the reigning definitions of value in this society. He believed that his own labor taking care of his employers' children was important and that the housekeepers who kept the home spotless and the gardeners, landscapers, and pool cleaners whose efforts made the grounds beautiful and pleasurable all did meaningful work. Yet all of these jobs were poorly paid, especially in contrast to the rich rewards that flowed to the celebrities, sports stars, and media moguls for whom the labor was performed.

Gomez developed a new artistic practice from his questions about what has value in this society and what ideally should have value. Perusing interior design magazines tossed away by his employers, magazines such as *Luxe*, *Dwell*, *Architectural Digest*, and *Elle Décor*, he discovered splendid full-color layouts of the kinds of appliances and pieces of expensive furniture that Gomez encountered every day in the luxurious homes where he worked. As he perused these magazines, Gomez "saw something that wasn't there"—the workers who tended to these dwellings every day (Lipsitz 2012). He began to insert his drawings of house cleaners, cooks, and nannies onto the pages of the magazines. These images questioned whether the commodities had value by themselves or if they took on value when used, cared for, and cleaned by low-wage workers. He wanted viewers to see that the kitchens and living rooms and bedrooms did not become beautiful by themselves.

Questions about value also led Gomez to create his cardboard cutout installations. He noticed that managers of stores that sold large appliances considered the boxes used to transport them to have so little value that they left the boxes outside to be picked up by garbage collectors. Yet from his point of view, the cardboard lying on the street was "cooler" than the products it once contained (Lipsitz 2012). Gomez saw that these big discarded pieces of cardboard could have great value for him as surfaces where an artist could place paintings. Valuing a piece of cardboard that was not valued by others and giving it respect seemed like a perfect medium for depictions of undervalued people who also deserved respect. With cans of brown spray paint Gomez drew the outlines of faces and bodies of Latinx workers. Then with other colors he created images of the people he knew from work, depicting them wielding leaf blowers, trimming hedges, cleaning pools, taking care of toddlers, and cooking meals. He took it upon himself to attach these acrylic-on-cardboard pieces of art to hedges, street signs, and bus shelters throughout wealthy neighborhoods in Los Angeles. His art made the invisible visible by repopulating the lawns and hedges, valet stations, and construction sites in affluent west side neighborhoods with two- and three-dimensional paintings on cardboard of workers without faces performing necessary but poorly compensated labor as gardeners, housekeepers, and valets.

Accompaniment and Improvisation

The works of expressive culture by artivistas intervene directly in the activities of everyday life. They create new social circumstances and subjectivities. The dominant culture's literature, music, theater, and paintings generally announce themselves as "art" that has been created self-consciously in conservatories, collected in libraries, galleries, and museums, or exhibited on theatrical stages. In contrast, Chicanx creations constructed for and at the grass roots aspire to something more than powerful personal expression, something more meaningful than vivid ornamentation of experience, something more moving than sad lamentation or ecstatic celebration of the human condition. Artivistas display extraordinary mastery of craft, but they deploy that craft strategically through interactive and participatory practices that call communities into being through performance. They create art as acts of interruption, as provocations that can wake people up (Watkins and Shulman 2008, 129). Through songs, sounds, signs, and symbols, Chicanx cultural workers feel and feed off of the pulse of the people. They assert and affirm collective dignity and determination. They embody and advance the ways of knowing and ways of being that resonate with what Boaventura de Sousa Santos describes as the oppositional postmodernism of the global south: an artistic and existential insistence on taking and making new paths in the face of displacement and dispossession (Mignolo 2011, 73; Santos 1998).

Son jarocho creator and performer Martha González points to the centrality of improvisation and accompaniment in her work. Raised in East Los

Angeles in a family that performed music together professionally, she studied ethnomusicology in college. Her research took her to Veracruz where she was exposed to the son jarocho revival there. González came to see the tarima as the focal point of Fandango, as the site where dancers (bailadoras) mark time, display balance and grace, and share the stage with others. The sounds made by their shoes striking against the wood, then intermittently sliding or shuffling across it, establish the complex core cadences for the Fandango. Appreciating especially the respect extended to women judged to be expert dancers, González set out to master the dancing form known in Veracruz by the name zapateado. Her many years of previous experience as a dancer made it relatively easy for her to learn the steps and other technical aspects of the form, but mastering its cadence or groove demanded something else: a careful listening and responding to the "conversations" taking place among the other dancers' steps, the musicians' notes and chords, and the vocalists' versos (González 2009, 367). Dancing on the tarima required cultivation of advanced understandings of accompaniment and improvisation: learning how and when to deploy the idiosyncratic subtleties that might not be seen or heard at all by novices but were perceived and highly valued by experts. By being fully in the moment and fully attentive to every sound being made around her, González let her dancing be guided by whichever instrument she wished to respond to at any particular moment, sometimes the requinto and sometimes the jarana.[4] "It all depends on who I want to have the conversation with at that particular moment in the composition," she explains (González 2009, 368).

Improvisation and accompaniment also permeate the performance art of Pedro Herrera. The character "Chingo Bling" itself is an improvisation crafted to forge new forms of accompaniment. Herrera created the persona of Chingo while he was a college student at Trinity University, a distinguished liberal arts college in San Antonio, Texas. He was a business administration student majoring in marketing who had previously attended an elite prep school in the east. Herrera's education put him on a path toward assimilation and upward mobility. Yet he drew his inspiration from people that he had known all his life who had been offered far fewer opportunities. In a revealing interview, Herrera compared the images he projected as Chingo Bling and the marketing practices he deployed as Pedro Herrera with the implacable determination to survive and thrive among Mexican women who must find ways of turning their everyday skills into monetary reward. "The hustle is American," he pointed out, "and so are those tamale ladies who work the parking lots at Wal-Mart, who keep their kids in the back seat of their cars, next to the cooler of tamales they made this morning and whisper—'tamales, tamales, tamales'—as you walk by" (Edge 2011). Just as these women turn their quotidian work making tamales into gainful employment, Chingo Bling uses the production and sale of tortillas as the informing metaphorical image of his foray into commercial culture. The words these women whisper in big box store parking lots inform the words that Chingo Bling sings and speaks onstage; they provide the model for his willingness to embrace and celebrate an identity that the dominant culture despises. In marketing his character, he sees himself accompanying the women whispering "tamales, tamales, tamales" to passersby.

Words whispered by low-wage immigrant women workers also influence the installation art of Ramiro Gomez. The inspiration for some of his early pieces came as he rode the bus to work listening to the conversations of women going to their jobs as cleaners, cooks, and nannies in houses like the ones where he was employed. Gomez felt that he did not even have to participate in these conversations to draw insight and inspiration from them. "I can hear, I can feel, I can connect," he explains, asserting that "hearing them talk about their jobs is enough to take that little knowledge into the things I'm creating. The next time I'm in the studio I remember that" (Recinos 2013). Those overheard words were part of the inspiration for Gomez's magazine pieces—improvised interruptions disrupting the visual frames used to display products for sale. Gomez drew images directly on the pages of the magazines, depicting housekeepers working inside these well-equipped kitchens, taking care to paint lightly so the drawings could be scratched off easily. "Those figures [immigrant low-wage women workers] are not meant to be in these magazines," he explains, "so I paint them in a way that highlights their transitory nature. Technically, because I don't do an underdrawing, nor apply a primer, the figures can be scratched out of the magazine I've interrupted. They only exist on the surface, and can actually disappear. They are ephemeral. In real life, people are constantly moving, and the workers I focus on move quickly in order to stay on schedule" (Vartanian 2013, 13). The ephemerality is crucial to the art because it reflects the unpredictability, uncertainty, time compression, and transience of working-class life. Interruption and improvisation in art mirrors the unpredictability of workers' lives and the flexibility and adaptability they need to develop in response.

Personal experience as well as observation shapes this art. Reflecting on his own job history, Gomez confides "I feel like a transient." Working at jobs that can end at the whim of the employer without any warning means that friendships among workers are constantly being disrupted and re-created anew. Coworkers can simply disappear one day at work because they have been dismissed or perhaps even deported. "My intentions are on highlighting the instability of jobs," Gomez explains, "My nanny hours were set, but sometimes my hours would be cut or added depending on the family's situation. When I started working, there was a housekeeper that would come in every Thursday and had been with the family for many years. I grew to expect her on Thursday until one day she didn't show up. Several weeks later, two new housekeepers appeared on a Thursday and I never heard from the previous one again" (Vartanian 2013, 17). Yet Gomez knew about job insecurity and unpredictable hours long before being hired as a nanny. His parents did not have the liberty to choose what jobs they would do in life. They had to take what was available, for as long as it was available. His father, Ramiro Sr., worked as a cook in a restaurant and as a gardener in a nursery before securing employment as a truck driver. His mother, Maria Elena, held jobs in restaurants, food processing firms, and a lamp factory before she became a school janitor. The art that Gomez creates flows from the hardships and injustices he has witnessed throughout his life. Gomez explains, "The people I paint are surrogates for my own family, people who are destined to work their entire lives and disappear without a trace in the world history books" (Vartanian 2013, 16). Limited-term employment, housing insecurity, and precarious citizenship status relegate low-wage workers to lives pervaded by what Mindy Thompson Fullilove calls "unexpectancy." "I wish there was stability," Gomez offers, "but that's not the way life works." Yet he adds, "You learn from instability"—to adapt, to improvise, to create, and to make your own path. Precisely because life is not stable, it is all that much more important to preserve in memory the things that are ephemeral in life (Lipsitz 2012).

By placing his art surreptitiously in unauthorized and unexpected public places, Gomez turns his art objects into events. On his travels to work he often encountered Latinx street vendors in Bel Air and Beverly Hills selling maps identifying the locations of the homes of film and television stars. Gomez wondered why a glimpse at a celebrity's home was worth money to people and whether those same people would even glance at the vendor selling them the map. He decided to paint pictures on cardboard of vendors selling maps to the stars' homes and install them in tourist populated areas, observing how long it took for people to recognize that they were seeing an image of a vendor instead of a real vendor. Gomez accompanied this installation with painted signs reading "real star," which he handed to vendors that he then photographed. In a similar attempt to call attention to the dignity of labor, Gomez created images on cardboard of valets and placed them outside restaurants and expensive homes where private parties were held. One read "I'm on a break: valet yourself."

The wealthy neighborhoods where Gomez worked seemed like contradictory entities to him. He describes them as locations that "exclude but invite" (Lipsitz 2012). They exclude through relentless racial profiling and policing, and through mortgage and insurance redlining. But they invite working-class Latinx inside every day to do the necessary work needed to operate and maintain the area's households and properties. Placing cardboard cutouts in public spaces enables Gomez to illustrate yet trouble this dynamic of exclusion and invitation. The cutouts affixed to support structures with wire do not damage any property. They rarely include any written messages. They are quite beautiful. Yet they do not belong where they are placed, even though they honor the identities of people who have been conditionally invited to enter this domain.

Gomez's cardboard cutouts are interruptions and improvisations. They stand freely in public places outside the circuits of commercial culture. "I place them there with no intention for a monetary exchange," he says softly, but resolutely. "It's street art to bring attention to those working in the area. They [the cutouts] are free to see and be taken. Which is often what happens with those. That practice allows me to get artwork out for free and available to everyone. More so, it allows me to insert art in a space that had none before" (Vartanian 2013, 16). Gomez's cutouts disrupt the spaces where they appear and provoke unpredictable responses. As Lyle Zimskind (2014) notes, "They stop us while we're viewing conventional scenes of ease and comfort and force us to look at the invisible hardships underlying them." From Gomez's perspective, his paintings are equally valuable if they remain on display for ten days or for ten minutes (Lipsitz 2012).

A strong commitment to accompaniment, improvisation, and inversion permeates Gomez's art. The medium of spray paint on cardboard turns the paint can that the graffiti tagger uses as an aggressively assertive sign of self-worth into a mechanism for affirming the beauty and dignity of workers. The discarded cardboard box that nobody seems to want becomes the canvas for honoring the worth of abandoned and discarded people. These inversions extend to the art itself. Gomez has come to prefer cardboard to canvas. "I love cardboard," he claims. "I'd always loved the feel of the medium, it's texture and its pliability. . . . Cardboard felt more natural to me, more casual, less indulgent than canvas: more immediate" (Weschler 2016,

18). Gomez paints workers without faces to evoke their anonymity in the eyes of those who employ them or pass by them on the streets. "They were always faceless," he explains of the workers in his cardboard cutouts, "in part to suggest the way they were taken for granted and overlooked, but in part also because somehow the viewer read more into them that way; they were less threatening, more inner-directed, and as such they more readily called forth the viewer's empathy. But they were never nameless. I always gave them names in the titles" (Weschler 2016, 9). These names are not simply invented; they are the names of the people Gomez met working as a nanny. His mural *Los Cuidadores* (The Caretakers) in a West Hollywood Park honors Daisy, Elsa, and Lucy. "Those were the real names of the women that I had pose for me, my old colleagues," he explains. Although Gomez never places himself inside the paintings, they represent his direct experiences. He absents himself from the images as a gesture of solidarity, as an affirmation of the spirit of accompaniment, as an acknowledgement that whatever difficulties he is going through, "someone else has it worse than me at any given moment" (Lipsitz 2012). This solidarity comes from recognition that his fate is linked to all of the low-wage service workers he depicts. When he sees the hatred directed at immigrants, at humans subsumed under the umbrella term of "those people," he feels "I *am* those people" and he tries to give them the respect he thinks they deserve (Lipsitz 2012).

The Middle Run

The huapango arribeño, Fandango, Chingo Bling's performances, and Ramiro Gomez's art comprise middle-run responses to long-term problems. The insults, injuries, and injustices that they respond to are not rectified merely by acts of convening in the spirit of *convivencia*, by proclaiming "They Can't Deport Us All" in a hip-hop video, or by drawings and cardboard cutouts intended to depict the value of undervalued people. Nor do these cultural creations gesture toward long-range solutions to problems caused by labor exploitation, language discrimination, housing segregation, unequal education, racial denigration, or mass criminalization and incarceration. Yet they establish insubordinate spaces for the middle run, places where people can improvise and accompany, come together and create, and perceive and protest the forces that divide, diminish, and degrade them.

The middle-run aims and aspirations of the Fandango movement reflect the powerful influence and appeal among Chicanx of the politics and principles developed in struggle in Mexico by the EZLN. Rooted in a combination of the liberation theology that guided Archbishop Oscar Romero and the Indigenous struggle against coloniality manifested in Idle No More, the EZLN developed imaginative new forms of improvisation and accompaniment. The movement's most quoted spokesperson, Subcommandante Marcos, attributed its nondogmatic flexibility and its ability to devise ever new forms of democratic deliberation and decision-making to the movement's capacity to improvise. "The only thing that we proposed to do," Marcos proclaimed, "was to change the world; everything else has been improvisation" (Holloway 1998, 161).

The EZLN used the ideals of accompaniment in the 1990s by convening encuentros (encounters) in public spaces where participants could engage in collective analysis of common problems. After decades of study and struggle together, the movement coalesced around concrete demands for procedural justice and autonomy. The degree of change that its adherents sought, however, required the participation of a broader group, of people who were both like them and unlike them. Rather than going out to recruit others to join their organization, they created spaces for hosting visitors and sharing strategies and knowledge, building many different kinds of relationships. Their aim was not to fuse all of these different currents of experience together into a unified totality but instead to create decentralized circuits of resistance and rebellion that promoted accompaniment among people walking down different paths (Callahan 2016, 283–284).

Members of Quetzal, a Los Angeles band prominent in the Fandango movement, attended a 1997 encuentro that placed Los Angeles artists and activists in direct dialogue with the EZLN. The experience moved the band members profoundly. It led them to seek out new ways of thinking about music and its place in community life. Five years later, Quetzal organized an *Encuentro/Chicano/Jarocho* in Veracruz (Zavella 2011, 211). The general idea of the encuentro responded to the efforts to promote popular democracy by the EZLN. Yet the situated circumstances and perceptions of Chicanx in Los Angeles led the musicians in Quetzal to envision a new kind of conversation, one that traversed national boundaries, that connected people living differently in distinctly different social circumstances in Veracruz and California to explore both their similarities and their differences. The encuentros led the members of Quetzal to think more carefully and more critically about the subject matter of the lyrics of their songs but also to consider new questions about the manner in which their songs were created, rehearsed, performed, recorded, distributed, and consumed. They vowed to compose their music collectively and to reach consensus on all questions in making decisions. As band member Quetzal Flores asserts, "The methods of organizing and the influence of the encuentro is embedded in what we do" (Zavella 2011, 207).

As highly skilled musicians and entertainers, Quetzal previously had been well on the way to commercial success. The group played a tour as the opening act for Kid Rock and attracted considerable interest from producers and labels. Yet they decided they wanted to live a different kind of life, one grounded in a different understanding of music. They decided to distance themselves from the normative practices of the entertainment industry and to make music collectively and collaboratively within and for aggrieved communities. One observer told them they were making a big mistake. He warned that Quetzal was squandering a great opportunity and that the band members were "shooting themselves in the foot" by walking away from the potential financial rewards of the music industry. Flores replied that his band's new direction did not feel like shooting himself in the foot but rather like shooting at the ground between his feet and blasting apart the chains that held his ankles together. Instead of being accountable to accountants, the members of Quetzal envisioned themselves as accountable to their community and to others. "We're accountable to people who are struggling, accountable to spitting out truths, accountable to living a life that is interconnected based on humanity and not marketing or greed," Flores explains (Zavella 2011, 208).

The Fandango functions as an insubordinate space cultivating collective capacity for democratic social membership in the middle run. It has also sparked the development of other middle-run projects, most notably Entre Mujeres, founded by Martha González of Quetzal. At the 2002 encuentro in Veracruz, González felt most powerfully drawn to meetings with women from different nations discussing the challenges of motherhood in an age of economic austerity and social disintegration. These conversations that started in Veracruz continued long afterward in the form of emails, phone calls, and occasional visits. Making especially deft use of social media and digital technologies, González coordinated a project with several of the women she met in Veracruz that established a new music ensemble, Entre Mujeres. This band eventually included fifteen different women from five different countries. Yet its participants rarely shared a physical space together. Generally unable to meet, compose, rehearse, or perform together in person because of the high costs of travel, because of the difficulty women in the global south face securing passports, and because of the familiar toxic blend of economic marginality and domestic centrality in many of the women's lives, Entre

Mujeres met online, mastering web technologies to compose and record music together. Composing and singing and playing songs about motherhood in the age of neoliberalism connected private worries to public issues. Composing songs through a translocal dialogue among women from different countries exposed both the particularities of each place and the circumstances that are shared in many different places. The women encountered each other as skilled collaborators connecting across national borders and creating a new kind of music. They came to know each other as individual virtuoso singers, musicians, and composers drawing on the unique musical cultures of their countries of birth and residence. Yet they also had much in common as women grappling with sometimes isolating and confining domestic and household responsibilities that might make their lives seem unbearably small if not for the reach across countries and cultures that they found in their music. Their work together offered a model of collaboration, cooperation, and capacity-building for the middle run.

The middle run might not seem immediately evident in the oeuvre of Chingo Bling. His lyrics and images respond to the immediate threat of mass deportation. Like any good marketer, he uses novelty and product differentiation to garner sales—of concert tickets, compact discs, MP3 files, T-shirts, tank tops, hoodies, hats, sweaters, earrings, and tamarind-flavored workout supplements. The political commentary in his interviews deploys concerns about current issues to draw attention to the products attached to his brand. Nearly everything he does is calculated to provoke the immediate sale of his products. The entire project may appear little more than a cynical marketing scheme. Yet in his capture of strains of insubordinate practices and ideas, Herrera has created an archive with great utility for the middle run. His images and lyrics hold in abeyance elements of the aggressive festivity of the massive immigration rights rallies of 2006. They resonate with the poetics of the determined survival strategies of Latinx communities, and through their humor they uncrown power and embolden its opponents. They draw attention to parallels between anti-Black and anti-Latinx racism and imagine mutuality and solidarity between the two groups. Intentionally or accidentally, wittingly or unwittingly, the ingenious reframing of concerns about immigration in Chingo Bling's art holds significance for the middle run. The song lyrics and the narrative videos he crafts to accompany them turn one corner of commercial culture into an insubordinate space, one of the few public places in U.S. society where the dignity and aspirations of low-wage immigrant Latinx workers are acknowledged and honored. Despite his prep school education and his business school credentials, Herrera cannot shake himself loose from the links that connect his name, phenotype, and personality to the collective fate of Latinx people in the United States in a moment of danger. Just as Black hip-hop artists such as Ice Cube and Chuck D—who were raised by middle-class professionals and who themselves attended college—decided to associate themselves and their art with the poorest and most despised parts of the Black community by deploying what Robin Kelley calls "ghettocentricity" (1994), Herrera and other educated Latinx artists display a bordercentricity that refuses to disavow solidarity with those who suffer.

This trajectory reflects a broader experience. Contemporary racialized capitalism invites talented members of aggrieved groups to leave rather than lead their communities—to accept the opportunities offered to the favored few deemed to be exceptional in order to rationalize and manage the abandonment of the many judged to be disposable. By remembering what he has been prompted to forget—the struggles of his undocumented immigrant parents and the basic decency and dignity of those demonized by anti-immigrant hatred—Chingo Bling's performances call into being a polity poised for action in the middle run.

The artistry of Ramiro Gomez may also seem preoccupied with immediate concerns and therefore unconnected to the middle run. His cardboard cutouts can have a public life of less than ten minutes before they are taken down and thrown away. The images of service workers that he inserts into advertisements in luxury home furnishing magazines are drawn so that they can be scratched away into oblivion. His emphasis on the unpredictability of immigrant working-class life can make it seem as if thinking about the middle run is a luxury unavailable to low-wage immigrant workers. Yet Gomez also connects his art to activism aimed at addressing proximate issues in the present and building democratic consciousness and capacity for the middle run. When actor George Clooney hosted a fund-raiser at his Studio City home for President Barack Obama's reelection campaign in 2012, Gomez decorated a nearby hedge with four cardboard cutouts of Latinx gardeners flanking a sign reading "We Are All American." The Secret Service ended that performance immediately by ordering the artist to take down his creation and move it to the remote area designated for "free speech" (Weschler 2016, 18). In another short-lived direct action, Gomez placed his creation "Los Olvidados" (the forgotten ones) in the Arizona desert. It depicted six immigrants, one pregnant and one holding a baby. He placed them gathered around a white cross as in mourning for one who had died during the difficult journey. Like his other cutouts, "Los Olvidados" was an

FIGURE 4.2. "After Work" by Ramiro Gomez. (*Reprinted with permission of Charlie James Gallery.*)

effort to take the painting off of walls and give it a life in the world where it might interact with the subjects it depicts (Recinos 2013). In 2013, Gomez brought his art to Washington, DC, as part of a mobilization in support of immigrant rights. Organizers of the National Day Laborer Organizing Network invited him to join hundreds of activists to fight against deportations (Montgomery 2013). He installed a cardboard cutout of a farmworker on the grass in front of the Capitol and placed another leaning against a rail outside a building that houses congressional offices. He displayed a cutout of an immigrant family to activists inside a Washington hotel meeting room and then took it to the White House where he tried to attach it to the fence surrounding the dwelling. It was almost immediately taken down.

Gomez's work is seemingly ephemeral and transitory, but it can still be important for the middle run. Everywhere he takes his art creates a new opportunity to connect with other workers in ways that call into question the social hierarchies of the art world. For example, the Denver Art Museum invited Gomez to participate in *Mi Tierra*, a group exhibition of work by artists of the western United States, which was on display from February to October 2017. When he visited the museum to plan his installations, he encountered Lupita Velazquez, who worked in the institution as a janitor. "I didn't know what it would turn into when I met her," he recalls, but the more they talked the more they connected and the more comfortable he felt (Leyte 2017, 1). Velazquez reminded him of his mother and the labor she provided as a custodian at a public school. He spent a day observing her work and decided to create an artwork that would pay tribute to her labor. He created a series of paintings depicting Velazquez's many roles in life as a worker, sister, daughter, and mother. As if to punctuate by contrast the transitory nature of both janitorial jobs and his own art about the people who hold them, he decided to install two figures of Velazquez cast in bronze outside the museum, using a monumental form for this first time in order to signify Velazquez's lasting contributions to the institution. As he was completing the piece, the museum's management changed janitorial contracts and Velazquez lost her job. Once again, the precarity and unpredictability of working-class life manifested itself. Knowing the turmoil that changing jobs meant for Velazquez, Gomez rededicated himself to the bronze sculpture as a way of making her a permanent presence in the museum. "It might seem like a simple figure, but there's nothing simple about an immigrant person's existence, especially in these times," he wrote on his Facebook page (Leyte 2017, 2). He followed the pattern he established in his cardboard cutouts by giving the sculpture the name Lupita, but leaving her face blank. He explained to a reporter, "Facelessness allows someone to dig a little deeper and explore within themselves" (Leyte 2017, 2). The piece honors a woman whose name is known to Gomez, but it also stands as a tribute to all the workers whose faces are forgotten by their employers and sometimes even by their coworkers because of the transitory nature of their jobs. The bronze sculpture created for the Denver exhibit will endure as a symbol of class and racial solidarity in the middle run. Even more important, however, this connection with Lupita Velazquez established a pattern. Gatekeepers in the

FIGURE 4.3. "Lupita Bronze" by Ramiro Gomez. (*Reprinted with permission of Charlie James Gallery.*)

art world now know that inviting Gomez to exhibit his work will lead him to make connections with their institutions' low-wage custodial workers, to place them in his art, and to talk with them about the meaning of art. He explains, "I don't only want to put domestic workers in my work; part of the work is to make them, the workers themselves, feel at home in the world of art" (Weschler 2016, 24). As the bronze sculpture of Lupita Velazquez endures physically in the world, the memories of conversations with Gomez and of his making images in response to them will persist in the consciousness of workers. The unlikely connections he forges invite workers to think of their relation to the artworks they guard and maintain while alerting collectors that not all of the art they prize has been constructed primarily for them. Gomez insists that his work is aimed at the workers he depicts. "I want to give them pause too, to let them know, in the midst of their daily round, that they too are recognized and worthy of being recognized" (Weschler 2017, 30).

Konesans

The cultural creations forged at this historical conjuncture by Chicanx artists display deep respect for ancestral traditions and knowledge but also deep determination to adapt them to contemporary circumstances. The Mexican and Mexican American past that is demeaned and denigrated in dominant discourse gets positioned as a source of wisdom and strength by huapango arribeño and Fandango participants. Chingo Bling and Ramiro Gomez honor the experiences and labor of their immigrant parents while tapping into a range of influences from Mexican cultural workers including corrido composers and mural artists. Yet these artivistas are not revivalists seeking to preserve old traditions but rather innovative and imaginative inventors looking to adapt traditional forms and turn them into something new.

Mexican American participants in Fandango immerse themselves in music with a long history in Veracruz. Their identification with the politics of the EZLN connects them to centuries of Indigenous resistance and struggle in Chiapas. In drawing on culture and politics from Veracruz and Chiapas they cast their gaze toward Mexico, but in an off-centered way. They are identifying with the regions in Mexico from which their familial ancestors were *least* likely to originate. They are embracing the music and politics of two of Mexico's most despised and mistreated groups: Afro-Mexicans from the eastern state of Veracruz and Indigenous people from the southern state of Chiapas. The Mexico honored in the Fandango is a subaltern Mexico replete with intercultural and interracial ramifications. Invoking the ideas of the EZLN inverts the prestige hierarchies of the Mexican national project. Within the modernization project favored by Mexican elites during the past century, Chiapas has functioned as a problem not as a solution. Although Mexican intellectuals have hailed the people of their nation as a *raza cosmica*, created through racial mixtures that provide a certain hybrid vigor, the racial project of the nation in fact has been an attempt to whiten the bodies and phenotypes of Indigenous people and persuade them to abandon their culture, to enter modernity not as a collectivity but as atomized and isolated individuals competing with each other in the capitalist marketplace. Indigenous culture in general and the Zapatista goal of democracy and autonomy outside the control of the Mexican state in particular directly rebuke the established projects of Mexican nationalism and racialized capitalism. Engagement with son jarocho and Zapatismo entails identification with Mexico in a way that is critical, privileging the plurality and diversity of the nation's people rather than the unity and homogeneity of its state-sanctioned culture.

The Fandango in the United States draws on, but differs from, the son jarocho revival in Mexico. "I do not strive to be *jarocho*," Martha González declares. "I do not try to emulate or imitate the *son*. Rather, I study the *son jarocho* and borrow from it, using it as a foundation for creating my own musical expressions. I draw greatly on the strong improvisational emphasis in *son jaro-*

cho fandanguero for my compositions" (2009, 374). The Fandango thus points neither to a return to the ancestral homeland nor to deracinated assimilation inside the United States. It takes what appear to be clear disadvantages— displacement and exile from Mexico as well as subordination inside the United States—and reconfigures them as advantages, as points of entry into a strategic translocal and transnational existence that requires a hybrid literacy, a mastery of the prestige hierarchies and cultural codes of both nations while offering uncritical allegiance to neither one. At the same time, participation in Fandango asserts an insistent and defiant commitment to the beauty and vitality of the Spanish language, an allegiance that defies the parochialism and prejudice of the insistent Anglophone monolingualism that prevails in most realms of U.S. society.

The Fandango movement honors and extends but also critiques and revises the cultural politics of the U.S. Chicano movement. In the 1960s and 1970s as masses around them mobilized for social change, musicians starting to call themselves Chicana/os changed their tunes and the names of their bands. The East L.A. ensemble known as the VIPs renamed themselves El Chicano. A Texas band, the Latinaires, became Little Joe y La Familia. "Viva Tirado" by El Chicano and "Las Nubes" by Little Joe y la Familia became anthems of the movement. In barrios across the nation, local musicians like Rámon "Chunky" Sánchez and Los Alacranes Mojados in San Diego wrote and performed corridos about local events, leading groups at marches and meetings in singing anthems such as "De Colores" (Rodriguez 2017). Compositions and performances resonant with Chicanismo continued to appear in the 1980s, as in "Con Safos" by Ruben Guevara and C/S and "Will the Wolf Survive" by Los Lobos.

The Fandango movement has been influenced by this heritage, but it also coalesces around things that are both newer and older, around crossborder translocal solidarities, around the dancing known as zapateado, around collective playing of jaranas and requintos, and around seeking and solidifying affiliations and alliances with other aggrieved groups. Moreover, the Fandango movement exudes a distinctly feminist dimension that makes its presence felt through the key roles played by women as bailadoras on the tarima and as composers, singers, and musicians. Compared to the comparatively minor roles played by women musicians at the height of the Chicano movement, the feminism of today indicates a profound generational shift. Quetzal Flores affirms "The whole East L.A. scene is into the mode of making a conscious effort to acknowledge the struggle of women and for us as men to act on that as well" (Zavella 2011, 210).

Fandango disturbs hierarchies of race as well as gender. Chicanx participants whose lives in the United States expose them constantly to the relentlessly anti-Black qualities of national political culture make a major statement when they look *to* and identify *with* Mexico's most African-influenced regional culture. The son jarocho music that provides the focal point of Fandango draws its name from the word "jarocho," which refers (sometimes disparagingly) to a mixed African-Amerindian person (Cuevas 2004, 68). Many Fandango participants believe that the word "fandango" probably came to Mexico from Africa where the Bantu word for fiesta is "fanda" (González 2009, 359). The tarima on which dancing feet stomp out complicated rhythms resembles similar instruments of African origin.

In Seattle, Los Angeles, and Santa Barbara (among other cities), African American musicians and rappers have become welcome participants in Fandango gatherings. The son jarocho musicians recognized their great debts to the African elements shaping the music of Mexico, but they have also been eyewitnesses to the power of Afro-diasporic culture north of the border. Martha González of Quetzal remembers seeing Black street dancers breaking, popping, and locking on the streets north of downtown Los Angeles near the William Mead Homes housing projects where she lived. She credits this exposure to the dynamism of hip-hop as her introduction "to the power of music and dance in community" (González 2014). Quetzal Flores, González's husband and fellow band member, identifies the target audience for their group's music as people who grew up listening to Mexican music but also to hip-hop and funk. "Without Black people and Black music, we would not exist in the same way. Living in close proximity and sharing the same experiences, it makes our lives richer, our experiences that much richer."[5] Acknowledging their connections to Black music constitutes an act of cultural justice for González and Flores, but it also functions as part of a conscious political decision to eschew narrow racialisms, to resist the processes in U.S. society that pit aggrieved racial groups against each other, and to create a new democratic public sphere grounded in the common concerns of similarly but not identically racialized communities. They have decided insistently to always be Chicanx—but never only Chicanx—because they believe each group can learn from the experience and collective resilience of others. Quetzal Flores explains how the invention and use of the tarima by Afro-Mexicans in Veracruz contains lessons valuable to all people. "As maniacal and genocidal as slavery was," Flores observes, "black culture survived and thrived. That's son. The slaves had drums: the Spaniards took them away. The slaves said 'All right, fuck you. I'll stomp on wood then,' and created this wondrous music. It shows how rich humans are. Human resilience will always prevail" (Zavella 2011, 209). Through improvisation and accompaniment, the dance platform became a political platform. The outlawing and confiscating of drums was designed to produce quiet and quiescence, but instead it only provoked people in bondage to invent other ways to make noise. Quetzal has consistently built on its intersectional connections to Black music and Black people to seek other affiliations and fusions. The band's respect for and friendship with Asian American cultural worker and activist Nobuko Miyamoto exposed its members to Japanese obon festivals. Miyamoto and the members of Quetzal quickly recognized the similarities between obon and Fandango. Both forms privilege participation over spectatorship. Both draw their aesthetic, affective, and political power from community collectivity and collaboration. Both feature a rhythmic complexity that is difficult to learn but impossible to forget. The members of Quetzal worked with Miyamoto to stage a FandangObon, a convening of two cultures but open to all, an exercise in accompaniment that foregrounded both the similarities and the differences of the two festivals. These deployments of son jarocho music as the focal point for multicultural fusions are race based but not race bound. They promote a radical consciousness based on polylateral relations among aggrieved communities rather than on bilateral negotiations between individual raced groups interacting with a putatively white center.

Like Fandango, Chingo Bling's music, comedy, and public persona craft a knowledge project as well as a cultural one. His decision to place the tortilla at the center of his iconography registers in a modest and unassuming way some tremendously important truths about the causes and consequences of Mexican migration to the United States. His artistry helps reveal the ways in which moral panics about *who* is undocumented obscure *what* is undocumented, namely the broader context of neoliberal trade agreements and structural adjustment policies whose ruinous consequences are responsible for the mass dispossession and displacement that produces immigrant exploitation and vulnerability. Thirty years ago, the United States imported virtually no mangos from anywhere in the world. Today, the United States imports more mangos than any other nation (Alvarez 2005). Yet most of the people who did not include mangos in their diet thirty years ago still do not do so today. A large part of the increase in mango consumption in the United States comes from immigrants who have arrived in the nation from Mexico and other mango-producing countries in Latin America, Africa, and Asia. They are in the United States in part because multinational agribusiness firms have taken control of agriculture in the global south. Big firms consolidated small landholdings into large estates, compelling the farmers they displaced to become transnational migrants.

Neoliberal structural adjustment policies and free trade agreements have influenced the tortilla in ways similar to what has happened to the mango. The government of Mexican President Carlos Salinas de Gotari promoted mechanized production of tortillas, giving large conglomerates like Gruma, which owns the Maseca company, huge advantages over small firms reliant on production by hand (Zemeño 2008, 29). Structural adjustment policies mandated by international financiers led to the destruction of Conasupo, the state-owned National Company of Popular Subsistence that administered subsidies holding down the price of tortillas in Mexico. As a result, the prices consumers paid for tortillas increased by 733 percent between 1993 and 2007, while Maseca took control of more than 50 percent of the national market (Otero 2011, 391). As the price of tortillas soared, tortilla consumers and producers migrated to the United States, only to encounter criminalization and low-wage labor (Bacon 2008, 24). Thus Chingo Bling's emphasis on masa is not an arbitrary gesture to local color but rather a register of a profound historical transformation central to the lives of Mexican immigrants but virtually unknown to the broader U.S. general public. While the movement of workers to jobs is hindered by regulation, surveillance, and incarceration, capital flows freely to the south. Subsidies and tax breaks for owners and investors, however, guarantee that profits can flow unimpeded to the north. The same structural adjustment policies and lending terms that require Latin American nations to end price supports for basic commodities also prohibit social welfare spending. Combined with consolidations of rural agricultural holdings that drive peasants and workers from their lands, these policies compel workers to migrate to the United States in order to survive.

Like the Fandango participants and Chingo Bling, Ramiro Gomez both builds on and challenges the legacies of the past. He points to the examples of the great Mexican muralists (Diego Rivera, José Clemente Orozco, and David Alfaro Siquieros) who made figures appear three dimensional, seemingly as if they were about to leap off the canvas. "In my compositions," Gomez asserts, "one of the pivotal elements is to represent figures so that the viewer feels like they're going to emerge, almost as though they want to break away from the wall" (Hart 2017, 65). Yet Gomez also registers his dissatisfaction with the legacy of the past by repurposing quotidian objects of commercial culture like the cardboard sleeves of old vinyl record albums, changing the way they look into how he thinks they should have looked. He goes through remainder bins at swap meets to look for images that he can improve by improvisation. Like his drawings on the pages of home decor magazines, these creations start with the "what is" and reveal the "what can be." For example, the cover of the album *Wildflowers* by Judy Collins depicts the blue-eyed Anglo folksinger as she appeared in 1967, wearing no makeup in front of wildflowers. Their yellow color accents the singer's brownish-blonde hair. Gomez takes his pen and gives Judy Collins a makeover, turning the 1960s icon of hippie beauty into a contemporary *chola*, a rebellious Chicanx teenager. This intrusion of something that does not belong, this attack on a space set up to exclude, imagines a world in which the daughters of the men and women he meets on his job as a nanny are considered as valuable as the white celebrities whose images circulate and are admired by society. He named this piece Rose Garden, in part as a play on the album's title *Wildflowers,* but also because Gomez feels that the father of a *chola* might well be a gardener, and he thinks that children are like roses; they are beautiful and they have thorns. When young people perceive they do not belong and are not valued, they might be motivated to seek status and recognition in party crews and gangs. Yet the way they construct their look, throwing out a style for other people to deal with, enables them to display through attitude and demeanor that while they may sometimes be broke, they are not yet broken (Lipsitz 2012). By giving the covers of discarded vinyl records his own "spin," Gomez questions the economy of value and shows the value that can be found in undervalued places and undervalued people.

Gomez's transgressive uses of public space, his artistry in rendering visible what racism renders invisible, and his willing insistence in affirming the humanity and decency of hard-working people defamed as parasites and loafers in dominant discourses all draw on the best traditions of the Chicano Art Movement to make powerfully important interventions in urban spaces. Yet in an era when immigrants come from Central America as well as from Mexico, the traditional symbols of Chicano art no longer suffice. Aztec eagles or portraits of Villa and Zapata do not speak directly to immigrants from El Salvador, Guatemala, and Honduras. At a time when anywhere from a quarter to a half of a million Mexican immigrants in California are native speakers of Indigenous languages, phrases in Spanish cannot be counted on as the lingua franca. Gomez's spray-painted images of faceless workers, however, invite the broadest possible engagement. The creative provocations that Ramiro Gomez creates exemplify the power of an art based on work and willingness. He creates an art that cannot be contained inside the walls of museums: it comes from and speaks to the collective consciousness of the people. He believes it belongs where they are. By appearing in spaces that exclude yet also invite, his art also underscores the interconnectedness of differently positioned economic and social groups.

Balans

In West African and Haitian cosmologies, crossroads are sacred places. They are sites where collisions may occur, where travelers can lose their way and take wrong turns. But crossroads are also places where vision extends in more than one direction, where decisions have to be made, where moral judgment and discernment are exercised. At the crossroads, the right thing can look like the wrong thing and the wrong thing can look like the right thing. There is danger at the crossroads, but also always possibility. The ethos of *balans* encourages travelers at the crossroads to forge unities out of opposites, to appreciate the dynamics of difference, and to change the world by action. Fandango performers and participants, Chingo Bling, and Ramiro Gomez stand at the crossroads and deploy *balans* to negotiate its challenges.

Through Fandango, the spaces of the stage and the dance floor host a unity of opposites, fusing Mexican and U.S. identities without giving priority to either one. Fandango performers enact a Mexican identity lived outside the borders of the nation. At the same time, they inhabit the U.S. ethnic and racial identity of Chicanx, seeking neither assimilation into the Anglo mainstream nor deracination from ancestral roots. While the Fandango is always Mexican, it is also often intersectional. Participants in the Fandango celebrate the Afro-diasporic dimensions of music from both the United States and Mexico, thereby rebuking the hierarchical racial orders of both nations. Fandangueros burrow in and build up inside the spaces of the Fandango but also prepare themselves to branch out to other insubordinate spaces and insubordinate subjects.

Fandango practices played a direct role in social justice mobilizations to legalize street vending in Los Angeles in 2014. The California Endowment's Building Healthy Communities initiative in conjunction with the Alliance for California Traditional Arts conducted an asset mapping project in the almost exclusively Latinx Boyle Heights neighborhood. In a neighborhood undervalued by policy makers and by private owners and investors because of its limited exchange value, the asset mapping project brought residents together to see, savor, and strengthen the positive aspects of life in the neighborhood. An array of musicians, altar makers, quilters, and visual artists working with the endeavor made visible the vast reservoir of talent, imagination, and creativity among the residents.

That demonstration of the value that resides in undervalued people in an undervalued place led to a political campaign in support of street vendors. Municipal officials had made street vending a crime because they imagined that the vendors harmed the area by taking business away from established firms, and by crowding the streets and calling out to passersby—which city officials worried would persuade some shoppers to avoid the area. The residents of the neighborhood, however, viewed street vending as an asset rather than as a liability. They valued vendors as suppliers of inexpensive healthful food, as people whose colorful carts and creative sales pitches enlivened the public sphere, and as a presence on the streets who might be called on in case of danger. Son jarocho virtuoso Cesar Castro and other musicians followed the practices of the Fandango to recruit street vendors and their supporters to write songs collectively about the virtues of vending. Savoring the ways in which playing music unites people who had previously been strangers in shared acts of accompaniment, these participants performed their compositions at community meetings and at an annual Christmas Posada celebration. One vendor noted how the campaign supplanted feelings of shame with affirmations of dignity and pride, because the music enabled people who had been previously ignored to be listened to and respected. The street vending workshops helped fuel a campaign to decriminalize vending and to set up a process for obtaining legal permits (Aguilar 2014).

Unlike the many different incarnations of Fandango, Chingo Bling's act is both a commercial enterprise and a political and cultural knowledge project. He stages a political provocation, a rehearsal for a world that is almost here, but not quite. Chingo Bling uses disguise, surprise, interruption, and inversion to flip the script, to question the reigning values of society, and to fill in what is missing and speak back to the Latino Threat Narrative. By pretending to inhabit and embrace the demonized identity of the coyote and the drug dealer, he finds a way to turn hegemony on its head. In his videos, it is employers shortchanging workers who are the criminals, immigration control agents who are the menacing presence, and the price of tortillas is more relevant than the price of drugs.

Ramiro Gomez deploys *balans* when he diagnoses spaces and intervenes in them. He finds parallel meanings in spaces of inclusion and exclusion. During travels to and from work Gomez noticed how space in racially segregated Los Angeles has a distinct temporal dimension. Neighborhoods whose residents are nearly all white people became Latinx hubs during the day because of the presence of service workers in and around them. Gomez perceived the hills along Mullholland Drive as "a funny part of town" because during the day "it's almost entirely Latino, but come five o'clock, the pick-ups and the vans will all head back down and the limos and the sports convertibles will come cruising back up, and the demographics will flip over entirely" (Weschler 2016, 14). Gomez's cardboard cutouts exposed and contested this serial spatiality. At night, when Latinx workers who labor on the west side and in the Hollywood Hills return to their homes on the east side, Gomez's installations in wealthy neighborhoods make sure that when the workers leave, their images remain, watching over the fruits of their labor and reminding residents of the value of their work (Weschler 2016, 14). A similar temporal and spatial inversion takes place in the office buildings downtown and along the Wilshire corridor. Occupied during the day by well-paid white executives who return to their homes on the west side when the workday ends, at night these buildings become filled with Latinx janitors who clean them and leave at dawn before the white workforce returns.

Gomez also employs *balans* in evaluating how his identities as Chicanx and queer can both coalesce and conflict. When California voters voided the chance for people of the same gender to marry legally in 2008 (later overturned by Supreme Court decisions affirming marriage equality), Gomez witnessed what he describes as a "whole upsurge of righteously indignant demonstrations." While he fully shared the demonstrators' frustrations, he recalls, "I couldn't help but wonder where all these people had been when it came to the question of the rights of immigrants. Why was their own right to marry the only thing that mattered to them?" On the other hand, Gomez knew from his own experience that immigrants could be homophobic; he "was not unaware that one of the main voting blocs that had pushed Proposition 8 through were the conservative Latinos so I was very much betwixt and between" (Weschler 2016, 13). That "in-betweenness" produces pain but also provides a privileged standpoint for social struggle and transformation.

The Metaphor of Two Mirrors

Two songs by Quetzal emblematize the two mirrors that Fandango performers and participants, Chingo Bling, and Ramiro Gomez hold up. "*Planta de los pies*" (the soles of the feet) captures beautifully and brilliantly its situated knowledge and serious aspirations. The song's title refers to the soles of the feet, the feet that dance on the tarima, but also the feet that migrants place one in front of the other as they ford rivers, cross deserts, and hike along back roads and highways, journeying to their country of arrival. At times in the song, the feet are planted where the singer is, inside the United States but looking back at Mexico. The unusual 11/4 meter of the song signals a temporal rupture, a break with tradition, communicated through an uneven rhythm that signals a disjunction, yet also a new conjuncture rich with possibility. The Spanish language lyrics of the song convey respect and affection for Mexico and Mexican music but with a certain distance. Translated into English they read "I'm here and not there." The singer confides, "although I highly enjoy the colors of your son . . . I feel my own groove, [and] well, Chicanos always invent" (Zavella 2011, 211–212). The lyrics voice the Chicanx perspective of being *here* (in the United States), not *there* (in Mexico). The physical location is also a psychic one. The narrator relates that while greatly pleased by son jarocho, she feels the need to dance to her own rhythm because as a Chicana, her life proceeds through improvisation and invention (Zavella 2011, 211–212). The groove or cadence refers to the unusual 11/4 meter of the song but also the tempo of life in Los Angeles and to the temporality of a historical conjuncture rife with interruption and uncertainty. As González writes, "In this song, I am addressing my need as a Chicana to express my own voice within the context of my Mexican heritage" (2009, 370). Pursuing neither deracinated assimilation into U.S. society nor a return to Mexico, *"Planta de los Pies"* treats the border as a generative site of binational consciousness rather than as a permanent and impermeable geographic or juridical boundary. The soles of the feet that ache and develop blisters on migrant journeys across deserts and mountains become joyously effective instruments for beating out new rhythms on wooden dance floors and platforms. Thus the feet whose march in new directions has placed migrants in novel physical and social spaces also become makers of musical sounds that beat out a rhythm signaling an oppositional imagination. Like the feet of people marching down a road together, the soles of the feet of dancers help move the body politic in a new direction.

The song *"Estoy Aqui"* declares "I am here," present in a world that has abandoned and forgotten so many people, here doing the work that needs to be done to survive and thrive. Musically, the song's core components come from the cumbia, originally an African-derived courtship dance from the Caribbean coast of Colombia but now long established as a staple of popular Latinx music across the hemisphere. Accompanied by an infectious rhythm and a captivating series of chord progressions that evoke movement, energy, and agency, the lyrics describe a colonia where houses are made of cardboard and tin. From this humble location, the first-person narrator asserts in Spanish that we are on our own, that no one will provide for us: no government, no king. The burdens of poverty are carried by the poor alone; no one feels their pain. Yet an insistent repetition of the words "estoy aqui" declares joyfully and triumphantly that being fully present in the world can bring good results. The narrator insists that she does not need anyone's permission to live and that the "what will be" lies hidden inside the "what is." In contrast to the grim conditions described by much of the song's lyrics, the narrator insists "I am rich with hope" and therefore does not shrink from the challenge. The speaker vows to show "the blindest of the blind" that "estoy aqui"—"I am here." This commitment to survival, subsistence, resistance, and affirmation finds the seeds of a new society inside the shell of the old.[6]

5 / Ferguson

When white police officer Darren Wilson shot and killed un-armed Black teenager Michael Brown—whom he had stopped for jaywalking on Canfield Drive in Ferguson, Missouri, on August 9, 2014—police personnel, prosecutors, and politicians responded callously and cruelly.[1] Ferguson police officers deliberately left the youth's bullet-riddled dead body on the street to fester in the hot summer sun for four and a half hours. When officers finally elected to remove the body, they did not call for an ambulance but attempted to stuff Brown's corpse into the trunk of an SUV until protests by onlookers forced them to call for an appropriate vehicle. They hastened to shuttle Wilson away to an undisclosed hiding place and declined to disclose the officer's identity to the press. The officials present on Canfield Drive that day refused to let Brown's family near the body. They repeatedly destroyed makeshift memorials that griev-ing residents and family members placed near the spot where Brown was killed (Taylor 2016, 153; Johnson 2016, 56).

In the days that followed the killing, groups of demonstrators chant-ing "I am Mike Brown" massed in the streets in spontaneous acts of im-provisation and accompaniment. They protested against the killing and the refusal of the authorities to bring the perpetrator to justice. City, county, and state officials responded with massive displays of intimidating force. One witness reported seeing some forty police cars speeding toward

Ferguson on Highway 70 immediately after the shooting. Demonstrators were confronted with an armed force assembled to keep them under control. The authorities may have believed this was the best way to keep the peace, but the people on the streets perceived the police presence as a taunt, a statement that Black people could do nothing about the killing of Michael Brown and other killings like it. When a few demonstrators broke some store windows, the authorities attacked anyone and everyone in the vicinity. Police officers dispatched to the scene came prepared to attack civilians. They used tape to cover the names and numbers on their identification tags so they could not be held accountable for the violence they intended to perpetrate. Some officers taunted the demonstrators by calling them "niggers" (Halpern 2015, 22). Wearing wristbands that proclaimed "I am Darren Wilson," the officers brandished guns and pointed them in demonstrators' faces. They fired rubber bullet projectiles into the crowds, launched tear gas and concussion grenades, and deployed pain-inducing acoustic devices designed to produce eardrum ruptures and loss of balance (Amnesty International 2014).

Investigations by journalists and public interest attorneys revealed what Black residents of Ferguson and surrounding municipalities already knew: the aggressive policing enacted by Officer Wilson in stopping Michael Brown was part of a conscious strategy by city officials to raise municipal revenues by detaining, harassing, charging, convicting, and fining the municipality's poorest residents. Black bodies in Ferguson functioned as what Jodi Rios aptly calls "a less-than-human, profit generating reservoir for the purpose of legitimizing and funding their own oppression" (Rios 2016, 66). Ferguson's mayor and Missouri's governor condemned the street protests but did nothing to stop the conditions that caused the initial confrontation, the killing, or the anger about it.

The Ferguson protest movement persisted for months. Night after night, people from diverse backgrounds filled the streets of Ferguson to proclaim that Black Lives Matter. They withstood wave after wave of attacks and mass arrests. The insurgency attracted regional, national, and international support. Sustained acts of improvisation and accompaniment turned streets, sidewalks, and parking lots into insubordinate spaces. The struggle gave rise to a wide range of new relationships that led to new projects designed for the short run but crafted as well to build capacities for contestation in the temporality of the middle run. Activists created a freedom school for adults, a software engineering class for teenagers, and a books-and-breakfast program for children and adults. The struggle displayed *konesans*, a collective intelligence honed in struggle that honored historical Black freedom struggles yet adapted itself to new understandings of the limits of legal reforms and electoral politics, of traditional definitions of leaders and leadership, and of the damage done to the community and the movement by misogyny and homophobia.

The struggle was sparked and sustained by one ingenious inversion suffused with the principles of *balans*. The shooting of Michael Brown, the public spectacle of his body lying in the street for four hours, and the massive display of police and military weaponry mobilized against spectators and mourners expressed the sovereign power of white supremacy—its unrestricted license and power. Like the long history of segregation, lynching, and slavery that preceded it, the spectacle staged by white power on the streets of Ferguson was designed to humiliate and intimidate, to flaunt white supremacy's arbitrary power to take Black lives, to force subjugated people to serve as compliant witnesses to their own subordination and dehumanization. The Ferguson protesters, however, turned the very symbol designed to silence them into a spur for collective affirmation and action. Jodi Rios, one of the movement's most astute and insightful chroniclers, explains that the protesters connected the spectacle of Michael Brown's body lying in the street to their own experiences of constantly being treated as bodies out of place—by police surveillance, stops, beatings, arrests, and jailings; by residential segregation and displacement; by relegation to living in abandoned and underserved places (Rios 2016, 65). Black women, and especially queer and otherwise gender-nonconforming Black women, played particularly prominent leadership roles in the movement, in part because of lifelong experiences with the disciplining of their bodies in public and private spaces. They felt deeply what Rios describes as "both the suffering and liberatory capacities of their inscribed flesh in their everyday lives" (2016, 71).

In response to a spectacle orchestrated by the police with the intention of shaming them as bodies out of place, the Ferguson activists positioned their bodies unapologetically out of place—on the front lines in the streets, face-to-face with police officers and National Guard troops. In defiance, they asked and answered questions through chants that went "Who Am I? Mike Brown!" and "Whose Streets? Our Streets!" They turned West Florissant Avenue, Chambers Road, and other thoroughfares where they had been ceaselessly stopped, searched, demeaned, and disrespected into insubordinate spaces of collective identification and mobilization. Their actions held up two mirrors for the world to view. One reflected the calculated cruelty of slavery unwilling to die; the other reflected masses in motion animated by their resolve and their non-negotiable rejection of the unlivable destinies to which they had been consigned.

Improvisation and Accompaniment

Witnesses at the scene viewed the display of Michael Brown's dead body sprawled in the street with blood draining from it as a spectacle meant for them. Police officers used dogs and drawn guns to keep the crowd at bay and to prevent Brown's family members from identifying the body and getting it removed from the street (Taylor 2016, 153–154). Witnesses perceived police indifference to Michael Brown's humanity and his family's grief as a message that "this could be you" or "that will be you if you get out of line" (Rios 2016, 70). They felt they had to respond. The uprising started with an improvisation. Michael Brown's stepfather, Louis Head, held aloft a homemade placard, a piece of cardboard on which he had inscribed the words "Ferguson police just executed my unarmed son" (Johnson 2016, 37). Young people took pictures of this sign and tweeted it to their friends. Using a variety of social media devices, spectators called others to the scene. What one eyewitness described as a "white hippie" showed up and walked along the street dragging a wagon that held a boom box blasting the sounds of Lil' Boosie's song "F— the Police" (Johnson 2016, 56). When neighborhood residents placed teddy bears and other objects near the spot where Brown was shot as an expression of their loss, an officer from the canine unit let his dog urinate on the memorial. When the deceased youth's mother, Lezley McSpadden, carefully arranged a line of rose petals to spell out her dead son's initials, an officer drove a squad car past the site to scatter the flowers and erase the homage to Michael (Taylor 2016, 154).

The diverse range of people who flocked to Ferguson forged new solidarities and loyalties. In the face of social death, they affirmed their dedication to life. In response to unremitting and unrepentant hate, they affirmed a politics of love, what Rios describes as "love of self, love of other, and, most importantly, love of Blackness" (2016, 72). Leadership shared among women of color, queer and trans, and men of color rejected the traditional politics of performed respectability characteristic of the civil rights movement and embraced fully the generative knowledge of people deemed to be deviant and outside of normative identities and roles (Rios 2016, 72). Black activist Kareem Jackson, who performs rap music professionally under the stage name Tef Poe, recalls how new identities emerged on the front lines of the struggle. "I have seen white gay men stand up beside me when we was getting guns pointed at us; Trans and gay people exist. I can't disown people that had my back when I had nothing to please you . . . on that first night, it was a woman from Palestine who taught us how to make gas masks out of plastic bottles" (Johnson 2016, 56).

The struggle escalated in direct proportion to the domineering arrogance of police repression. No one in authority expressed any sadness or sorrow about the killing. Mass arrests were designed to clear the streets and suppress all signs of dissent. The commander of state National Guard units sent to Ferguson described the citizens exercising their constitutional rights on the city's streets as "enemy forces" and "adversaries" (Walters 2015). Armed agents of the state escalated rather than defused tensions. They provoked confrontations. Referring to attacks on business establishments and police vehicles, one nineteen-year-old demonstrator explained "all of these things happen after the police provoke it. What they want to do is impose their will" (Taylor 2016, 156). Yet these efforts often backfired. The more the police pushed, the more protesters resisted. Johnetta Elzie recalls her transition to a more active and aggressive stance. "Using my voice to chant loudly along with other protesters seemed to be enough but it wasn't. Instead, I decided to yell directly at the police. I decided to dare the police to look at the faces of the babies and children their dogs were so ready to chase down." This stance infuriated the officers. Elzie relates, "As more people began to look directly at the police and yell their grievances, the more aggravated they became" (Taylor 2016, 156). The officers were less concerned with protecting public safety or maintaining public order than with demonstrating white immunity and impunity. The demonstrators refused to knuckle under to that desire.

Ferguson protestors and their allies recognized that like Eric Garner, Trayvon Martin, Taniesha Anderson, and so many others, Michael Brown's killing was what feminist Rita Segato in another context describes as an expressive death, not simply a utilitarian death (2010, 75). It was structured to send a message. Leaving the body in the street and bringing massive force to the scene was a performance by white authorities designed for Black spectators. It flaunted and celebrated the ability and inclination to protect the killers of Black people from legal accountability. This was an end in itself, an impunity offered as part of the rewards of whiteness, not only to the proximate perpetrators from law enforcement but to white citizens invited to identify with them. As Segato argues, we should not think of unprosecuted killings as mere *consequences* of impunity, they are also *producers* of it (2010, 79). Like lynchings, police and vigilante killings are not designed

FIGURE 5.1. Flower Memorial to Michael Brown on Canfield Drive, Ferguson, Missouri, August 30, 2014. (*Gino Santa Maria/Shutterstock.com*)

merely to punish particular victims, they are public displays of power intended to silence, suppress, and intimidate entire aggrieved groups.

The killing of Michael Brown, and the absolute refusal to concede the legitimacy of protests against it, was a performance in another sense: a spectacle designed to entice whites to reaffirm their views of Black people as nonpersons. In addition to the material and psychic rewards that whiteness provides by itself, the spectacle of unaccountable police killings serves a particular purpose in a neoliberal society that depends upon violent competition and portrays caring for others as an intolerable burden. The flaunting of white immunity and impunity invites white spectators to take sadistic pleasure in the suffering of those humans designated as "other" and therefore as entities who deserve no empathy. Totalitarian regimes throughout history have recruited those they rule to identify with the brutality of the state. In this society, a body left to decompose in the sweltering summer heat on a Ferguson Street has a relationship to the bodies of humans killed by U.S. drone strikes around the world, to the children ripped from their parents' arms and locked up in cages in immigrant detention centers at the U.S. border, and to the "enemy combatants" tortured at Guantanamo and a variety of secret sites around the globe. Acts of brutality that have little strategic utility for preserving public order, managing immigration, or ending acts of terror have enormous value as cultural performances designed to make the public numb and compliant. As Watkins and Shulman astutely note, "such arousal may even be welcomed as a contrast to feelings of inner deadness. Symbolically, violence viewed from afar may memorialize in the outer world the kind of dissociative splitting in the inner world that has killed off capacities for feeling" (2008, 73).

If the sole concern of the Ferguson protesters had been the 90-second encounter between Darren Wilson and Michael Brown, a short-term solution would have sufficed. This option was in fact pursued; the protestors demanded repeatedly that Officer Wilson be charged with a crime and made to stand trial for it. Even this modest step proved impossible. St. Louis County prosecutor Robert McCulloch contorted and distorted the grand jury process to make sure there would be no adversarial preliminary hearing and no indictment of Officer Wilson. Yet even if the killer could have been indicted, convicted, and sent to jail, or if the clock could be turned back to the day before Michael Brown was killed, Black people in Ferguson would still have found themselves oppressed economically, politically, and personally. Participation in the uprising brought home to them emphatically the degree to which short-term solutions would be insufficient. The killing of Michael Brown distilled and crystallized the pains of collective experiences that spanned decades.

The insurgency did not take place because Michael Brown's death seemed exceptional, but precisely because it seemed so ordinary—even expected. Michael Brown was consigned to premature death long before he died. The school district in which he was enrolled when he entered kindergarten had not been fully accredited for ten years. During his school years, the district never received more than five points on the state's fourteen-point scale that required six points for accreditation (Norwood 2016, 98–99). The projected life expectancy in the 63136 zip code where Michael Brown lived is 70.4 years, 21 years less than the projected life expectancy of residents in the affluent and mostly white west county suburb of Wildwood. In nearby Kinloch, in the 63140 zip code adjacent to Ferguson, life expectancy is only 55.9 years (Bernhard 2016). The 20 percentage point gap between Black and white unemployment rates in St. Louis exceeds that of any other major city (J. Rogers 2015, 46). Moreover, Michael Brown lived and died in the midst of what so many of the protestors recognized as their experience: life as unwilling participants in a one-sided war on Black people waged every day though employment discrimination, housing segregation, food insecuri-

ty, transit racism, and aggressive predatory policing. Their persecutors profited from their subordination. In 2014 alone, revenues raised in Ferguson by
fining poor people for trivial offenses like jaywalking, leaf debris on lawns,
driving with an expired city sticker, changing lanes without signaling, or the
vague and ever elastic charge of "failure to comply" contributed some $2.5
million dollars to the city's coffers. In comparison, minimal property taxes
on the 152-acre campus of Emerson Electric, a Fortune 500 company that
reports sales of $6 billion per quarter, brought in only $68,000 in revenue
for the municipality in 2013 (Johnson 2016, 50).

The Middle Run

Like the participants in Idle No More and the creators of works of Chicanx
expressive culture, activists in Ferguson created insubordinate spaces where
acts of accompaniment and improvisation deepened democratic capacity
for the middle run. Veteran activist Jamala Rogers, best known for her
leadership in the Organization for Black Struggle, appreciated the spontaneous, decentralized, and democratic character of the demonstrations
but also found that the Ferguson rebellion imbued her with a new sense
of urgency about how to sustain the movement's energy and imagination
in the future. The uprising signaled the existence of a turning point from
which there could be no turning back. What she terms "the Ferguson effect" made Rogers feel that "unless we do something in a very accelerated
way, a very intentional way, and a very united, coordinated way, then my
assessment is that we're headed for really ugly times" (Green et al. 2016, 16).
The perverse and punitive actions by the state and the courageous resistance
against it that he saw in the struggle led Tef Poe to a deeper appreciation of
thinking in terms of the middle run. One evening as demonstrators congregated in a fast-food parking lot in the midst of night-after-night battles
with the National Guard, county police, and city police, Poe felt obliged to
apologize to two women comrades for having in the past placed so much
emphasis on electoral politics. "I was part of the regime that told you that
a ballot could remove this," Poe told the women. He realized fully at that
moment that voting was at best a short-run answer to long-run problems.
It was not useless, but it was also not sufficient. "I do believe that voting is
a weapon," Poe conceded. "But I do not believe that oppressed people have
to consistently go back to the system to correct those wrongs" (Green et al.
2016, 18). Months later, Poe surveyed with satisfaction and pride what had
been achieved through the books-and-breakfast program: "There's political

education going on," he noted. "We're teaching people about what's actually happening. We're giving books to kids that otherwise wouldn't get books. Some people are eating that otherwise wouldn't eat. People are meeting people they otherwise wouldn't meet" (Green et al. 2016, 19).

Working in the temporality of the middle run transformed the meaning of militancy for Poe. In the short run, in face-to-face battles with the police, militancy meant the willingness to face attacks and be willing to fight back: to battle for the right to occupy urban space on the people's terms. It might also mean a campaign to get a particular official in or out of office. In the middle run, however, militancy meant something else. Poe explains that most people think militancy means picking up a gun, but in the programs the movement established to build Black consciousness and bolster Black solidarity—projects for the middle run—militancy meant working with a breakfast program consistently and conscientiously, deciding who would cook the food, who was going to wake up at 6:00 A.M. to go shopping, who was going to bring the books to the event. It meant, according to Poe, "delegating responsibilities and being committed to those responsibilities in rain, sleet, hail or snow" (Green et al. 2016, 27).

Konesans

Ferguson activists interpreted the killing of Michael Brown, the exculpation of Officer Wilson, and the brutal repression of their movement as a logical continuation of a history they knew well. The young people were joined in their demonstrations by longtime St. Louis activists including Percy Green and Jamala Rogers. Their direct action tactics, slogans, signs, and symbols reflected advanced knowledge of past local, national, and global freedom struggles.

Yet while respectful of the past, the participants in the Ferguson insurgency refused to be chained to it. Like Idle No More, the EZLN, and Chicanx artivistas, they embraced new ways of knowing and new ways of being as liberating forces in themselves, not just as tools for securing augmented rights-based recognition from the state. They refused to perform respectability for the eyes of their oppressors, to audition for approval, to prove themselves fit for freedom; instead they insisted on their right to freedom now, to talk their everyday talk, wear their everyday clothes, look the way they wanted to look, and especially for queer participants, love whom they wished to love. They rejected in their own ranks and in the larger society outside it pressures to conform to heteronormative, cisgendered, and mascu-

FIGURE 5.2. Armed police confront unarmed demonstrator in Ferguson, August 11, 2014. (*Scott Olson / Getty Images News / Getty Images*)

linist hierarchies. They did not "follow" leaders—they led themselves. They did not submit meekly to arrests, offer their bodies up to be beaten, or believe they had to act peacefully and respectfully to people coming into their neighborhoods to kill them. One of their slogans proclaimed, "This Ain't Your Mama's Civil Rights Movement" (Green et al. 2016, 9).

The young people who forged themselves into forces of resistance might have expected approval and support from their elders. For years Johnetta Elzie had heard complaint after complaint from members of older generations that the young people do not fight for anything or care about a better world. At the apex of the Ferguson uprising, she observed, "We've proved them to be wrong" (Taylor 2016, 161). Yet the assertion that this was a new civil rights movement offended many liberals and was used repeatedly to discredit the Ferguson insurgency. Critics portrayed the demonstrators as criminals and hoodlums. At Michael Brown's funeral, Al Sharpton blamed the demonstrators for the violence on West Florissant Avenue, belittling the people who stood firm in the face of rubber bullets and teargas being fired at them (Taylor 2016, 160). Critics chided the demonstrators for taking to the streets instead of launching voter registration campaigns and trying to elect new municipal officials. They were unmoved when Tef Poe observed that "a few folks have been coming to Black people's doors for three hundred years about why you all ain't voting. Maybe it's more responsible to analyze why people aren't voting and bring mechanisms to them that will spark some type of political interest in them, and then when the time comes we should vote, then we vote. But we don't just go vote for some Tom, Dick, or Harry just because it's time to vote. White people don't do that. But we as black people are told that's how we can get free. I can ask the Palestinians what voting gets you" (Green et al. 2016, 18–19).[2]

Journalists inquired repeatedly about why the Ferguson demonstrators did not follow in the nonviolent footsteps of Rosa Parks and Martin Luther King, Jr. In fact, the demonstrators may have known more about the traditions of the Black freedom movement than their critics. Historian Robin Kelley notes that Parks was not the first or only Black woman to protest segregation on the buses: while the Montgomery Bus Boycott of 1955–1957 publicized her example and mobilized around it, the movement also sprang from the actions of the dozens of Black women in the preceding years who sat down in seats reserved for whites, who argued with drivers and conductors, and who sometimes fought physically with white passengers (Robinson 1997, 141). The critics remember Dr. King's "Letter from a Birmingham Jail" but forget that it took angry Black youths hurling rocks and bottles at firefighters to convince Attorney General Robert Kennedy's Department of Justice to send federal marshals to enforce the law in that city. The critics imagine that the students could replicate the nonviolent lunch counter sit-ins at which demonstrators were beaten and humiliated for seeking the right to order a meal, when the situation facing Black people in Ferguson was more like the circumstances that compelled the Deacons for Defense and the Black Panther party to engage in armed self-defense. As Ashley Yates from Millennials United in Action argues, "The youth knew something very early that the older generation didn't. We knew that the system had already failed even before they began to show their hand publicly. We knew that not only was the murder of Mike Brown unjustified, it was another example of how the systems in place made it acceptable to gun us down" (Taylor 2016, 162).

Balans

In their many diverse acts of accompaniment and improvisation, the Ferguson movement repeatedly turned hegemony on its head. Participants understood that Officer Wilson confronted Michael Brown because he had been assigned to police bodies considered out of place and make arrests so that fines imposed on Black people would fill the city's coffers. They responded as bodies out of place, joining together in the streets and on the sidewalks in festive and resistant congregation. Their place-based resistance had been years in the making. Poe remembered standing at the corner of West Florissant Avenue and Chambers Road when he was thirteen and thinking, "This isn't normal. I can't even walk to the barber shop to get a haircut without being harassed by a cop. I remember standing there one day on that corner and I just looked up at the sky and I was like, I don't know what's going to happen here, but something is going to happen here. I don't know what. I don't know when. I don't know how. But this is so unsustainable that it has to explode one day. And it exploded" (Green et al. 2016, 17–18).

Another deployment of *balans* emerged from being treated as colonized subjects. Black people in Ferguson were patrolled by armed law enforcement officers and National Guard troops riding in mine-resistant armor-protected vehicles, wielding weapons originally intended for use in Iraq and Afghanistan against opponents of the U.S. presence in those nations. Protesting citizens were expected to bear the brunt of what colonized people around the world have faced from the oppressors who occupy their territory, a battle for complete victory and total dominance. That is why the officer leading the National Guard troops in Ferguson referred to them as "adversaries" and "enemy forces." Yet that very ascription won them unexpected partners in accompaniment. When Palestinian activists in territories occupied by the Israeli army saw images tweeted from Ferguson, they recognized that the same instruments of counterinsurgency that had been used against them were being used against the uprising in Missouri. Immediately they sent tweets to the Ferguson activists with instructions about self-defense, advising them to stay close to the police so the police could not launch the gas without endangering themselves, to always run against the wind, and to refrain from rubbing their eyes. One Ferguson activist had viewed pictures posted online by activists in Gaza weeks before Michael Brown was killed. She identified with the people she saw suffering repression but never expected that the place where she lived would soon "become Gaza" (Taylor 2016, 162). Philosopher and social justice activist Judith Butler notes how the militarization of police forces controlling people of color in U.S. cities has in fact been facilitated largely by "weapons and training sessions supplied by states such as Israel and Bahrain" (Butler 2015, 234). Butler explains that these colonial links unwittingly promoted decolonial solidarities among previously disparate peoples. Activists in Gaza sent their helpful information to street demonstrators in Ferguson, but they also offered political support. One tweet read "Hashtag Palestine, Hashtag Ferguson: Palestine knows what it means to be shot for your ethnicity" (Butler 2015, 237–238). That solidarity tempered the Ferguson activists' desires for full citizenship and social membership inside the U.S. nation with recognition of the U.S. role as an imperial power in the world constantly at war with people of color.

Another instance of *balans* in the Ferguson movement entailed holding street protests inside suburban big box stores and throughout downtown shopping areas in the St. Louis area. Resenting how aggressive policing in Ferguson and other North County municipalities caused Black motorists and pedestrians to be fined relentlessly, with these fines used to finance city expenditures, the demonstrators found ways to raise the costs of white supremacy by disrupting business as usual, by staging demonstrations that closed the streets to traffic and by promoting boycotts of downtown businesses during the Christmas season. Percy Green explains, "For me, racism is like you are bringing a business proposition. It always has been. Even slavery was a business proposition. So the way I see it, you make it more costly. . . . Make the status quo more costly to exist. . . . Make it a liability rather than an asset. Why should businessmen or why should the establishment make change when they can still continue to make their profit?" (Green et al. 2016, 14).

Two Mirrors: What Good Is a Mirror if It Hides the Truth?

Like the accompaniment and improvisation of the Idle No More movement and the creations made by Chicanx artivistas, the Ferguson movement is at one and the same time a political project, a cultural project, and, importantly, a knowledge project. Just as Idle No More needed to challenge the principle of *terra nullius* and the myth of discovery in order to restory Canada, and just as Chicanx artivistas needed to displace and replace the Latino Threat Narrative, the Ferguson movement needed to promote new ways of seeing in order to create new ways of being. They held up two mirrors to the world, one reflecting terrible oppression and the other revealing a new world on its way. Yet the pictures they showed were seen in distorted form by many outsiders, as if they were reflections in a fun house mirror. Most of the dominant knowledge producing institutions of our society go to great lengths to make people *not* see what is clearly in plain sight. They produce experts in legitimation and justification. Their impoverished explanations for the existence and persistence of racial oppression teach people to live with evil and ignore it. The enduring realities of racial oppression that should demand honesty and accountability instead produce pervasive denial and disavowal.

Expert Knowledge as a Racial Project

Opportunities and life chances in U.S. society remain color bound, but dominant discourses about race require people to pretend to be color blind. The spaces structured in dominance in scholarly journals and college classrooms where humanities and social science instruction, apprenticeship, and expression take place are parties to the problems that Black people face in Ferguson. Dominant traditions of colonial knowledge embraced by credentialed scholars in gatekeeping institutions create the frameworks that distorted public perceptions of the Ferguson movement and other social movements like it.

The killing of Michael Brown and the responses to it evidence many failures: a failure of police procedure, a failure of prosecutorial ethics and accountability, and a failure of political and religious leaders. Less evident, but equally important, are the ways in which the crisis in Ferguson reveals a colossal failure of the humanities and the social sciences. This may seem like an odd claim. The categories, concepts, and contexts of academic research appear to be far removed from the immediate perceptions of people in the midst of crises like the one in Ferguson. We can be certain that Officer Darren Wilson did not read John Locke, Immanuel Kant, or G.W.F. Hegel before firing bullet after bullet into Michael Brown's body. It is safe to assume that Prosecutor McCulloch and Governor Nixon did not need to peruse the writings of Daniel Patrick Moynihan or James Q. Wilson to guide their exculpation of Officer Wilson and their criminalization of his victim. Yet every scene of argument is a space shaped by the promiscuous movement of ideas across discourses and social divides. The things that police officers believe about themselves and others, like the decisions that prosecutors and politicians make about which people deserve protection and which deserve prosecution, are deeply rooted in concepts and practices that are constructed, nurtured, sustained, rationalized, and justified in the humanities and social sciences. Especially at play in the Ferguson crisis were the humanities' concepts of interiority, projection, and methodological individualism and the social sciences' understandings of difference, deviance, and dependence. People who may never read books or articles from the humanities and social sciences nonetheless lead lives governed by the categories learned and legitimized in them. Although not directly referenced by any of the participants in Ferguson, the ideas of Kant, Locke, Hegel, and other humanists, and of Daniel Patrick Moynihan, James Q. Wilson, Samuel P. Huntington and other social scientists shaped the behaviors and beliefs that caused the crisis in Ferguson and shaped the deeply unjust and immoral responses to it.

Ferguson as a Failure of the Humanities

Core concepts from the humanities helped shape the ways in which participants and observers understood and explained the events in Ferguson. To make such a claim is not to recommend dispensing with the tools that the humanities provide but rather is meant to provoke exploration of how the emancipatory promise of humanist knowledge is undermined by its practices and to identify how new and better ways of knowing are emerging at the grass roots among people compelled to deal with its contradictions.

Three key items in the humanities tool kit stand at the center of the failures of the humanities in Ferguson: interiority, projection, and methodological individualism. Interiority entails the creation and cultivation of a private psychic subject seeking protection from engulfment by a threatening social aggregate. Projection displaces doubts and anxieties about the self onto demonized others. Through projection, aggression becomes rationalized as preemptive self-defense. Methodological individualism treats social relations as solely the accretion of actions by autonomous individuals rather than as the creation of social structures and systems. It focuses on individual intentions and behaviors as if they take place in a vacuum.

Interiority in Ferguson

The inner fears and feelings of the white police officer Darren Wilson took center stage in accounts of the Ferguson uprising, while Michael Brown was assumed to have no interiority worth noticing. Wilson's statement that he was afraid during his confrontation with the unarmed teenager was accepted as justification for the killing. The six-foot-four officer who weighed 215 pounds presented himself as so frightened by the unarmed overweight teenager in shorts, a T-shirt, and flip-flops that he had to fire his gun at the youth over and over, a total of twelve times. Wilson initiated the confrontation by driving up to the youth, grabbing him by the arm from inside his squad car and telling the young man to "get the f— back on the sidewalk." He pursued Brown when the youth tried to run away and then fired his gun repeatedly once the suspect turned toward him. These were not the only actions available to the officer. Wilson was driving a squad car equipped with a radio on which he could call for backup. His car was equipped not only with a gun but with mace and a retractable baton. Yet in the officer's account, which was accepted fully and uncritically by his supervisors, the prosecutor's office, the press, and his public supporters, he was the victim and Brown was the aggressor. This distortion of reality could be seen as sensible only because of a racialized narrative that pitted a fully acknowledged human with an interiority deserving respect against a symbol of non-humanity presumed to have no feelings or fears.

Like the core scenario of Hollywood westerns where settler colonial aggression against Indigenous people becomes understood as frontier defense, Officer Wilson perceived himself as threatened by the natives of hostile territory. A white officer who resided in the nearly all-white suburb of Crestwood, Wilson was patrolling a Black neighborhood in a city that was two-thirds Black. Wilson claimed that his interior fear stemmed in part from being in Southeast Ferguson, an area that he described as filled with gangs, guns, and drug activity. If that was indeed the case, perhaps public safety would have been better served if Officer Wilson would actually have been looking out for gangs, guns, and drugs rather than stopping a teenager for allegedly jaywalking. Moreover, the official crime statistics for St. Louis County reveal that the Black neighborhood in Ferguson that so frightened Officer Wilson experiences levels of drug use and violence no different from many of the white neighborhoods in suburban south St. Louis County where Officer Wilson lived.

It was not the actual threat to Officer Wilson that guided his actions on August 9, 2014, but rather the significance of the racial demography of the neighborhood inside his mind. "It's not a very well-liked community," Wilson told the grand jury. Then perhaps realizing that his statement had just revealed his deep bias against the neighborhood and its residents, the officer reversed the equation and said, "That community doesn't like the police" (Clarke and Castillo 2014). If indeed the community did not like the police, it may have been because Darren Wilson and his fellow officers were under orders to raise revenue for the municipality by making nuisance stops and to provoke confrontations so that they could add on charges such as failure to comply and resisting arrest that would increase the fines that residents like Michael Brown would have to pay.

Michael Brown's interiority was treated quite differently from Darren Wilson's. Just ten days after the killing, the *New York Times* published a story by reporter John Eligon alleging that Michael Brown "was no angel" (2014). Eligon noted that the eighteen-year-old lived in a neighborhood with "rough patches," that he had dabbled in drugs and alcohol, that he got into at least one "scrap" with a neighbor, and that he sang rap lyrics that "were in turn both contemplative and vulgar." This narrative did not explore whether these descriptions created a particularly unusual profile for an eighteen-year-old youth. It did not mention that Michael Brown had parents and a grandmother who loved him, who affectionately called him Mike Mike, and who admired his skill with computers. The story did not say that despite never having had the opportunity to attend a fully accredited school, Brown graduated from high school and had enrolled in a technical training institute to study heating and cooling system installation and repair. Eligon's story was not concerned with the interiority of a mother who had just had her eighteen-year-old son's life taken or of a father seeing his dead child in the street (Johnson 2016). Instead, John Eligon decided to investigate whether Michael Brown was an angel.

The upshot of Eligon's story was that Brown's "failure" to be an angel undermined the legitimacy of grief about his death. This is an extraordinary formulation. Given the premise of this story, one might expect reporter Eligon to have a lucrative career writing comparable features about other deaths. Perhaps he could investigate whether any of the people killed on 9/11 were angels or whether John F. Kennedy and Robert Kennedy were sufficiently angelic to merit having their deaths treated as grievable. He might find his next journalistic "scoop" in the Bible, which reveals that Jesus Christ dabbled in wine, consorted with criminals, and on at least one occasion got into a scrap with money changers in the temple. Perhaps Eligon could use that evidence to argue that the crucifixion was really no big deal. Such stories would be considered deeply offensive and gravely inappropriate, and rightly so. But in relation to the death of Michael Brown, Eligon's absurd premise proved perfectly acceptable to the nation's most respected newspaper.

The standard of angelic status apparently expected of Michael Brown was not applied to Darren Wilson. He too was a person with some rough patches in his history, in both his upbringing and his adult life. During his freshman year in high school, problems at home led Wilson to stop attending school and to start spending much of his time with youths known to be troublemakers (Halpern 2015, 4). The officer's mother, Tonya Dean, was caught writing bad checks and pleaded guilty to charges of stealing and forgery. She spent money recklessly and plunged her family deeply into debt.

Dean repaid some of what she owed by stealing it from new victims. She lied repeatedly, telling unsuspecting marks that she was an heiress. Yet Dean's white skin protected her from serving time in jail. She was convicted of crimes but sentenced only to probation, an option not offered to the many Black residents of Ferguson who were sent to jail in 2014 for being too poor to pay fines imposed on them for petty offenses after being arrested and charged by Officer Wilson and his colleagues (Halpern 2015, 4; Leonnig, Kindy, and Achenbach, 2014). Officer Wilson had a sketchy family life, got into trouble as a teenager, and as a fully grown adult got into a "scrap" of his own with the former partner of his second wife, a man who was the father of her four-year-old son—and who at one point assaulted her, pulling her hair and punching her in the face, and attacking Wilson as well (Collins and Bates 2014).

Wilson also used vulgar language, perhaps not singing along with rap lyrics but rather while in pursuit of his duties as a police officer sworn to protect and serve the public. In court depositions related to civil litigation given after his grand jury testimony, Wilson admitted that on the day that he killed Michael Brown he had shouted at the youth to "get the f— back" and had grabbed Brown's arm through the window from his sitting position in his patrol car. He also admitted that in the past, he had used the word "nigger" to describe Black people (Lowery 2017). Yet John Eligon's story in the *New York Times* did not see fit to discuss why Darren Wilson's use of profanity was less significant than Michael Brown's rap lyrics, or whether the criminal background in Officer Wilson's family, his previous record of police work in an expressly anti-Black setting in another suburb, or his shooting at Michael Brown twelve times proved that Darren Wilson was "no angel." Wilson did not need to be an angel, however, to secure sympathy and support; he only had to be white (Leonnig, Kindy, and Achenbach 2014).

The privileging of Darren Wilson's interiority over Michael Brown's was supported by a long history of the coloniality of power central to the traditions of the humanities. The creation of Western modernity proceeded through conquest, colonization, and slavery. In official papers of state, but also in paintings, plays, poems, novels, and historical narratives, Europeans presented colonial conquest not as plunder but as noble and ennobling work necessary for the spread of civilization. The murdering, torturing, starving, burning, and looting carried out by Europeans became depicted as a sad burden to be endured by the conquerors only because of the alleged savagery of the conquered. The Europeans' own interior state of mind as they carried out this burden fascinated them endlessly. The subjectivity of those they brutalized and killed interested them not at all. Hannah Arendt observes how this pattern persisted as an exculpatory trope in the 1930s and 1940s when it was used by Heinrich Himmler in justifying Nazi brutality. Arendt explains, "Instead of saying what horrible things I did to people!" Himmler framed the issue as "what horrible things I had to watch in pursuance of my duties, how heavily the task weighed upon my shoulders!" (Arendt 1994, 106).

Darren Wilson and his supporters viewed the events on Canfield Drive on August 9, 2014, through the self-pitying lens that Arendt found in Himmler. Wilson appealed for sympathy from the grand jurors by speaking about his internal state of mind, about how frightened he was, about how small and powerless he perceived himself to be, and about how demonic Michael Brown seemed to him. Yet he granted no personhood to Michael Brown, referring to him as "it." One year after the shooting, a reporter asked Wilson if he ever reflected on what kind of person Brown was. "Do I think about him as a person?" Wilson inquired, and then answered his own question. "Not really, because it doesn't matter at this point." Wilson did complain, however, that Brown's parents had filed a civil suit against him for killing their son, "so I *have* to think about him" (Halpern 2015, 27). His own inconvenience at possibly being held accountable for the life he took loomed large to Wilson; the suffering of the Brown family because their son's life had been taken did not matter to him.

The roots of Wilson's rationalizations and the full embrace of them by journalists and the justice system echo many of the traditional moves of the humanities. John Locke's theory of contract presumes the existence of separate and independent persons who come together reluctantly and hesitantly at a particular point in history to form a social contract. Similarly, the psychic subject created by humanistic expressive culture imagines itself as always already autonomous. It looks inward and resists putative incursions by others. A sustained social pedagogy encourages people to perceive themselves as self-regulating individuals and to cultivate the interior qualities and external appearances needed to function as a rights-bearing subject of the law and a rational and acquisitive actor in the market. Narrated in literature through the novel, naturalized in visual art through perspectival paintings and portraits, and used to form the imagined autonomous agent of moral philosophy, the interior subject of the humanities substitutes affect for action. It seeks sensations to feel, not practical work to perform. The suffering of others may provoke sympathy and pity but not intersubjective solidarity. Each realm of expressive culture and each dimension of social life tells the same story. This apparatus requires enormous cultural labor to invent and sustain, but its ubiquity makes it seem as if it is not an invention at all.

Literary scholar Nancy Armstrong explains the formative role played by the eighteenth-century novel in creating the particular interior subject of modernity. The structure and narrative voice of the modern novel wrote interiority into being by presuming that it already existed, by presenting the self-reflective individual subject as both the narrating voice presenting stories and the implied and inscribed recipient of them (Armstrong 2005, 3). Like the market subject of contract theory, the interior psychic subject of the novel seeks individual fulfillment and resists collective associations and obligations. The social aggregate becomes coterminous with the threat of monstrous collectivity, an engulfing otherness, a mob that threatens individuality (Armstrong 2005, 25). Edward Said shows the connections between this modern subject and the colonial matrix of power. He analyzes a wide range of canonical novels to reveal how their narrative and ideological tensions build reader engagement and investment through a geography of dominance that is global in scope. "Without empire," Said asserts, "there is no European novel as we know it" (Said 1994, 244; Feldman 2015, 155). Social historians Leonore Davidoff and Catherine Hall demonstrate how contract theory and literary interiority came to shape and reflect idealized narratives about the patriarchal, propertied middle-class family as a haven in a heartless world, as a protected realm of intimacy and affection in an otherwise ruthlessly competitive and cruel capitalist society (Davidoff and Hall 2003). Musicologist Susan McClary establishes the ways in which the symphony and other forms, figures, and devices of Western art music metaphorically connected agency and autonomy to a besieged yet heroic masculine subject (McClary 1991). Intellectual historian and philosopher Donald Lowe shows how the emergence of typographic culture and its attendant visual regimes encouraged the perception that objective knowledge existed independently of knowing subjects, elevating dispassionate distance over intersubjective empathy, proximate experience, and engagement (Lowe 1983). As Robert Scholes warned—in his Presidential Address at meetings of the Modern Language Association in 2004—in actual practice "the humanities not only fail to humanize, they may actually dehumanize, by putting a concern for texts in the place where concern for other human beings ought to be found" (Scholes 2005, 726).

The interiority promoted by the humanities offers the illusion of autonomy and independence, yet it remains utterly dependent upon phobic fantasies about the social connections it rejects. The bourgeois subject perceives itself to be under attack, constantly fending off external aggression and corruption. It seeks safety from the crossing of borders and the blend-ing of categories. Yet it is obsessed with the others it disavows. It secures its identity more from what it is not than from what it is. Anxieties about social disorder and criminal violence in the outside world have social utility. They provide justification for the suffocating closures of bourgeois domesticity; they become a rationale for giving uncritical support to the state violence that protects class rule and empire. Lowering others by describing them as different, deviant, and dependent artificially elevates selves that can be seen in contrast as morally virtuous and self-sufficient. The more degraded and threatening the world seems, the more justified bourgeois interiority be-comes. The properly ordered private home and neighborhood are imagined as antidotes to public disorder and deviance. The self-interested, avaricious, acquisitive, and conscienceless market actor proclaims itself as morally virtu-ous by stoking moral panics about the thief and the thug. The investor and owner who profit from exploiting others become in their own eyes virtuous producers through repeated depictions of the poor as parasites and perverts.

The physical geographies of suburbs like Ferguson replicate the moral geography that reflects and shapes the interiority of the humanist subject. City planners and developers created bedroom communities in St. Louis County as an escape from the imagined vices of the city. Free-standing owner-occupied houses were placed a suitable distance from neighbors in the county, contrasting sharply with the row houses and multiple family dwellings in the city. A paucity of public places and connecting through streets combined with a plethora of private neighborhoods and cul-de-sacs made suburban space different from the gathering places and avenues tra-versed by streetcar and bus transit inside the city. Zoning regulations and mortgage lending practices pitted each suburban neighborhood in competi-tion with others as residents tried to trap amenities and advantages within their jurisdictions and to export hazards and nuisances to other places. A resulting ethic of defensive localism and hostile privatism fuses economic self-interest with the interiority of the humanist subject creating a mutual-ly reinforcing feedback loop between social structures and culture. In this ecology, Black bodies ascribed as out of place trigger defensive and aversive fear in the interior worlds of whiteness.

Projection in Ferguson

Projection displaces onto others the uncomfortable truths one does want to acknowledge about the self. It has been deployed consistently and repeatedly in colonial knowledge projects to blame the colonized for the violence and brutality committed against them by the colonizers. Europeans claimed to be modern by portraying the peoples of Africa, Asia, and Latin America as premodern and primitive. Positioning the inhabitants of the territories marked for conquest and colonization as ontologically and rationally deficient justified their exploitation, enslavement, and extermination. When the people targeted for domination resisted, they were considered monstrous, so monumental force was deployed to defeat them. Rather than taking responsibility for the brutality of conquest, Europeans deployed a complex cultural apparatus to blame the victims and excuse the victimizers. Phobic fantasies of monstrous Blackness erased the barbarism committed in the name of civilization by depicting the people of the global south as savage, immoral, and impervious to pain. Such fantasies are used to justify the almost all-white Ferguson police force acting like an occupying army patrolling a municipality with a population that is two-thirds Black. Such fantasies fuel the demonization of Black people by officers claiming to be fearful in the face of the subjectivity of Black people.

Phobic projection permeated Darren Wilson's grand jury testimony as well as the narratives advanced by his supporters before and after it. Wilson described himself as helpless in relation to Brown. Referring to the teenager as "it" rather than "he," Wilson related, "It looks like a demon," adding that as he grappled with Brown's arm from the inside of his squad car, "I felt like a five year old holding on to Hulk Hogan. Hulk Hogan. That's how big he felt, and how small I felt just grasping his arm" (Goldwasser 2016). Wilson expressed no regret for the incident, no sorrow for the death he caused, only self-pity for having been exposed to a threat and relieved when it ended. As he watched Brown die, Wilson recalled, "the demeanor on his face went blank—the aggression was gone, I mean, I knew he stopped, the threat was stopped" (Goldwasser 2016).

Identification with Wilson and his phobic projection received public support. Once Officer Wilson's identity as the killer became public, police officers' unions, family members of officers, and spokespersons for racist right-wing hate groups rallied to support him. They quickly raised half a million dollars and sent it to Wilson, even though he had been charged with no crime and never would be, had no legal defense fund, and never asked for these donations. Wilson was able to buy a new home with the bounty he received from these supporters (Halpern 2015, 3). They carried signs in demonstrations that read "We Love and Support You Darren," "We Are

Your Voice PO Wilson," and "I Love the Police." These statements are quite different from describing the shooting as a misunderstanding, a regrettable tragedy, an escalation of a situation that could have been handled more calmly, or even a legally justified act of self-defense. Why would people who did not know him "love" Darren Wilson? Why did the signs portray him as in need of a helping "voice" when he had not been charged with any crime or targeted for internal disciplinary action and it was clear that the chief of police, the police union, the mayor, the city council, and the county prosecutor were doing everything possible to prevent Wilson from even having to be questioned under oath in an adversarial courtroom proceeding? These signs were not really designed to provide support for Officer Wilson but instead were used to protest the protestors: to present innocent white people as oppressed by demonstrations claiming a racist injury and to recruit other white people to that position. One sign at a demonstration supporting Officer Wilson directly taunted the people protesting the killing. Mocking the slogan "Black Lives Matter," the Wilson supporter displayed a sign that read "Police Lives Matter." No police officer's life had been taken or even threatened. Yet the mere assertion by the Ferguson protesters that the life of Michael Brown was worth grieving and that his killer should be brought to justice was inverted by projection into a threat against police officers' lives.

Another sign supporting Wilson proclaimed, "Reason Must Prevail Not Emotion," as if the officer who claimed to be frightened by a demon and to feeling like a five-year-old being picked up by a giant was a paragon of reason, while demonstrators who wanted a trial where evidence could be introduced and the killer cross-examined on the witness stand were rationally and ontologically deficient beings motivated only by emotion. Other signs displayed in demonstrations supporting Officer Wilson were suffused with projection. One read, "I don't support a race: I support the Truth." As a statement on a sign held by a white man in a crowd of white people seeking to have a white officer not stand trial for killing a Black man, the disavowal of racial intent strikes an oddly unconvincing defensive note. The premise of the sign is that the participants in the Ferguson uprising were reflexively and unthinkingly antiwhite, that Wilson was being persecuted because he was white, and that to charge a racial injury is to be inappropriately race conscious. Yet this purported devotion to not supporting a race was not evident in Ferguson during all the years that the all-white city council and the nearly all white police force engaged in conscious and deliberate racial profiling in making vehicle stops. While comprising 67 percent of the population, Black people were targeted for 86 percent of the stops by Ferguson police. White people who comprised 29 percent of the population accounted for only 12.7 percent of those detained. Fifty-nine times the police took more than thirty minutes to search the vehicles of Black motorists. Only one search of a white driver's car took as long as thirty minutes. Yet the white drivers and pedestrians stopped by Ferguson officers possessed contraband 34 percent of the time compared to 21.7 percent of the similarly detained Black people targets of the police (Arch City Defenders 2014).

The placard proclaiming "I don't support a race" also read "I support the Truth." This statement no doubt refers to the contested claims about whether Michael Brown had "surrendered" before he was killed. Officer Wilson and his supporters insisted that Brown did not have his hands up in the position of surrender when he was killed and stated that the findings of the Grand Jury, of an investigation by the U.S. Department of Justice and by investigative reporters verified that claim. Witnesses testified to the grand jury, however, that Michael Brown did have his hands up in a position of surrender when he was killed (Mirzoeff 2016) and this view was taken up by protestors in Ferguson street demonstrations who held their hands high above their heads and chanted, "Hands up. Don't shoot."

The grand jury proceedings did show that Brown was in a posture of surrender: he had one arm and hand above his head; the arm not lifted above his head had been broken and its hand had been wounded by a shot (Brown was suffering as well from a punctured lung with a two-centimeter hole in it). One might argue that no matter how many hands were up, the "truth" is that Brown was in a posture of surrender and was certainly not a threat to Wilson. In any case, the officers and a prosecutor who challenged the story of Brown's surrender were resolutely determined to do what they could to exonerate the officer. No one interested in Michael Brown's side of the story got to question Officer Wilson under oath.

Moreover, constructing the "truth" of the surrender story as instead a matter of *either/or* serves the useful political purpose of framing the demonstrators as "lying." Relying on interview testimony and forensic evidence, an investigation by the Department of Justice found that the claim that Brown had both "hands up" *could not be proved.* Journalists from the *Washington Post* and other mainstream news outlets took this to mean that because the claim could not be substantiated that it was a *lie.* Yet such is not the position typically taken by prosecutors and the press when police officers make claims about a brief and violent incident that cannot be substantiated. Under such circumstances the conclusion drawn by the authorities and the press is *not* that the officers lied but that it is difficult to rely on eyewitness testimony and personal recollections in such cases.

No matter what the truth of the "hands up story," actually standing in support of "the truth"—as the sign holder professes to do—would entail a whole host of obligations that the sign holder would certainly eschew. When Officer Wilson was first questioned by friendly police officials, he stated that he had no knowledge that Brown earlier that morning might have been in a slight pushing match with a store owner and might have taken some cigarillos without paying for them. When he testified to the grand jury, however, Wilson swore that the report of the "robbery" is why he stopped Brown. This was probably not a discrepancy that the sign holding supporter of "the truth" would want cleared up. The Ferguson chief of police released a videotape of the incident at the store in order to smear Brown's reputation and provide a possible alibi for the officer. He claimed that he was not trying to help Officer Wilson's case; he had been compelled to release the video because of a Freedom of Information Act request. Yet no such request had been submitted. The sign held by the truth seeker gave no indication of demanding truth from the chief of police. Moreover, the investigation by the Department of Justice revealed that Ferguson police officers routinely lied about their actions and covered up each other's breaches of proper procedure. Surely, this is a matter to which a defender of the truth would attend.

Another sign lifted up in support of Officer Wilson said "It's about the Rule of Law." In general parlance the rule of law is about getting one's day in court, having evidence assembled fairly, facing accusers, and having a judge or jury reach a verdict after an adversarial proceeding where the arguments are tested. None of that was done in response to the killing of Michael Brown. Instead, the rule of law was perverted and undermined by the prosecution and the police. The grand jury proceeding was conducted in secret, while Prosecutor McCulloch consistently leaked testimony favorable to Officer Wilson to the press. The prosecutors led Wilson through a series of carefully designed exculpatory questions. The officer did not have to undergo cross-examination. Prosecutors instructed the grand jurors to decline to indict on the basis of a state statute that had already been declared unconstitutional. The grand jury was not informed how the rule of law had been openly flaunted by the Ferguson Police Department. The racial profiling carried out by the department expressly violated the Safe Streets Act and the Fourteenth Amendment. Stops without probable cause violated the Fourth Amendment. One young Black man was ticketed and fined for giving "false information" to a police officer because he told the office that his name was

Mike but the officer found that his driver's license referred to him as Michael. Evidently the rule of law celebrated in the pro-Wilson demonstrator's sign does not include constitutional rights for Black people.

The political and psychic power of projection is revealed in Ferguson particularly through the differential deployment of discourses of personal responsibility and accountability. The alleged failures of Black people to demonstrate personal responsibility and accountability are used to warrant draconian policies and aggressive policing against them. For example, when the investigation by the Department of Justice revealed patterns of illegal racial profiling that prevailed in Ferguson—with racial disparities in police stops, arrests, convictions, fines, and jail terms—police and court officials claimed that the disparities had nothing to do with white racism but instead stemmed from the lack of personal responsibility and accountability among Black people. Systematic projection—displacing devalued traits and anxieties onto demonized others—justifies their criminal treatment. Such projection assumes the robust presence of a white accountability. However, examination of the careers and comments of only a few prominent officials, judges, and police officers calls into question this implicit assumption of a healthy white accountability.

For example, Mary Ann Twitty was the white city clerk in Ferguson who administered a system of collecting unjustly leveled fines paid by the disproportionately Black population of Ferguson in such a way that people went to jail, lost their jobs, got evicted from their homes, and sank into irreversible debt. The Department of Justice found these practices in violation of the law. It was discovered that Twitty had also circulated a number of racist emails. One of the emails she sent included a picture of Ronald Reagan feeding a baby chimpanzee, with a caption calling it a rare photo of Ronald Reagan babysitting Barack Obama in 1962 (MacNeal 2015). Another email claimed that aborting the fetuses of Black women would be a good form of crime control (Halpern 2015, 14). When her practice of circulating racist emails was made public, Twitty was fired. But her response was not to take personal responsibility for her actions: instead she claimed that the emails were funny and complained that she was being picked on unfairly. "They ruined my life for the sake of what was going on in Ferguson. I think it's sickening. It really just upset me," she exclaimed in a display of self-pitying interiority (MacNeal 2015). Twitty claimed that she was the real victim. "It took me a while," she proclaimed, "to get over the feeling of being raped and thrown under the bus" (MacNeal 2015). Her indignity was short-lived, however. Twitty was soon hired by another North County municipality,

Vinita Park. Twitty's behavior and comments do not demonstrate a white commitment to personal responsibility or accountability that could justify differential treatment of Black people.

Another example is municipal court judge Ronald Brockmeyer, who fined thousands of Ferguson residents and ordered hundreds sent to jail when they could not pay their fines. When Brockmeyer himself received a traffic ticket for running a red light in a nearby municipality, however, he turned to Ferguson's city manager for help and got the ticket fixed. Brockmeyer himself fixed tickets given to police patrol supervisors in Ferguson (United States Department of Justice 2015, 74). A Ferguson city council member at one point notified municipal officials that Judge Brockmeyer consistently failed to listen to testimony in his court, to review reports, to read the record of the criminal histories of defendants, or to allow witnesses with relevant information to testify. The council member was told in response that the money that flowed to the city's coffers from Judge Brockmeyer's court did a great deal for the city, so the judge's behavior should not be questioned (United States Department of Justice 2015, 15). Brockmeyer used his position as a judge routinely to demand his version of personal accountability from Black defendants, but he had his own problems with accountability. He failed to pay federal taxes for years, amassing an unpaid debt to the government in excess of $170,000. Brockmeyer did not spend one day in jail for this massive debt but continued to send to jail Black people who owed Ferguson less than $100. Judge Ronald Brockmeyer did not take personal responsibility for his conduct in court or for his failure to pay taxes, nor was he held accountable for it.

The projection of unaccountability onto others protects white political interests and shores up the legitimacy of white failures of accountability and personal responsibility. This practice was exhibited in the arguments of St. Louis police union representative Jeff Roorda and Missouri Lieutenant governor Peter Kinder in response to the report by the Department of Justice. The Department of Justice found that the Ferguson police department's racial profiling and harassment violated Section VI of the 1964 Civil Rights Act, the Safe Streets Act of 1968, and the First, Fourth, and Fourteenth Amendments to the Constitution. Its report found that the racial practices of the Ferguson police compromised rather than protected public safety (United States Department of Justice 2015). There are many responses to the report that could have demonstrated a robust commitment to accountability and personal responsibility on the part of white officials. For example, Roorda and Kinder could have urged reflection and reform in the face of the evidence of the report. They could have urged a rethinking of Ferguson's all-white city government bureaucracy. They could have suggested revisiting the decision to raise revenue by having Ferguson's nearly all-white police force racially profile Black people and charge them with as many offenses as possible. They could have suggested reforming police policies, so Darren Wilson and his fellow officers would not be encouraged to provoke suspects and escalate street encounters in order to create additional charges of "failure to comply," a subjective offense routinely added to other alleged violations—even used alone as a charge if no other violation could be fabricated. Instead Roorda extended the scope of his projection, insisting on the complete innocence of the police department, while comparing the investigators from the Department of Justice to "a band of marauders" (Mann 2015). Similarly, Lieutenant Governor Kinder charged that the Department of Justice was staffed by Marxists and Black radicals intent on "fanning the flames of racial division" (Mann 2015). In the eyes of Roorda and Kinder, no personal responsibility or self-reflection was required of the police or the city policy makers. Projection allows people who themselves refuse to accept personal responsibility to project their own character flaws onto the people they oppress.

Officer Wilson displayed projection explicitly in his descriptions of Michael Brown and other Black residents of Ferguson. Immediately after telling a reporter that he did not think about who Michael Brown was as a person, Wilson contradicted himself and demonstrated that projection provided a means to frame the youth according to standards that he himself did not meet. "Do I think he had the best upbringing?" Wilson said, asking himself a question the reporter had not asked. "No. Not at all," he insisted (Halpern 2015, 27). Wilson projected a tumultuous home life onto Brown as justification for killing him, despite Wilson's own problems at home throughout his life. It was Officer Wilson whose mother was a convicted felon. It was Wilson who ceased attending his classes in high school, and who associated himself with people known to be troublemakers. In another part of the same interview, Wilson described Black youths in Ferguson as immersed in a "pre-gang culture, where you are just running in the streets—not worried about working in the morning, just worried about your immediate gratification." He went on to assert with confidence, "It is the same younger culture that is everywhere in the inner cities" (Halpern 2015, 11). The suburb of Ferguson, however, can only be described as an "inner city" if everywhere that Black people live is the inner city.

That "inner city" culture was so offensive to him, Wilson claimed, that he decided to dwell twenty miles away from Ferguson in the nearly all-white suburb of Crestwood because he and his family needed "that buffer" and "a chance to get out of that element" (Halpern 2015, 11). Wilson would not live within the city limits of the municipality that employed him. His own home life in a sheltered suburb away from "that element," however included the violent confrontation with his second wife's former partner. The poor upbringing and turbulent family life that Wilson cited as an explanation for treating residents of Southeast Ferguson as criminals out of control applied to him as well. If Wilson was held to the standard projected onto Michael Brown and his community, then his own logic dictates doubting the veracity of his accounts of the incident where he took the life of another family's son.

Methodological Individualism in Ferguson

Racism can be a matter of private prejudice and individual animus, but it also permeates social structures and systems in ways that consign raced people to premature death while imposing impediments to their physical movement and economic mobility on the basis of the artificial, arbitrary, and irrational category of race. Methodological individualism functions as a form of racial suppression by portraying systematic, structural, and institutional racism as the product of innumerable isolated actions by presumably independent individuals. The act of denying structural causes also serves to delegitimize structural solutions. It makes the project of ending racism cost-free for white people, enabling them to disavow the advantages they receive from their group identity while insisting that victims of racism remedy their condition individually by finding ways to work around the unjust impediments placed in their path.

Methodological individualism has a long history. In his exhaustively researched and brilliantly argued analysis of the links between nineteenth-century slavery and the system of racialized capitalism that it created, Walter Johnson demonstrates that slavery's defenders attributed the horrible brutality of the system to the misdeeds of a few bad actors. They claimed that rapes and beatings were misdeeds by individual slave owners. They celebrated (and exaggerated) their own alleged acts of paternalism and kindness, representing slavery as a largely voluntary agreement between the humans held as property in bondage and the humans who profited from their subordination. Johnson writes: "They broke the system of slavery into hundreds of thousands of isolated sets of human relations between individual masters and individual slaves and argued that the violence of slavery was a matter of generally benevolent human relations gone awry, of the personal failings of particular owners, of bad masters who gave slavery a bad name, not an inevitable feature of the system itself" (Johnson 1999, 217–218).

Darren Wilson displayed methodological individualism in downplaying police misconduct. He conceded that the Ferguson Police Department included a few bigoted officers but insisted he was not one of them. Wilson did not acknowledge as significant the structural conditions framing his own work as a police officer. Before he joined the Ferguson police force, for example, Officer Wilson had been employed as a police officer in Jennings, a suburb with a population that was 93 percent Black but where 43 of the 45 police officers were white. Racial tension between the white officers and the Black public became so inflamed that the city was forced to fire its entire police force (including Wilson) and close the department. Wilson also did not find relevant his record of "pedestrian checks" that included stopping and searching Aaron Simmons on February 27, 2014, forcibly removing Simmons's hands from his pockets. Even though Simmons had no contraband in his pockets, he was charged with "failure to comply" and when brought to the police station was pushed against a wall. Wilson saw nothing unusual or untoward about the Ferguson department's practices of racial profiling, commenting, "You can make those numbers fit whatever agenda you want" (Halpern 2015, 13–14).

Wilson admitted that there had been anti-Black racism among police officers in the North County at some unspecified time in the past, but he concluded that only elders who had lived through those specific experiences could charge racism. "People who experienced that, and were mistreated, have a legitimate claim. Other people don't." He saw no cumulative effects or continuing patterns that might make Black people suspicious of the police. Framed this way, each incident of racial abuse, no matter how egregious, ends at the moment it ceases and concerns only the individuals directly involved. Wilson presented himself as an example that Black people should emulate in their thinking. "What happened to my great-grandfather is *not* happening to me. I can't base my actions off what happened to him," Wilson volunteered (Halpern 2015, 8).

Yet what happened to Wilson's great-grandfather, grandfather, and father has a great deal to do with what has happened to him throughout his life. He was raised in exurban St. Peters, Missouri, which today has a population of 49,914 white people and only 2,226 Black people, a gap that was even wider in the years when Wilson lived there.[3] Restrictive racial covenants, mortgage redlining, and exclusionary zoning has kept generations of Black people from residing in places like St. Peters and Crestwood, where Wilson lived on August 9, 2014 (Gordon 2008, 59, 146). While Wilson's ancestors were eligible for free land given out by the Homestead Act and government-subsidized home mortgage loans, the ancestors of the Black residents of Southeast Ferguson were denied access to assets that appreciate in value and could be passed down across generations, were crowded into means-tested public housing units, and suffered from serial displacements because of urban renewal, mortgage foreclosures, and evictions. If Wilson's great-grandfather had been Black, Wilson would have been less likely to be able to secure employment as a police officer in Jennings or Ferguson where white officers were hired almost exclusively. This racial privilege had implications for career advancement. Wilson sought work in majority Black cities because the aggressive and coercive policing that takes place there is good for the careers of white officers. "If you go there and you do three to five years, get your experience, you can kind of write your own ticket," he boasted (Halpern 2015, 4). The interiority that fears monstrous Blackness and the projection that depicts oppressed people as savages needing to be controlled subsidizes the rewards of white methodological individualism. It gave Wilson a credential that could help him advance in police work. Similarly, Ronald Brockmeyer and other municipal court judges in Ferguson and other North County cities received exorbitant salaries for their part-time work. For about twelve hours of work per month, the presiding judge in Bel-Ridge is paid $18,600, the prosecuting attorney receives $25,000, and court clerks take home $38,350 per year. Ferguson funneled $221,700 to the personnel of a municipal court for three sessions per month, an hourly rate of $2,950. The judge appointed in nearby Florissant received $50,000 per year for presiding over two court sessions per month.[4]

Officer Wilson acknowledges the existence of no structural forces giving him advantages in life, and similarly he sees the problems of the people he policed as purely personal. When reminded of the absence of jobs for Ferguson residents, Wilson replied, "There's a lack of jobs everywhere. But there's also a lack of initiative to get a job. You can lead a horse to water, but you can't make it drink" (Halpern 2015, 10). He thought that residents could cope with the challenges they faced in Ferguson if they were imbued with good values at home. Yet despite presuming that he had those excellent values himself, Wilson and his wife refused to live in Ferguson and chose to live in the mostly white suburb of Crestwood, twenty miles south of Ferguson because they needed "a chance to get out of that element" (Halpern 2015, 12). Wilson himself refused to live in the places where, he claimed, Black people could thrive if they only had his values. Nor did he notice the obstacles that might be in their way if they wanted "to get out of that element."

Methodological individualism focuses attention on the 90-second encounter between Darren Wilson and Michael Brown at the expense of understanding the ninety-year history that led to the confrontation of August 9, 2014. It occludes the histories of Black displacement, dispossession, and disposability that have been chronicled so effectively by Walter Johnson, Clarence Lang, Jodi Rios, and Keeanga-Yamhatta Taylor (Johnson 2016; Lang 2009; Rios 2016; Taylor 2016). It has no room for Thomas Shapiro's evidence about how racialized real estate and lending practices caused home values to plunge in Ferguson in the wake of the recession of 2008, how banks foreclosed on homes in Ferguson at a rate four and a half times the national average, how the state of Missouri's Tax Increment Financing laws and the statewide Hancock amendment channeled millions of dollars of property tax subsidies to wealthy individuals and corporations, leaving cities like Ferguson to rely on revenues raised through fines (Shapiro 2017, 85–87).

Some of the racist obstacles confronting Black people in places like Ferguson are individual and intentional. Yet it is the collective, cumulative, and continuing vulnerabilities of past and present racial discrimination that determine the capacity of individuals to cope with the conditions they confront. Michael Brown's mother, Lezley McSpadden, worked for low wages, sometimes holding two jobs at a time, so she could feed, clothe, and raise a son who graduated from high school, who loved computers, who did not have a police record, and who did not get into trouble (McSpadden 2016, 4–5). Like most low-income parents, McSpadden's problems stemmed not from a lack of responsibility but from a lack of resources. Michael Collins of the Center for Financial Security at the University of Wisconsin observes that this is typical among families headed by low-wage workers, who in general do "very, very well given the very meager resources and high expenses they have. But there comes a point in time when there's just nothing there. There's no more income, there's no more savings, and the options are pretty limited, because you don't have a social network, you don't have the legal and other resources available to you to find a solution" (Kiel and Waldman 2015, 13–14). In a similar vein, the Department of Justice investigation of the Ferguson Police Department found the claim by Ferguson officials that

Black people lack personal responsibility to be a product of the municipality's blatantly racist culture. The report noted, "Our investigation revealed African Americans making extraordinary efforts to pay off expensive tickets for minor, often unfairly charged, violations despite systemic obstacles to resolving those tickets" (United States Department of Justice 2015, 74). City officials and the police department actually produced the criminal records they condemned Black people for having by criminalizing poverty and making it virtually impossible to get out of indebtedness to the city, causing residents to lose jobs and get evicted from their homes.

Ferguson's practices of producing indebtedness and then blaming it on the personal irresponsibility of the indebted have also been deployed with devastatingly destructive consequences all across the nation in the form of debt collection practices by municipal agencies and private corporations. The harm enacted by these practices falls disproportionately on people of color. Court-ordered debt collections take place twice as frequently in Black neighborhoods as in areas of white residence. A study by researchers for the public interest organization ProPublica found that the disparity did not stem from a lack of personal responsibility among Black people but rather from the ways in which past and present expressly racist obstacles to asset accumulation leave Black people with fewer resources to fall back on when financial crises emerge (Kiel and Waldman 2015, 2).

Legacies of racialized housing and lending practices in the United States have resulted in Black and white people with exactly the same incomes having widely disparate amounts of wealth (Oliver and Shapiro 2005, 99–126). The typical white household possesses $141,900 in wealth while a comparable Black household owns only $11,000. Between 2008 and 2012, in the St. Louis area alone debt collectors seized some $34 million, most of it from people living in Black neighborhoods (Kiel and Waldman 2015, 4). The emphasis on personal responsibility that methodological individualism envisions and endorses not only fails to assess the causes of collective problems accurately but also produces the very lack of agency it purports to prevent.

Thus the core concerns of the humanities—interiority, projection, and methodological individualism—are very much present in the ways in which the conflict in Ferguson came into being and has been subsequently interpreted. The impact of the humanities on Darren Wilson, Robert McCulloch, Jeff Roorda, and the other participants in the public framing of the Ferguson events was indirect. A more direct connection can be made between the humanities and a group of actors more distant from the streets but intimately involved in the scene of argument where similar events are described and interpreted in legal terms. For decades and even centuries before the killing of Michael Brown, decisions by the U.S. Supreme Court established within law the very mechanisms whereby the killer could be excused and his victim condemned.

Interiority, Projection, and Methodological Individualism in the Law

The practice of law sets the rules by which society operates. Although aggrieved groups routinely turn to the law asking for justice and are sometimes successful, legal practice is innately conservative. The importance of precedent in legal reasoning makes the present dependent on the patterns and practices of the past. The centrality in law of property rights and individual rights works to preserve and protect the unfair gains and unjust enrichments secured by white supremacist policies in the past by treating them as a baseline norm that must be left undisturbed. One clear manifestation of the historical mission of the law to preserve order rather than to dispense justice rests in the impossibly high standards of proof needed to convict any police officer of killing unarmed suspects. The Supreme Court's ruling in the 1989 *Graham v. Connor* case set a precedent that made officers' claims of being afraid a valid defense.

Beyond *Graham v. Connor*, however, decades of Supreme Court decisions produced and reinforced the structural conditions that created the clash between Michael Brown and Darren Wilson on August 9, 2014. Unequal education and school segregation, employment discrimination, unfair taxation, voter suppression, and vote dilution permeated the atmosphere in Ferguson. Black people would not have been concentrated in Southeast Ferguson in such a visible and vulnerable way if the Supreme Court had supported the 1968 Fair Housing Act more enthusiastically over the years. Similarly, if the court had been more critical of the 1994 Violent Crime Control and Law Enforcement Act, Black families would have suffered fewer of the devastating consequences of mass incarceration—including family fragmentation, disruption of social networks, interrupted work histories, and the ways in which a previous conviction inhibits access to jobs and housing. The Supreme Court's decision in the 2007 *Parents Involved Case* reinforced the forms of school segregation and unequal education that Michael Brown faced. Its ruling in the 2009 *Ricci* case drastically narrowed the scope of the affirmative action remedies that could have opened up jobs for Black people on Ferguson's police force. The *Citizens United* decision of

2010 increased the political influence and power of precisely the kinds of wealthy contributors to political campaigns responsible for Missouri's Hancock Amendment with consequent pressure on small municipalities to raise revenue through user fees and fines. In 2013, in *Shelby v. Holder* the court gave approval to the very kinds of voter suppression and dilution practices that resulted in the all-white city council that set policies for Ferguson, a city with a population that is two-thirds Black. In each of these cases, all of the justices on the Supreme Court agreed that there was a distinction between impermissible de jure segregation by law and de facto segregation by circumstance. Liberals and conservatives disagree about what policies fall into each category and which remedies are legally permissible. Yet they share a commitment to believing that the two realms are separable and to holding sacrosanct the interiority of the rights-bearing subject of the law and the property-owning subject of the market. Moreover, many of their rulings rely on projections that portray members of aggrieved groups as the sources of their own problems and that depict their efforts to secure justice as a form of "reverse racism." Other rulings treat desegregation not as justice for aggrieved people of color but merely as a temporary punishment for whites who have been caught discriminating too crudely. The notion of a distinction between de jure and de facto segregation is constructed only by ignoring a large, unrefuted, and irrefutable body of evidence demonstrating the mutually constitutive and mutually reinforcing intersections of state and nonstate actors in creating racial stratification and subordination (Lipsitz 2005; Roithmayr 2014; Rothstein 2017).

The justices no doubt learned to frame issues of social justice in terms of interiority, projection, and methodological individualism from many different sources, but among them is the humanities education they received in elite institutions of higher learning. In college the judges who decided the *Parents Involved*, *Ricci*, *Citizens United*, and *Shelby* cases majored in the humanities and attendant areas of the social sciences. Chief Justice John Roberts majored in history at Harvard, as did Justice Antonin Scalia at Georgetown and Justices Sonia Sotomayor and Elena Kagan at Princeton. Justice Stephen Breyer studied philosophy at Stanford, while Justice David Souter did so at Harvard. Justice Clarence Thomas majored in English at Holy Cross. Justice Ruth Bader Ginsburg majored in government at Cornell, as did Justice Anthony Kennedy at Stanford and Justice Neil Gorsuch at Columbia. Justice Samuel Alito majored in interdisciplinary liberal arts at Princeton.

What did these jurists learn from their undergraduate courses? They encountered the writings of the great philosophers of the Western tradition: Kant, Locke, Hegel, Hume, as well as the many scholars and artists influenced by them. Training according to the knowledge traditions of the West, steeped in the legacies of the coloniality of power, taught them to view the world through the lenses of interiority, projection, and methodological individualism. They came to be present-minded and to accept the unjust legacies of the past as a baseline norm that should not be disturbed. When injustices can be proven, they are still seen as isolated and aberrant rather than systemic and structural. People whose rights have been violated need to prove that their injuries stem from overt and intentional acts by clearly identified individual perpetrators, not from historical patterns that have locked them out of opportunities and life chances. This is a system designed to frame injustice as only a matter of personal guilt rather than as a matter of collective responsibility. It works to preserve the privileges and rewards of whiteness. This outcome is not by accident. As we argue here and in Chapter 6, the authors of the foundational premises and practices of the humanities derived their ideas in the midst of Europe's vexed confrontations with peoples that it perceived to be "other."

Kant argued that the Indigenous peoples of the Americas could simply not be educated and that while Black people could be educated, it was only possible for them to become servants. He advised that dispensing physical punishment to Black slaves required a split cane rather than a whip because of the Negro's thick skin (Eze 1997a, 116). Kant contended that "humanity is at its perfection in the race of the whites." He added that the inhabitant of the temperate zones of the world where Kant was born and lived "has a more beautiful body, works harder, is more jocular, more controlled in his passions, more intelligent than any other race of people in the world" (Kant 1997, 63, 64). In *The Philosophy of History*, G.W.F. Hegel described Black people living in the same era that he lived in as "the natural man in his wild and untamed state" (2001, 111). He claimed that Black people lacked the capacity for reason and as a result deserved to be enslaved. Hegel dismissed Africa as a continent without history, as not part of the modern world, and as devoid of movement or development. Yet in a characteristic contradiction, Hegel also asserted that this continent that he claimed not to be part of the modern world was *terra nullius*, an empty land whose riches could be rightfully plundered by Europeans (Eze 1997b, 9–10). David Hume contended that Black people were naturally inferior to people of all other races, and that Europeans and Amerindians differed from one another as greatly as human beings differed from animals (Hume 1985; see also Garrett and Sebastiani 2017). He assumed that an erudite Black poet from Jamaica whom he encountered was like a parrot, simply repeating words he did not understand (Eze 2000).

It is not that these sections of the writings of Kant, Hegel, and Hume were emphasized or absorbed uncritically by the future Supreme Court justices. Most modern thinkers would reject the racist conclusions voiced in them. Yet even if the explicit conclusions of the great philosophers of the Western tradition are rejected, their way of framing questions exudes the idea that seeing peoples as different from one another requires deciding which is better and which is worse, instantiates an unjust history as an uninterrogated baseline norm, and approaches problems through the lenses of interiority, projection, and methodological individualism. Destructive on its own as an epistemology grounded in ignorance, humanities thinking also provides the core categories that make the social sciences useful to the coloniality of power.

Ferguson as a Failure of the Social Sciences

No less than the humanities, the social sciences came into existence as knowledge projects functioning as forms of social control. Anthropology and geography emerged from the practices of empire. Economics developed as a way of rendering the predations of capital as natural and beyond critique or correction. Political science and sociology came into being as tools for the efficient administration of grossly unequal societies. The statistical methods that occupy a place of privilege across the social sciences developed their core contours inside eugenics, a racist field of inquiry focused on identifying superior and inferior social groups.

John Burgess, who played a key role in establishing political science as an academic discipline in the United States, viewed the field's mission in expressly racist terms. He declared that "American Indians, Asiatics and Africans cannot properly form any active, directive part of the political population which shall be able to produce modern political institutions and ideals" (Vitalis 2015, 36, quoting Burgess 1895, 406). When U.S. military forces assisted in the overthrow of the monarchy in Hawai'i, Burgess provided technical advice to the provisional government in order to establish U.S. colonial role over the islands. He proposed voting and representation requirements designed to ensure white rule over the domain (Vitalis 2015).

The first scholarly journal for political science established in 1910 was titled *Journal of Race Development*. In 1922, it was renamed *Foreign Affairs*, and to this day remains one of the central journals in the field (Vitalis 2015,

18–20). This link between domestic racism and overseas imperialism continued to inform the discipline in the succeeding century. In a 1968 article in that very journal, *Foreign Affairs,* Samuel P. Huntington, professor of government at Harvard and one-time president of the American Political Science Association, proposed saturation bombing of the Vietnamese countryside as a way to force peasants to move to areas controlled by the U.S. military. In the 1970s, Huntington advised the Trilateral Commission that the major problem facing the United States was that it tolerated too much democracy (Crozier, Huntington, and Watanuki 1975). In *The Clash of Civilizations* (1996), Huntington presented crude, inaccurate, and racist depictions of Islam, and in *Who Are We?* (2004) he argued for the inassimilability of Latinx immigrants, charging that they threatened the essence of the national culture, which he claimed was and must remain exclusively Anglo-Protestant.

The framing of problems by sociologists reveals how the conventions of social science research have long been linked to systems of control. Drawing on the ideas of philosopher Friedrich Schiller, Max Weber envisioned the project of sociology as the "disenchantment of the world," as the rejection of superstition and belief in favor of rational inquiry, the production of objective knowledge, and a commitment to rational problem solving. This framework proved useful to elites seeking to manage social problems and threats to the social order in an era of colonialism, urbanization, industrialization, and nation building. Key concepts in sociology, especially difference, deviance, and dependence, have played prominent roles in public policy and policing, and competing understandings of them were at the heart of the troubles in Ferguson.

Social science studies of social relations were structured in dominance from the start. The first two sociology books published in the United States—George Fitzhugh's *Sociology for the South* and Henry Hughes's *A Treatise on Sociology*—were insistent defenses of slavery. As the scholarship of Aldon Morris, Stephen Steinberg, and Khalil Gibran Muhammad delineates, academic sociology became institutionalized in the United States in an era suffused with racial hate and fear, at a time shaped by Jim Crow segregation, overseas imperial expansion, mass migration, and eugenic explanations of social differences (Aldon Morris 2015; Muhammad 2010; Steinberg 2007). Key founders of the discipline, including Robert Park and Charles Henderson, established sociology as a managerial field. Their work accepted the existing social order as legitimate, as an uninterrogated baseline norm needing protection from disruption and difference. In this work, social problems become attributed to the stranger, the other, the different, the deviant, and the dependent, not to the processes that compel people to suffer for *being perceived* as strangers, others, different, deviant, and dependent. As Khalil Gibran Muhammad explains, "Inequality based on exploitation, coercion, duplicity, and genocide" became "subsumed within an understanding that the oppressed were dominated because of their own inherent weaknesses" (Muhammad 2010, 24).

Thus, protecting structures of unjust domination from critique necessitated an approach to social problems that concentrated on studying how and why allegedly deviant and deficient individuals failed to assimilate to dominant norms. These ideas infiltrated social practice in many different ways as the informing logic shaping medical diagnosis and treatment, social welfare policies, immigration law, and policing and incarceration. For example, pioneers in the study of psychiatry in the nineteenth century treated the desire by slaves to run away to freedom as evidence of a mental illness they named "drapetomania." Articles in medical journals argued that Black people who showed disrespect for white property suffered from dysaesthesia aethiopis, an "illness" that could be treated best by severe whippings. Writing in the journal *Psychoanalytic Review* in 1914, J. E. Lind surmised that Negroes were psychologically unfit for freedom (Metzl 2009, ix). As late as 1968 an article appeared in *Archives of General Psychiatry* claiming that listening to speeches by Malcolm X and participating in groups that opposed white supremacy produced a "protest psychosis" in Black people, a mental illness characterized by the symptoms of "delusional anti-whiteness" and "hostile and aggressive" feelings (Metzl 2009, xiv).

As in political science and psychology, research paradigms in sociology originated in racist assumptions. At the University of Chicago in the second decade of the twentieth century, Robert Park advanced the concept of the assimilation cycle in an attempt to assess the proper pace at which the outsider would lose all signs of difference and become like those on the inside. Park described this as a natural and inevitable process, even though it had never actually happened. He disguised his prescription as description. Park and his students had no room for rumination about when, why, and how insiders should change *their* exclusionary and oppressive practices. Sociological studies did not consider that aggrieved outsiders might want to change the system, not merely enter into it. By making the "difference" of the oppressed the heart of what constitutes a social problem, other social structures and relations became validated as *not* problems. Inequality, injustice, exclusion, exploitation, subordination, domination, suppression, and oppression escaped scrutiny, assessment, and critique.

As with the humanities, many of the premises and practices that shaped the discipline of sociology in these earlier works have been critiqued, rejected, and disavowed. For example, very few scholars today directly use the assimilation cycle of Robert Park. But the patterns of the past still shape the presumptions of the present. Sociological research still focuses disproportionately on the stranger, the other, the different, the deviant, and the dependent. Informed by social science, public policy still proceeds from the premise that it needs to prevent challenges to order rather than to create justice.

Social scientists have continued this pattern in the present. When anti-immigrant hysteria reached a new level of viciousness in the early 2000s with the introduction of H.R. 4437 in the United States Congress and the emergence of legislation at state and local levels expressly designed to preempt the federal responsibility for immigration law, sociologist Ivan Light counseled local municipalities to create ordinances vigorously regulating occupancy, building codes, rental contracts, and employment to drive away immigrants from their locales. Focusing on southern California, where voters gave overwhelming approval in 1994 to an unconstitutional anti-immigrant ballot initiative written and championed by white supremacists, where activists in overtly racist anti-immigrant vigilante groups secured elective office throughout the 1990s and early 2000s, and where racist police and vigilante violence took place again and again, Light contended that racism played no role in efforts to drive Latinx people out of the region. Instead, he claimed that the nuisance ordinances were motivated by a sincere and generous desire to maintain "a standard of human decency" in living conditions and to reduce poverty by forcing immigrants to move away from a region where wages were low and housing was unaffordable. He did not mention the ways in which the militarization of the California border with Mexico compelled migrants to enter other states, but instead "credited" nuisance policing with forcing Latinx migrants from the state.

From Light's perspective, blatantly unconstitutional forms of harassment that violate civil rights laws, interfere with freedom of contract, impede the ability of workers to bargain freely over wages and working conditions, and create chaos in the lives of some of society's poorest and most vulnerable men, women, and children, become noble acts of paternalism. Light's endorsement of the use of nuisance laws to deny freedom of residence to Latinx immigrants helped build support for those exact policies in the regions outside of California. Thus the immigrants displaced by the policies that Light championed became displaced again and again as municipalities in New Jersey, Pennsylvania, and the states of Georgia, Alabama, and Tennessee used draconian and expressly racist enforcement of legally dubious ordinances ostensibly regulating housing occupancy, traffic, trespassing, and solicitation as pretexts useful for driving Latinx immigrants from their jurisdictions. Social science knowledge in this case provided justification for winking at unconstitutional and racist pre-emptions of federal immigration law and for diverting police resources away from protecting the public safety in order to preserve the unfair gains and unjust enrichments of whiteness without having to admit racist intent (see Light 2006, 2007; Varsanyi 2008).

Its early emphasis on the weaknesses of the oppressed served to establish core contradictions inside sociology that plague the discipline to this day. Although putatively the study of social structures, the field's protection of dominant practices from critique encourages explanations and policies that focus on individuals. The "welfare reform" legislation of 1996 supported by both political parties in the United States—cruelly named the "Personal Responsibility and Work Opportunity Act"—has produced drastic increases in concentrated poverty and human suffering. It accounts partially for why the Ferguson city government and police force could attribute their exploitation of the Black community to that group's lack of personal responsibility. This move to "end welfare as we know it" has been a major failure. It is directly responsible for increasing the concentration of poverty in places like Ferguson and nearby areas of North St. Louis County and the city of St. Louis. Its practical failures, however, are excused because it has been an ideological success. It corresponds to and reinforces the ideology of an earlier influential work of social science: the 1965 Moynihan Report that held that Black poverty is caused by nonnormative family identities rather than by racism, low wages, unemployment, educational inequality, residential segregation, mass incarceration, and environmental racism.

The logic of the Moynihan Report permeated Darren Wilson's explanations of the situation in Ferguson, for example, when he surmised that Michael Brown did not have the best upbringing. Proclaiming that good values need to be learned at home, Wilson offered as an example a Black single mother in Ferguson whose teenage children broke into cars, dealt drugs, and fired guns. He blamed this on the mother's inadequate parenting. In fact, the woman in question was physically disabled, blind, and raising her children on her own. Wilson noticed no material obstacles facing the family because of poverty and disability, focusing solely on what he perceived to be the individual problem of inadequate mothering by a Black woman as he had been coached to do all his life by educators, journalists, and politicians following their sociologists of choice (Halpern 2015, 10).

The Moynihan Report's condemnation of Black women and its erasure of structural racism appealed to President Barack Obama as well. His My Brother's Keeper initiative—along with his repeated public scolding of absent Black fathers and inadequate Black mothers— reveal the deep hold of this formulation on the political imaginary and public policy. The fact that Obama (like Moynihan) was himself raised by a single mother and went on to what most people would consider a career success did not diminish his profession of faith in properly gendered home life as the magic antidote to the poisons of racial subordination and class oppression. Tukufu Zuberi notes the harm perpetrated by this innately antisociological frame that was developed and legitimized by social scientists. He argues that explanations emphasizing culture serve the same purpose that explanations grounded in biology did in the era of eugenics. In this shift from one type of essentialism to another, "a focus on unproductive behavior of the unassimilated," Zuberi argues, constitutes "a return to viewing the Negro as a [peculiar] problem" (2011, 1577).

Sociology's past also permeates the practices and policies of the present in the form of "broken windows" policing. Developed by social welfare scholar George Kelling and political scientist James Q. Wilson, this strategy entails stopping, arresting, charging, and jailing poor people for minor "quality of life" offenses such as loitering, littering, jaywalking, or sitting, lying, or sleeping in public (Kelling and Wilson 1982). The theory is that these minor offenses demonstrate disrespect for law that undermines neighborhood pride and accountability and thus leads to more serious crimes. "Quality of life" is a cruel misnomer for these policies because they damage the quality of life among the very people they purport to protect (Hayden 2013). In practice, broken windows policing merely criminalizes the survival strategies of poor people. It creates additional disorder in their lives by disrupting their daily rounds, taxing their time, and saddling them with unpayable debts. This was precisely the policy in place in Ferguson where people went to jail routinely because they could not pay fines for a broken taillight, a noisy muffler, high grass and weeds on front lawns, jaywalking, failure to provide proof of insurance, driving with an expired license, and failing to answer a summons—even if that summons went to a previous address. Like the public policies guided by the assumptions of the Moynihan Report, broken windows policing treats symptoms rather than causes. What has been broken are not the windows but rather the promises of the

1866 and the 1964 Civil Rights Acts, the 1968 Fair Housing Act, and the Thirteenth, Fourteenth, and Fifteenth Amendments to the Constitution: promises of full citizenship and social membership that are guaranteed in theory but not in practice (Camp and Heatherton 2016).

The influence exerted on how elected public officials, police officers, and policy makers framed the Ferguson uprising through the concepts and categories forged by social scientists Daniel Patrick Moynihan and James Q. Wilson reveals how the knowledge producing institutions of society play a role in the subordination of aggrieved populations. Moynihan received his doctoral degree in history and held academic positions in political science and government departments. Yet he composed his report as assistant secretary of labor in the presidential administration of Lyndon Johnson. His stance on the alleged deficiencies of the Black family played a key role in his prominence as a spokesperson for what Keith Feldman aptly names racial liberalism: a confluence of views that include viewing affirmative action as reverse racism against whites and opposing U.S. support for reparations for the harms perpetrated by European imperialism in the global south (Feldman 2015, 23–57). Wilson received his Ph.D. in political science, taught in the government department at Harvard, and served as president of the American Political Science Association. Yet he articulated many of his key ideas promoting nuisance policing and mass incarceration as the chair of the Johnson administration's task force on crime.

The demonization and criminalization of Black people and the shaming and blaming of Black mothers served as technologies protecting white privilege and power in Ferguson. These frameworks formulated in scholarly settings guide, justify, and excuse the mechanisms used to treat Black people as nonpersons. In general public discourse, they obscure from view the profound knowledge possessed by Ferguson activists about dispossession and displacement, about state violence and municipal governance as instruments for gouging the poor and subsidizing the wealthy. As knowledge projects, the ideas articulated by Moynihan and Wilson resemble the ones used to suppress Indigenous knowledge and aspirations during the Idle No More Uprising and to occlude the profound knowledge and social analysis emanating from the practices of Chicanx artivistas. The Idle No More movement recognized coloniality as a form of social, environmental, and epistemological control. The same system that blocks the natural flow of rivers and streams, that extracts natural resources from the ground ruthlessly and recklessly, that categorizes whole groups of humans as either superior or inferior, rests on a foundation of knowledge compartmentalization, specialization, and administration (Watkins and Shulman 2008, 30). The scholarly traditions in the humanities and social sciences that organize knowledge around expressly national histories, economies, literatures, languages, and political systems make people ill-equipped to understand the cognitive mapping and political practice of Chicanx artivistas whose creations cross borders and speak to pressing translocal and transnational realities.

This chapter has argued that the crisis of Ferguson emerged on a terrain of inequality established by the continuing legacies of coloniality, supported by the failure of the humanities and social sciences to insufficiently interrogate and revise modes of thinking still shaped by their emergence as part of the justification of the colonial matrix of power. On the streets of Ferguson, a broad coalition with queer and trans Black women in the forefront included people who were men and women, straight and gay, cisgender, queer, and transgender, young and old, employed and unemployed, religious and not religious, white and not white. They came together in accompaniment to protest the callous and cruel behavior of those in power, to refuse an unlivable destiny, and to find something left to love in a society that makes people seemingly unlovable. They improvised a collective consciousness that challenged the hegemony of humanist interiority, projection, and methodological individualism and social science understandings of difference, deviance, and dependence.

The killing of Michael Brown by Darren Wilson distilled and crystallized lifelong experiences of systematic subordination and unjust criminalization and dehumanization. Rios argues that participants were galvanized into action by "the spectacle of Michael Brown's flesh—lying heaped and face down on the pavement, stripped of corporeal rights, exposed, and expanding in the sweltering summer sun for four and a half hours as his mother pleaded with the officials to remove his body so she could be near her son . . ." (Rios 2016, 65). This death reminded many participants of their perpetual pushing back against their being disciplined as bodies out of place. They responded with a politics of love. For them, Black Lives Matter was about more than the right not to be shot down in the street, it was about living—and loving— freely and fully. "The demand is simple: Stop killing us. However, the call to reimagine one's humanity in direct relationship to one's capacity to love fluidly and unconditionally is profound" (Rios 2016, 72).

The polities, politics, ideas, and imaginaries forged on the streets of Ferguson amount to much more than the personal, provincial, or parochial responses of an aggrieved group to an unlivable destiny. They express ways of knowing and ways of being with emancipatory potential for everyone. If they are to be heard and understood, however, it will require a revolution in the composition, practices, and mission of the knowledge-making institutions of society, a possibility explored in the next two chapters: the first on coloniality and neoliberalism as knowledge projects, and the second on accompaniment as a practice inside academic institutions.

6 / Coloniality and Neoliberalism as Knowledge Projects

This book argues that improvisation and accompaniment can create insubordinate spaces, places where a collective capacity for social justice can be developed and deepened. To do so, however requires countering the enduring consequences of two major knowledge projects: coloniality and neoliberalism.[1] As knowledge projects, coloniality and neoliberalism have shaped worldviews, modes of thought, and the ways research questions are asked and answered both inside and outside the academy. This chapter explores some of what needs to be displaced if social justice is to take place. It underscores what is at stake in the practices of accompaniment and improvisation highlighted in this book by enabling a contrast between decolonial options and the ways of knowing and being learned and legitimated inside dominant cultural and educational institutions and practices.

Coloniality

What Aníbal Quijano has aptly named the "coloniality of power" continues to structure social relations and knowledge formations all around the world, even though it has been more than five hundred years since the European invasion of the Americas, more than two hundred years since the Haitian Revolution, and more than a century since the Mexican Revolution. A powerful and pervasive matrix of colonial power, Quijano explains, determines definitions *of* and control *over* production, reproduction, violence, and knowledge (2000, 557). In most places in Asia, Africa, and Latin America, wars of national liberation successfully terminated the formal practices of colonialism and created new nominally independent nations, albeit nations replete with their own often uninterrogated unjust and hierarchal structures. Long after formal colonial administrative institutions have been dismantled, however, coloniality as a way of life continues to structure the world's economic and political alignments as well as its dominant ways of knowing. Civic leaders and scholars alike persistently deny the formative and continuing roles played in the modern world by Indigenous dispossession, slavery, and colonialism. They resist honest and open assessment of the ways in which the colonial patterns of the past pervade the present.

In the United States, coloniality enables the continuing suppression of Indigenous self-determination and explains the direct rule that perpetuates the status of Puerto Rico as the world's oldest continuous colony. The inadequate relief efforts by the U.S. government in response to Hurricane Maria in Puerto Rico in 2017 formed only one more chapter in a long history of misrule. Coloniality even goes beyond colonialism, however. It informs the policies that boost the profits of U.S. pharmaceutical firms by pricing patent medicines beyond the reach of AIDS sufferers in Africa (Comaroff and Comaroff 2012, 41, 45, 173–190). It manifests itself in neoliberal economic policies that impose austerity on El Salvador, Guatemala, and Honduras, forcing the flight of desperate unaccompanied children to the U.S. border seeking refuge. It endures in the continuing occupation and administration of some eight hundred military bases around the world, like those in Okinawa—where the combined histories of U.S. and Japanese imperialisms work in concert to place forty-five thousand U.S. military personnel and their families on thirty-seven bases that take up 20 percent of the landmass of that island (Soble 2016).[2] Coloniality manifests itself in the incarceration, interrogation, and torture of prisoners covertly in secret sites around the world, and overtly in Guantanamo, where people designated nebulously as "enemy combatants" are denied basic rights of due process including the ability to face their accusers and to learn the exact charges lodged against them. The colonial matrix of power helps explain why U.S. military forces dropped more than twenty-six thousand bombs on Afghanistan, Libya, Yemen, Somalia, Pakistan, Syria, and Iraq in 2016 alone, with almost no public notice, much less debate (M. Benjamin 2017).

While coloniality is a political, economic, and military structure, it also has served as a very successful knowledge project with continuing influence in the present. The coloniality of power subordinates Indigenous people and people of the global south pedagogically as well as politically. For example, the map of the world routinely displayed in U.S. classrooms and textbooks inaccurately inflates the size of Europe and North America, while locating those regions visually in the center of the world. A product of the projection designed by Gerardus Mercator in Flanders in 1569 at the start of the age of European imperial expansion, the Mercator map makes the 18.9 million square miles of the Northern Hemisphere appear larger than the 38.6 million miles of the Southern Hemisphere (Bonnett 2008, 93; Goldman 1994, 377; Schechner 2013, 41).[3] It promotes a spatial imaginary of a global "east" and "west"—an orient and occident—calculated in relation to England, the presumed central point in the world marked by the prime meridian located in Greenwich (Quijano 2000, 544). The binary division of the world between East and West is a colonial invention that only makes sense from a Eurocentric perspective. Travel from Japan (known as part of the orient or East) to the United States (known as part of the occident or West) requires a move to the *east*, while travel from the United States to Japan entails heading *west*. Divisions of space provide the basis for distinctions by race. The places thought to be inhabited originally by people in the global east and south become defined as nonwhite and therefore other, elsewhere, peripheral, and nonmodern. Yet the settler societies of Canada, the United States, New Zealand, and Australia become designated as "white," in a move that erases the original Indigenous inhabitants.

The unacknowledged continuing presence of coloniality does not go completely unchallenged by artists, academics, and activists. This is evident not only in the activities discussed in earlier chapters but in repeated contestations through protests, arguments, and art. For example, the widespread dissemination of Europe's narcissistic grandiosity through the Mercator map provoked artist Alfredo Jaar to respond with an installation in 1990 titled *Geography=War*. A native Chilean who spent eleven years of his childhood and adolescence in Martinique, Jaar's piece configures the globe differently from the standard classroom map. He uses the image of the world created by the 1974 Peters projection, which presents the physical proportions of the global north and south more accurately than the Mercator projection (Goldman 1994). While emphasizing how formerly colonized areas around the world are both physically large and economically significant (especially to the prosperity of the north), Jaar's artwork also reveals the south's political and economic subordination. He presents maps and photographs that trace the trail of toxic waste materials from northern industrialized nations to dump sites in Koko, Nigeria, where Europe's garbage poisons African air, water, land, and people (Anderson Gallery 1991).

In a related work, Jaar challenges the cognitive mappings and conversational habits that permit the term "America" to be used to designate not the entire hemisphere but the United States alone. His 1987 installation *A Logo for America* appeared on a spectacolor light board above a U.S. military recruitment office in New York's Times Square. In sequence, a map of the United States appears followed by a caption crawling across the screen that reads: "This is not America." Then an image depicts the U.S. flag followed by the caption: "This is not America's flag" (Leval 1992, 79–80). Jaar's artwork calls attention to the conceit (in more than one sense of the word) that leads people in one country to appropriate the name of the entire hemisphere for only one nation. It also demonstrates how asymmetrical power relations enable European and North American fictions to assume the status of social facts. The hemisphere is designated nearly universally by a version of the name of Amerigo Vespucci, a European who wandered around it aimlessly, accomplished little on his journey, but brought back enslaved Indigenous people to Europe and has since been credited as a "discoverer" of the "new world" (H. Thomas 2013, 49, 188, 190).

Jaar's provocation hints at broader truths. The Native inhabitants of the Western Hemisphere are still designated as "Indians" because Christopher Columbus, an Italian seafarer sailing under the Spanish flag, mistakenly believed that he had arrived in India. That error is preserved in perpetuity as if it were an accurate fact. Columbus's mistake is applied as a label to describe Indigenous people who are denied the dignity of naming themselves. The descendants of people who called themselves Chinchas, Aymaras, Mayas, and Aztecs are known today as "Indians" dwelling in a place designated as America. On the other side of the Atlantic, people descended from ancestors who called themselves Ashantis, Zulus, Yorubas, and Bakongos are known as "Africans" (Quijano 2000, 551–552). This nomenclature is at heart an exercise in racial formation. By occluding the singular self-definitions and separate histories of peoples in the Americas and Africa, by blending diverse and plural histories into the unified totalities of "Indians" and "Africans," the colonial matrix of power creates racialized "others" whose ascribed shared difference justifies conquest, slavery, colonization, and exploitation (Quijano 2000, 552).

Colonial knowledge framed Indigenous people as nomads and savages, relegating them to an imagined state of nature where they do not deserve sovereign rights. As delineated in Chapter 3 of this book, colonial violence derived its ideological justification from the legal doctrine of *terra nullius*, which means empty land or territory owned by no one (Moreton-Robinson 2015, xx). The land was judged to be empty, even though people had lived on it for at least ten thousand years. Europeans claimed that the Indigenous inhabitants could not own the land because they had not "improved" it— which meant turning it into a generator of return on investments. There-fore Europeans could seize the land for themselves. The relational lie of Indigenous savagery, juxtaposed against the equally tenuous claim of white "civilization," transformed colonial theft into legally secured property rights based solely on the cultural practices of the invaders (25, 56).

A nexus of place and race emerged from colonial thinking, a nexus inflected with class distinctions that persist over time yet get reconfigured every day. Quijano observes that it was the colonization of America that produced the modern meaning of race, but the concept "has proven to be more durable and stable than the colonialism in whose matrix it was estab-lished" (2000, 533). Coloniality lives on in the economic subordination of people of color that relegates them to labor market segments where they cannot bargain freely over wages and working conditions. It pervades the present in the socially shared practices and perceptions that turn the con-nection between whiteness and property into a settled expectation (Harris 1993). As Quijano explains, "The fact is that from the very beginning of the colonization of America, Europeans associated nonpaid or nonwaged labor with the dominated races because they were 'inferior' races" (2000, 538). The histories of the reservation, the plantation, the barrio, and the ghetto— as well as the demographic features of the country club, the corporate board room, and the gated community—demonstrate how the hierarchy of race became firmly inscribed through coercive control of place.

The coloniality of power shapes conceptions of time as well as space. European space dictates the terms of global time. As Walter Mignolo illus-trates, the zero line of longitude that divides East and West in Greenwich, England, marks the beginning of the universal solar, nautical, and astro-nomical day. The zero line of longitude produces a concomitant *zero point epistemology*, a way of knowing that gives priority to Europe. Just as the uni-versal day is presumed to begin at midnight in England, colonial knowledge conceives of universal history as the linear and chronological development in time of European modernity (Mignolo 2011, 168–170). The dominant histories of the world presented in textbooks, taught in classrooms, and re-iterated constantly in development projects continue to locate the origins of civilization in Greece, trace its migration to Rome, and hail its incarnation as "modernity" in London, Paris, and New York. One would not know from this narrative about the historical reach and scope of Islam, about the architecture, science, and technology of China, India, and Egypt, or about the complex cultures and beliefs of the Benin, Maya-Aztec, and Tawantin-suyo societies. The temporal imaginary of the colonial matrix of power relies on a fabricated but putatively universal linear progression from antiquity to feudalism to capitalism. According to this narrative, Europe developed first and more fully than anywhere else in the world and therefore stands at the apex of modernity. The rest of the globe is presumed to be not yet modern (Quijano 2000, 541). As Walter Rodney has demonstrated, however, the construction of "modernity" in Western Europe and North America depended on the expropriation of land, labor, and resources from Asia, Africa, and Latin America and on imposing forms of serfdom, dependence, and debt peonage on the global south. Africa was not originally "underdeveloped," Rodney demonstrates, but rather had underdevelopment thrust upon it by European modernity (Rodney 1982).

As we explained in Chapter 5, the great philosophers of the Western tradition worked within and contributed to the coloniality of power. John Locke placed the protection of property and contract theory at the center of his philosophy of liberty. Yet the liberty that gave this great theorist of freedom the leisure to think and write came from relegating living Africans to the status of property as slaves. Those held in bondage were contracted over by "owners" including Locke's patron, the Earl of Shaftesbury, Anthony Ashley Cooper. Locke profited personally from investments in the slave economy and helped write the South Carolina constitution that protected racialized permanent hereditary chattel slavery in perpetuity. In order to rationalize and excuse the relegation of living humans to the status of property owned by others, Locke defined Africans captured for the slave trade as people who deserved enslavement because they were prisoners taken in a just war (H. Thomas 1997, 451). Locke does not specify how greed and lust for profits can be connected to justice, nor does he explain how profiteers engaged in the slave trade can be characterized as soldiers in a war between nations. When Locke wrote about the free contracting subject of the law, he meant only white Europeans like himself, not the people who Charles Mills describes as the Black African held in bondage by contracts made between white men or the Red Native whose land had been taken to establish the contract system that held the white settler state together (Mills 2014, 33).

The autonomous, self-interested contracting market subject conjured up in theory by Locke did not actually exist. Free property-owning individuals did not come together at some distant point in the past to cede limited authority to a central society. Human life was originally and organically social. People with property did not obtain their wealth by improving empty land. They got rich by enclosing common areas and driving off those inhabiting them, by obtaining monopoly control over the mechanisms of finance and transportation, by exploiting their employees and cheating their customers, and by engaging in programs of overseas conquest, plunder, and slavery. Precisely because the free property-owning individual did not actually exist, it had to be contrived into existence through an amalgam of imperial knowledge projects in philosophy, law, literature, and religion. This autonomous individual was a fabrication, a false subject that came into being as a social fact only through the construction of equally false objects—the purportedly "primitive" Indigenous people of the Americas and Africa. North Americans and Europeans claimed for themselves the ability to name "other" places and people. They generated notions of universal freedom premised on designating the majority of the world's population as inhabitants of places that rendered them innately unfit for freedom. In the process they created whiteness as a racial cartel, a structured advantage that ensures that white people's lives will be treated as innately more valuable than the lives of others.

As was the case with Locke, the philosophical writings of Immanuel Kant, the prime theorist of moral philosophy, flowed from the pen of an individual living and thinking in the West in the age of empire. The knowing modern subject capable of moral judgment that Kant theorized in his work emerged from experiences grounded in colonial thinking. Kant's philosophy and anthropology conflated race with place and time, denying the coevalness of existence and relegating people from the global south to an earlier and more primitive stage of human development (Escobar 1995; Fabian 1983). Historical and contemporary discourses of development have long relied on this very translation of geography into chronology. This discursive move has deadly material effects. As Mignolo explains, "The rhetoric of modernity is a rhetoric of salvation"—by conversion yesterday and development today. Implementing what this rhetoric proclaims, however, requires marginalizing or destroying what gets in the way of modernity (2011, xxiv).

The imperial project required a concomitant knowledge project realized through the development of the disciplines. Nearly all of the disciplines in the humanities and social sciences emerged initially out of acts of war, plunder, political repression, and economic exploitation. Fantasies of racial difference were developed to justify European dominance. Intellectuals explained and excused Europe's brutally cruel yet immensely profitable acts of Indigenous dispossession, enslavement, and colonization through knowledge systems designed to solve white problems and soothe white consciences.

The core premises and practices of nearly all scholarly disciplines contain clear traces of their colonial origins. Even seemingly neutral tools such as the map, the museum, and the census came into being as technologies of empire, as mechanisms for establishing, legitimizing, and preserving social differences, not merely for displaying, exhibiting, and measuring them (B. Anderson 2016, 167–190). Unease about the physical and social differences between Europe and the rest of the world produced the disciplines of geography and anthropology. Musicology developed as a formal discipline devoted to the ideals, figures, devices, and practices of Western art music while relegating the overwhelming amount of music produced in the rest of the world to the subfield of ethnomusicology (Kajikawa 2019), which derived its originating impulses from the imperial projects of anthropology. Classics and oriental studies originated in efforts to ground the imperialism of modern Europe in the legacy of the Roman Empire, to establish Europe as decidedly different from—and superior to—the civilizations of Africa and Asia. Economics emerged in the age of empire as a discipline devoted to representing commercial behavior as the product of general laws and individual psychology rather than as practices rooted in specific social structures and institutions (Wallerstein 1996, 17). Ideologically grounded theories masquerading as science became mobilized to justify the unequal consequences of racial subordination and as an excuse to blame them on the alleged deficiencies of its victims (Lyman 1993; Steinberg 2007).[4]

Coloniality provided the informing logic that naturalized nationalism in departments of language, literature, and history, where the juridical and geographic boundaries of individual nation-states delimited objects of research. By making nation-states the proper unit of study and object of analysis, these studies occluded Indigenous knowledge systems and cultures as well as many different kinds of movements across national borders. They erased the long history of human affiliation and association not defined by state power (Robinson 2016). Making human history the chronology of separate states obscured how dispossessions of Indigenous peoples routinely made the state possible. Vertical mapping within nations impeded recognition of the horizontal networks that gave national elites more in common with each other than with the vast majority of people in their own nation. Canonical literature and literary studies constructed, legitimized, and naturalized a bourgeois subject grounded in phobic relations with the social aggregate, a subject recognizable to itself only through a defensive embrace of possessive individualism (Armstrong 2006). Philosophy came into being in the age of empire as a way of cordoning off thought from action through a firm refusal to be intimate with the world (Mills 1997).

The epistemologies of coloniality are not merely academic matters. Deployed through politics, law, science, and expressive culture, they divide the people of the world along binary axes, separating the definers from the defined, the modern from the premodern, the waged from the wageless, the protected from the vulnerable, the exceptional from the disposable, and the fully human from the not quite human. In these typologies, everyone is included, but not everyone has the power to include. As Walter Mignolo emphasizes, the key to these binaries rests in the racially marked colonial distinction between "humanitas" and "anthropos." The people positioned as humanitas define and inhabit the spaces of modernity, have access to power and wealth, and derive benefits from the exploited labor of others. The goals of humanitas are to control and to possess. Humanitas promises growth, development, and inclusion for all, but arrogates to itself alone determination of the course of development and the nature and proper pace of inclusion. People relegated by humanitas to the status of anthropos are the objects of knowledge but not its subjects. They are producers of wealth but not the recipients of it. They are low-wage labor, demonized cultural "others," and lesser citizens. They are displaceable, disposable, and deportable. Although their productivity makes possible the high-consumption lifestyles of their oppressors, they are condemned as parasites. Humanitas does not construct anthropos as homogeneous but all classified as anthropos are relegated to a subordinated position in relation to humanitas. In the eyes of humanitas, anthropos is always rationally and ontologically deficient (Mignolo 2011, 82).

Yet for all its reach, scope, and power, coloniality is not invulnerable. Like all other hegemonic systems of knowledge and power, it is unstable, ever changing, and riddled with contradictions. Its aspiration to control everything and to preclude even the possibility of opposition should not be confused with its actual workings. As Cedric Robinson argues, the self-promoting discursive practices of coloniality masquerade as if they were natural and inevitable outcomes of encounters with difference, yet in actual practice they are contrivances that "tend to wear thin over time" (Robinson 2007, xiii). The coloniality of power obscures and distorts alternative and oppositional knowledge formations, but it never completely erases them. In its imperial ambition and administrative overreach, it often produces the very opposition it seeks to preclude. Aggrieved social subjects cannot fully escape from or live completely outside of the systems of knowledge and power that control them. They can, however, expose these systems' existence, examine their internal logics, and exploit their contradictions through creative contestation.

Neoliberalism

Neoliberalism is an artificial but necessary political label for representing a conjuncture of economic policies, political projects, and social pedagogies. It refers to a dynamic process, not a static entity (Hall 2011). This evolving and morphing conjuncture coalesces around the ideas that the market should be the center of social life, that belligerent and brutal competition will ensure the survival of the fittest, and that self-interest "frees" people from obligations and responsibilities to others.[5] In a market society, all the institutions—even charities and churches and unions and universities—must be incorporated into the market and guided by its principles of accumulation. In a society compliant with neoliberal principles, no area of human endeavor is immune from the imperatives of marketing and profit making.

Neoliberalism emphasizes individualism and the "privatization" of responsibility through the interpellation of people as individual entrepreneurs of their own selves. People are framed as solely responsible for their own life outcomes and positioned as free of responsibility to others and to what might be considered a community or "public good." Bronwyn Davies and Sue Saltmarsh note that in neoliberalism, "Populations are administered and managed through the production of a belief in each individual in his or her own freedom and autonomy" (2007, 3). They point to Nikolas Rose's arguments demonstrating that it takes an enormous structural apparatus to create these seemingly "natural" conditions (Rose 1999). Dominant discourses treat this structural apparatus as both necessary and invisible, constantly "hailing" subjects through the ideological discourses of institutions and cultural products (see Althusser 1971). The advocates of neoliberalism understand the process of social pedagogy well. From entertainment to advertising to education, they seek to shape institutions, structures, and spaces that run by themselves and reproduce themselves and that generate not only market-oriented opinions but market-oriented personalities and dispositions as well.

Neoliberalism presents itself as an apolitical, nonideological, and essentially technical project based on objective principles of efficiency. The free market fundamentalism of neoliberal hegemony imagines people to be market actors who are atomized engines of self-interest unencumbered by the particularities of time, space, and social identity, as free individuals unaffected by tradition and history, and as isolated, independent, and purely self-interested monads. This conceives of all realms of human endeavor as market transactions and elevates the time, space, and subjectivity of the market over all other identities, spatialities, and temporalities. It produces a particular way of life and particular kinds of social subjects and subjectivities.

As a social pedagogy, neoliberalism pervades the psyches and self-conceptions of individuals. It produces miserable conditions and miserable people. The kinds of unequal societies that neoliberalism creates have more violence, more cases of mental illness, more crime, and more disease than comparatively more equal societies (Wilkinson and Pickett 2010, 40, 66, 67, 81, 135). Unequal societies promote intense status competition and personal anxiety leading people to embrace self-enhancing and self-promoting measures. Richard Sennett argues that an institutional order that abandons the needy and forces everyone into brutal competition creates a society where there are high levels of anxieties, fears of irrelevance and uselessness, and a diminished amount of informal trust among people (2006, 181). In an unusually perceptive study, psychoanalytic researcher Lynne Layton argues that the neoliberal conjuncture's shrinkage of state support for jobs, housing, health care, and an adequate standard of living promotes anxiety and leaves people feeling that they have to craft individual rather than collective solutions to social problems and distress (2010, 308). Layton shows how the extreme vulnerability that people feel, coupled with neoliberalism's incessant divisions of people into categories of superior and inferior, fuels "backlash" movements of hatred directed toward vulnerable others (2010, 309).

In a neoliberal culture, people become outwardly less modest, more boastful, cruel, and insensitive to the suffering of others, yet inwardly they become more vulnerable, poorer at personal relationships, unwilling to admit mistakes or faults, and implacably resistant to criticism. One study found that two-thirds of U.S. college students in 2006 displayed levels of narcissism higher than what had been the *average* in 1982. Unlike neoliberal structural adjustment policies that enact their most severe consequences on the weakest and most vulnerable members of society, the psychic damage done by neoliberal culture spans all social classes. In fact, antisocial traits are not randomly distributed throughout society but are disproportionately found among the more wealthy individuals. People with less wealth are more likely to help others and to join social networks organized for mutual aid.

The people with more wealth, however, display higher levels of entitlement, reduced sensitivity to the suffering of others, and increased tendencies for unethical self-serving behavior (Piff 2014, 35). Studies show, for example, that people from wealthy families are more likely than others to feel entitled to their advantages and are less likely than others to exhibit compassion, cooperation, and trust (Piff 2014, 40). These findings help explain how talk radio and internet blogs in the past three decades have become the province of what surely must be the most belligerent, brutal, surly, and self-pitying group of "haves" in the history of the world. An extensive apparatus of institutions promotes self-confidence and self-care, yet researchers have found a direct correlation between high self-esteem and insensitivity to others, as well as an inability to establish and maintain relationships and decided propensities for racism and violence (Wilkinson and Pickett 2010, 37).

Even the physical places of neoliberal society are structured in dominance. Homes, schools, workplaces, and entertainment venues have been organized to produce particular kinds of people. Tax codes and the rules and regulations that govern the activities of homeowners' associations teach people that their dwellings are investments and that maximizing wealth is the central premise of residential life. Fears of outsiders, of cross-class social contact, and of potential losses in property values impel homeowners to hoard opportunities by securing amenities and advantages for their area while exporting hazards, nuisances, and costly obligations to places with less powerful residents (Lipsitz 2011, 25–50). These practices concentrate and exacerbate poverty while placing every sub-unit of governance at war with every other sub-unit. Schools are seen not as crucibles for democratic citizenship but as business enterprises where investors seek maximal profits and consumers are left to compete to secure advantages in crafting their own personal brands (Giroux 2013; Lipman 2011). Television programs, motion pictures, social media platforms, and print journalism increasingly hail viewers and readers as isolated individuals filled with resentment and spite.

The practices that shape spaces structured in dominance reflect a culture of competitive consumer citizenship that expanded in the 1970s as a result of right-wing mobilizations against school desegregation, fair housing, fair hiring, progressive taxation, and environmental protection (Lipsitz 2006). This culture encourages people to see themselves as investors, accumulators, and owners who are always in competition with others rather than as workers, neighbors, and cocreators of a common existence who have reciprocal responsibilities and obligations. The culture of competitive consumer citizenship establishes itself as a collective common sense through a series of public policies that promote particular behaviors: for example, regressive tax cuts—including low property, inheritance, and capital gains taxes for the wealthy, which in turn require the working class and the poor to pay higher user fees, fines, and sales and payroll taxes. State power provides the wealthy with unfair gains and unjust enrichments through decreased expenditures for social services paid out of general tax revenues, reorganization of federal and state spending to subsidize the successful, and two-tiered systems of education, transportation, and retirement savings effected by voucher systems, toll roads, tax subsidies for private retirement accounts, and state abdication of collectively bargained pension obligations. The cultural logic writ large in state practices becomes writ small in the consciousness of individuals as attention and effort is increasingly directed away from collective civic life and toward managing increasingly fragile and diminishing individual wealth portfolios.

The acceptance of competitive consumer citizenship as the prevailing common sense of society has shaped and reflected rapid increases in economic inequality—a massive transfer of wealth to the very rich coupled with stagnant and even declining real wages for the majority of the population. This inequality has cultural consequences. It produces particular kinds of people. Without a strong counterculture like the kinds that emanate from insubordinate spaces, this culture of competitive consumer citizenship will remain the default position guiding public policies and personal lives for the foreseeable future. It leads to misguided policies like President Obama's My Brother's Keeper initiative, which aims to build self-esteem among Black boys, unconscionably leaving out girls as if racism is only an injury to male gender privilege. Moreover, in this program, the self-esteem of young Black boys is to be enhanced by their being mentored by wealthy and successful adult men. Yet research in social psychology indicates that it is the wealthy who most need to learn sensitivity, cooperation, and mutual respect. Perhaps young Black boys and girls should be called on to mentor wealthy and successful adult men.

The pedagogies, policies, and personality disturbances of the neoliberal conjuncture foment anxiety, suspicion, and fear, which are used to recruit people to participate in practices that keep them compliant with dominant powers. Phobic fantasies of demonized monstrous "others" occupy the center of the political and cultural imaginary. Political leaders who cannot persuade the public to support their policies can secure power by fomenting fear and promising protection. Fear is thus politically productive for predatory capitalism. People are manipulated to support the very policies that disempower them, by an avalanche of anxieties about terrorism, immigration, crime, disease, religious difference, sex and gender nonnormativity, gun violence or gun control, bilingualism, downward mobility, and the desegregation of neighborhoods and schools. For many white people, fear of falling has a distinctly racial dimension because their whiteness has made them beneficiaries of multiple forms of structured advantage secured through residential and school segregation, employment discrimination, and systematic failure to enforce civil rights laws. Any gains for communities of color are seen as unfair impingements on white expectations of never being disfavored in competition with nonwhites. Laws and policies that actually enact a measure of equality are condemned as "reverse racism," a charge that reveals the trauma that privileged people feel from perceptions of diminished overrepresentation. Politicians, journalists, filmmakers, and writers treat white fears as serious concerns that need to be addressed. At the same time, the much more legitimate and empirically verifiable fears felt by members of aggrieved racial groups because of displacement, deportation, poverty, eviction, incarceration, unemployment, police brutality, and pollution are dismissed as the whining of special interests seeking special favors. The contradiction comes into clear relief in the language of politics and public policy that portrays food stamps, housing vouchers, and social security benefits as special "entitlements," while policies that subsidize the truly entitled—tax increment financing, the home mortgage deduction, and bailouts of bankrupt corporations—are hailed as good for all.

The more that neoliberal policies fail, the more fear they produce. Nearly every attempt to secure safety without questioning the primary premises of neoliberalism increases danger. Military attacks aimed at inducing regime change in the Middle East produce more rather than fewer terrorists. Racialized mass incarceration and the collateral consequences of criminal convictions destroy social cohesion in aggrieved communities and close off gainful legal employment to millions, creating the preconditions for increased crime. Denying diagnoses, condoms, clean needles, and treatment to AIDS sufferers spreads rather than combats the disease. Fining poor people for delinquent city and state auto license fees and then jailing them when they cannot pay the fines results in their losing jobs, getting evicted from their homes, and taking out loans they cannot afford to pay back, a cascade that drives them deeper into penury and leaves them even less able to purchase license plates and stickers. Moral panics about crime—evident even while crime steadily decreases—incite purchases of guns that kill toddlers and spouses and wind up in the hands of killers who find glory in opening fire at movie theater audiences, elementary school classrooms, and audience members at country music concerts.

Fear does not have to be the primary response to crisis. Thomas Dumm demonstrates that the word *fear* has antecedents in the word *far* (1987, 148). It was originally a designation of travel over a great distance. It has connections to the word *fare*, which signals the cost of travel. It is the price of the ticket. In the Middle Ages, to travel meant to be removed from protection and exposed to danger. Dumm explains that the connotative meaning of fear encourages people to seek a safe condition, and evidence of this abounds in contemporary life. Suburban dwellers wall themselves off in gated communities. They move away from socially created hazards, nuisances, and problems to escape and to evade accountability and responsibility. In 2017, the majority party in the U.S. Congress and the president proposed building a physical wall to separate Mexico from the United States. Misogynists, homophobes, and racists seek to be relieved of encounters with difference by complaining about "political correctness" so they can feel perfectly comfortable and safe in sadistically demeaning their targets. Some college students and teachers seek to create "safe spaces" of their own imagining that they can be protected in the classroom from having to see or hear any of the vile and poisonous social pathologies that run rampant in society at large and that entire communities must cope with and contest every day.

Desires for safety are understandable, but, in an interconnected modern world constructed through predatory plunder, they are an illusion. Efforts to move from exposure to protection, Dumm argues, simply establish "new dangers that tighten the vise in which the human species is now trapped" (1987, 148). The designation of the pursuit of profit as the core activity in society ultimately means that no one is safe and that everyone is imperiled. There can be no once-and-for-all resolutions of the crises that surround us and no return to a private peaceful existence once the present crises are solved. There will never be an end to all of this. If there is peace to be found, it will have to be crafted in the midst of struggle.

Neoliberal culture portrays the world as divided between those who are deemed to be exceptional and those who are dismissed as expendable. It leads people to believe that while all the suffering in the world may be sad, somehow through clever conduct and self-care a lucky few can ensure that it will not touch them personally. They scramble to become part of the small number of people who can secure recognition and reward rather than the great majority consigned to endure anonymous suffering. The dead bodies of refugees on Mediterranean shorelines and of migrants in the Arizona desert, the corpses floating in the floodwaters of New Orleans after Hurricane Katrina and lying on the hills of Puerto Rico after Hurricane Maria—and the lives cut short by AIDS, drought, hunger, and war—may be noted, but not grieved, by people living in the places that they consider to be inside the realm of the exceptional. As Jean and John L. Comaroff observe, however, the exclusions and sacrifice zones of capitalism are integral rather than peripheral to its inner workings (2012, 46). When undocumented immigrants are demonized, it becomes easier to take away the rights and resources of those with documents. When houseless people are portrayed as failures responsible for their own poverty, it becomes easier to excuse the predatory practices of a banking industry that secures surplus profits by driving millions of mortgage borrowers from their homes. When prison officials are given license to subject the "worst" prisoners to indefinite isolation, this punishment soon becomes routine treatment meted out to thousands of inmates. When low-wage workers and the unemployed have been belittled as unworthy parasites preying on the labor of producers, it becomes easier to attack teachers and municipal workers by taking away their pensions and denying them the right to be represented by unions. Once foreigners designated as enemies can be captured, tortured, and killed with no accountability and civilians considered collateral damage in wars around the world can be ignored, sadistic desires to see others squirm and cower and even be killed can be unleashed on the home front.

Without a strong conscious counterculture to combat neoliberal culture, fear and hate will remain at the center of the ways in which people experience the world. The emotional charge of fear inhibits the imagination of alternatives. It functions to justify the most vile and violent feelings and actions. It leads people to cultivate degrees of contempt, callousness, and cruelty that make hierarchy and exploitation seem natural, necessary, and inevitable. Yet fear can also be a source of knowledge and an impetus for action. Accompaniment can be an antidote to fear and a crucible for creating people capable of creating a world diametrically opposed to the premises and presumptions of neoliberal pedagogy.

Despite seeming control over every major social institution, the claims and appeals of the neoliberal conjuncture are riddled with contradictions and rife with disappointments. Attempting to clean up the wreckage caused by its own policies makes neoliberalism today largely a matter of managing, explaining, and excusing failure. As a social, economic, and political project, neoliberalism proves to be massively inefficient. It wastes and misallocates resources. It pledges empowerment but produces abandonment. It speaks in the name of opportunity and innovation but produces social exclusion and economic stagnation. The failures of neoliberal measures require cultural institutions to take on new functions. They are assigned the tasks of portraying the disintegration of social relations and social institutions as a victory for personal autonomy. They celebrate trivial consumer choices as satisfactory substitutes for political agency. They shift accountability for social crises away from powerful institutions by mobilizing blame and shame against society's most vulnerable individuals and groups. Dominant institutions and those who administer them encourage people to substitute vengeance for justice. They foment incessant moral panics based on exaggerated fears of difference and perpetually mobilize anger and resentment against an ever-increasing roster of domestic and foreign enemies.

During the past three decades, neoliberals in the United States have advanced the cause of privatization through a series of moral panics focused on the putatively bad behavior of demonized groups that are frequently coded as nonwhite, non-normative, and/or female: racial minorities, immigrants, welfare recipients, the houseless, inner-city youths, single mothers, religious minorities, and people with sexual identities that differ from the heteropatriarchal ideal. Moral panics about the spoiled character of public spaces and public institutions are promoted to justify neoliberal ways of "saving" them through market-based "reforms" like privatization. The fact that these reforms always fail to produce positive results—and, in fact, help destroy the very institutions they purport to save—does not discredit them. The failures of neoliberal reforms are attributed to the personal deficiencies (and racial identities) of the populations purported to rely on public services and institutions. When privatized reformers fail to contribute to the "public good" as they have promised and been paid to do, when they have *not* expanded opportunities and have *not* improved outcomes, racism works as a pivotal way to rationalize the failure of those reforms and to authorize new, ever more draconian neoliberal schemes with their accompanying rise in surplus profits for the few. Racially inflected rounds of blaming and shaming absolve capitalism and capitalists of any accountability for the stagnation of real wages, the impoverishment of the public sector, social services cuts, mass incarceration, unemployment, and the enormous and ever-expanding gap between the superrich and everyone else. These campaigns focus attention instead on the putative deficiencies of members of aggrieved groups. People who control virtually nothing are then blamed for virtually everything. In the process, the people who control nearly everything are blamed for nearly nothing (Salaam 2009). Thus neoliberal logic itself is impervious to failure: if any new privatization program does not deliver the promised "public benefits," the blame for the failure is always placed on those who should have been helped and were not: they are judged to be unfit for freedom.

What counts as "failure" under neoliberal logic has a shifting role: individuals can fail, will fail, and can be positioned as deserving to fail because they have not accommodated themselves to their proper tasks as consumers and entrepreneurs. Public employees and their institutions can fail and be punished if they do not satisfy mandated standards. In contrast, however, privatization schemes can never fail because their focus is always on the short-run interests of capital. The failure of vouchers or charter schools, privatizing public services, and cutting services for the poor and the disabled are essentially inadmissible evidence under neoliberal logic because the "success" of a privatization scheme is immediate. These schemes "succeed" as soon as investors and owners are given access to public funds, and that success continues until those public funds are depleted. What appears to be a failure to contribute to the "public good" is no failure at all for investors and owners authorized to loot public resources and to "write off" any failures as a tax loss. Public institutions are evaluated and disciplined in terms of their "intended" goal of improving the public good, but privatization schemes are evaluated in entirely different terms. Maximizing profit requires developing illusions of "value" through structures of publicity, leading to the cheating and misrepresentation routinely found to accompany high-stakes testing, charter schools, and other forms of educational privatization (Anderson and Applebome 2011; Asimov 2007; Severson 2011; Winerip 2011). But such revelations are not treated as a challenge to privatization. For in neoliberal logic, the ideology that authorizes privatization is untouched by the collapse of any single scheme of privatized exploitation, which is treated as a singular event. Investors and owners, having increased their wealth through the profits gained from public funds, simply move their capital onward, reconstituting themselves as new companies or brands. Properly framed in the neoliberal paradigm, nothing succeeds as much as failure. Each new disaster created by neoliberal policies creates a crisis that can be used to advance another round of privatization.

The contradiction between the world that neoliberalism imagines and the world in which we actually live is just one of many contradictions that plague the free market fundamentalist project and render it inherently unstable politically and ideologically. Neoliberalism produces many of the very problems it purports to solve. It requires political legitimacy and popular acquiescence, yet it creates chaos constantly in the lives of the public, which has to grapple with its regimes of disciplinary subordination. It fabricates a grossly deluded description of the economic and social world in which we live. Rather than the sum of interactions among free market actors, our world has in fact been shaped in innumerable ways by systematic exploitation, racial stratification, and gendered subordination created and sustained by inherited wealth, hierarchical divisions of labor, coordination among oligopolies and cartels, and the "locked in" advantages that accrue to dominant social identities (Roithmayr 2007).

Social Justice Scholarship as Contestation against Coloniality and Neoliberalism

Over the past two decades, the work of a number of academic fields with a history of concern for social justice—such as American, ethnic, feminist, and sexuality studies—illustrates both the bold promises and stark problems that attend to efforts at countering the colonial and neoliberal knowledge projects. What we might call the social justice scholarship of these academic fields attempts to grapple with the pervasive presence of the knowledge projects of coloniality and neoliberalism. This work draws necessarily on disciplinary paradigms, but it also recognizes how the history of the disciplines makes it necessary to call into question how scholarship has been framed by the colonial and neoliberal knowledge projects. The work of these fields tends to directly contradict the neoliberal pedagogy that elevates market times and market spaces over all other temporalities and spatialities. In recent decades these fields have become generative sites of improvisation and accompaniment by researchers focusing on race, ethnicity, gender, sexuality, class, dis/ability, and, more recently, coloniality and Indigeneity.

The field of American Studies provides a useful window into the complications of transforming fields necessarily shaped by colonial power. For example, American Studies' traditional focus on the U.S. nation and its national cultures as the logical and even inevitable framework of research is a legacy of the colonial matrix, a product of the processes of urbanization, state building, and empire in the nineteenth and twentieth centuries. White Anglo-Protestant elites in the United States accepted the zero point epistemology and the distinctions between humanitas and anthropos at the heart of the colonial project. They presumed that the educational system in the United States should embrace, honor, and emulate the cultural achievements of the imperial states of Europe. Through that lens, Indigenous dispossession, slavery, and imperial expansion were treated as inevitable and necessary components of the spread of the greatness of Europe to the New World. This perspective fit organically inside the nascent college system of the United States, which was financed, as Craig Wilder's research reveals, in no small measure by the profits made from the slave trade, plantation labor, and expropriation of Native American lands (Wilder 2013).

Yet many scholars in American Studies have worked to decolonize knowledge and consciously counter the hegemony of the neoliberal knowledge project. The field's formative attention to the particularities of place and the challenges of change over time–once a project structured in dominance–have now become subversive to the neoliberal project because these objects of analysis reveal the existence of alternatives to market time's infinitely renewable present and its seductive speculative futures. The avaricious and acquisitive economic subject privileged by neoliberalism has no need for tradition, history, culture, or moral judgment. But the focus on the poetics and politics of place in American Studies challenges the unlimited fungibility and interchangeability of space needed by the market mentality. As Doris Sommer and Pauline Strong explain about the arts and humanities in general, an attention to particularity can be a source of opposition to theoretical dogmatisms like those that undergird neoliberalism. They note that creative and artistic practice and criticism invite people "to tarry with detail and form," a detour that promotes multiple interpretations and delays conclusions in such a way as to promote collective deliberation and contemplation (Sommer and Strong 2016, 67–68).

Konesans and *Balans* in Academic Debates

Just as they do in Idle No More, Chicanx cultural production, and the Ferguson mobilization, *konesans* and *balans* can guide academic studies that challenge the knowledge projects of coloniality and neoliberalism in productive ways. The wisdom of the past connoted by the term *konesans* has value if deployed critically and creatively. Despite being structured in dominance, historical struggles over citizenship, social membership, and national identity have often led to unexpected emancipatory outcomes. Some scholars, however, advocate wholesale rejection of existing paradigms. They refuse to work with or against the assumptions of the nation-state, fearing that state-centric practices have too often foreclosed other possibilities. Yet this anti-statist framework suffers from the same illusions and delusions about purity that underwrite the nation-state itself. The concept of *balans* encourages a *both/and* rather than an *either/or* perspective on structures of sedimented power. It is indeed an error to imagine that social justice can be secured solely by seeking rights from the state. Yet it is equally wrong to imagine that the state does not need to be addressed, engaged, and confronted. Many all-encompassing indictments of received knowledge as inherently colonizing and racializing projects are fully justified and need to be articulated openly and repeatedly. Yet as is often the case with broad critiques, these run the risk of making a caricature of a complex reality, of accepting the grandiose aspirations of colonial thinkers as if they had been fully achieved or were even achievable. Elites throughout history have found that asserting domination is far easier than implementing it. Much will be lost if we let the magnitude of colonial pretensions erase the plenitude of decolonial practices.

There is a benefit to inhabiting, exploring, and critiquing tactically and strategically the contradictions of coloniality and neoliberal capitalism from the inside and to understanding their tools as devices that not only inhibit but can also enable. In attempting to find the right tools for the jobs we have to do, we cannot afford to discard completely any previous paradigm of knowledge simply because we are dissatisfied with the present that it has helped to create. As Malcolm X counseled his followers: when people are fighting for survival and freedom "there's no such thing as a bad device" (Guralnick 2005, 537).

Academic research, teaching, and studying in contemporary universities and colleges are activities fraught with peril. The knowledge regimes and social relations of coloniality unwilling to die and neoliberalism are not only "out there" in the minds and practices of clearly identifiable enemies but also "in here," meaning inside the physical and discursive spaces scholars inhabit. They cannot be worked around, but they can be worked through.[6] As Homi Bhabha argues, "The state of emergency is also always a state of *emergence*" (2008, xxiv). In a time of crisis, however, it is not always easy to distinguish the emergent from the residual or to discern exactly what is dying and what is being born. At any given historical moment, many temporalities exist inside the same time. Even when people occupy the same location, their cognitive mappings can be different. Inside academic fields concerned with social justice, these multiple times and places can become sources of conflict and division.

A sense of *balans* can keep academic inquiry principled and productive. In times of conflict, confusion, and disorder, sharp disagreements will arise. Scholars are not going to find many areas of easy and uncomplicated agreement in an era of dramatic transformation and change. There is no one formula for scholarly and political work; no one-size-fits-all solution exists for the problems that the people of the world face. Scholarly debates may oscillate wildly between fervid hopelessness and naive hopefulness—neither of which will succeed as imagined because both perspectives contain part of the truth, but only part. Competing impulses and interpretations of politics, ethics, and research can provide scholars with temptations to resort to convenient but flamboyant authorizing gestures that announce their own projects as a clean break from the corrupt foundations of the field to which, they argue, others still cling. Under these circumstances, differences of opinion and interpretation can too easily be framed as incommensurable moral hierarchies. There is room, however, for humility on all sides. Fields concerned with social justice have always profited greatly from the fact that they do *not* speak with one voice and that people participating in its dialogues are *not* the same. The differences that hurt can also help if scholars develop an imagination of unity that does not require unanimity or uniformity. Opposites do not need to be antagonists. They both may represent valuable parts of the truth.

Because a neoliberal society needs to create neoliberal subjects that are pliable to the demands and desires of a market society, it does not need or want critical readers, creative thinkers, or lifelong learners. In this context, fields concerned with social justice are certain to come under concentrated and sustained attack by vested interests threatened by the potential power in these areas of inquiry of repositories of collective memory, practices of ethical instruction, and propensities for identifying and honoring new publics, new polities, and new politics. The current balance of power is likely to produce heightened struggle but repeated defeats. Defeats can lead to demoralization. Demoralization can lead to division and mutual blaming and shaming. Being hurt can make people want to hurt others. Injured individuals and groups see a mirror of their own subordination in the eyes of the people closest to them. They can come to perceive people who might be allies as enemies, to be repulsed by the powerlessness they see around them and in the mirror, and to long for escape from association with those similarly aggrieved and with their problems. Unable to confront directly the people and institutions that actually cause the suffering, social justice seekers can quickly turn on each other. A radical divisiveness already permeates lived experience and popular culture. This encourages everyone to imagine that making others *lesser* can make themselves *greater*. Scholars in fields concerned with social justice might easily succumb to an affective politics that provides momentary satisfactions and feelings of superiority in the short run but that in the middle and long run will disempower struggles against neoliberal conditions. How scholarly communities carry these burdens will determine a great deal about their futures.

Scholars often see themselves as merely *enduring* neoliberal hegemony rather than *dwelling within it*. Yet even those of us who identify its failings *inhabit* neoliberalism. The academy is not an innocent victim of neoliberalism but rather one of the institutions where it has been generated, learned, legitimized, and implemented. Parts of the subjectivities of scholars have been produced by discourses that may seem "natural" to them yet ultimately work against scholarly and political goals of antisubordination. Scholars who feel like victims of neoliberal hegemony may actually be working as its cocreators through the form and content of their academic arguments, their teaching, and their pursuit of recognition and reward. In consequence, they may fail to identify how neoliberalism works to promote invidious competition even within the politics of debates that appear on the surface to make radical oppositional claims.

Philip Deloria observes that market pressures can lead many graduate students and junior faculty to believe that they will not succeed in the profession if they honor the past in any way, if they do not claim to be overturning past scholarship completely and replacing it with "a new political intervention, a new methodological innovation, a new paradigm that redefines the very questions being asked" (2009, 14). Yet this fetishization of novelty is a core premise of neoliberalism. Under these conditions, researchers can be tempted to reduce social and intellectual differences to simple oedipal conflicts. While the young may attempt matricide and patricide, veteran scholars may charge younger generations with betrayal of foundational research principles and purposes. There are very real structural imperatives that pressure scholars to take this path. But one of the most important lessons to be learned from the history of fields concerned with social justice is that destructive pressures can be evaded, inverted, subverted, and resisted.

Researchers and teachers cannot assume that they are already prepared for the impact of neoliberal thinking on their scholarship or that their teaching and writing activities are immune to neoliberal influences. The discourses scholars inhabit seek to shape not merely *what we think* but, more important, *how we think*. Although scholars have examined the assumptions of neoliberal argumentation in popular culture and public discourses, they have devoted less attention to the infusion of neoliberal assumptions inside the form and content of their own scholarly arguments. Readers tend to focus on what scholars argue, what dangers the content of their arguments signal for us, and what satisfactions or dissatisfactions emerge from reading them. In doing so, scholars may incorporate without examination neoliberal assumptions about how arguments should be conducted, what should count as successful argumentation, and what kinds of evidence should be necessary to criticize or shut down a line of argument.

Neoliberal assumptions may frame scholarly debate within the terms of consumerism by celebrating new topics and focusing on slight realignments of theoretical arguments. This search for the new emerges "organically" not because problems have been solved or debates have been exhausted but because the appearance of change speaks to desires promoted by neoliberalism for novelty, diversion, and distraction. Neoliberal consumerist assumptions may encourage scholars to look at academic arguments that have long histories yet enduring relevance with jaded, bored, and impatient eyes. This taken-for-granted consumerist mentality has enormous political consequences for the relationship of academic arguments to arguments about social justice taking place in broader public arenas. What could be more useful to neoliberal hegemony than "oppositional" scholars who routinely declare the work of other "oppositional" scholars hackneyed and banal? What could be more useful for neoliberalism than the establishment of bored detachment and imperious disdain as significant affects in a scholarly field that would otherwise be attempting to counter histories and cultures of subordination? To absorb, ignore, or fail to challenge neoliberal stances that may pervade scholarly debates is to render our scholarly work intellectually and politically marginal at a time when it can provide vital alternatives. Some of those alternatives reside in the improvised academies described earlier in this book that emanate from the work of Idle No More, Chicanx artivistas, and Ferguson activists.

The exigencies of these times need not create a sense of despair or defeat for scholarship about social justice. Instead, scholarship's role in rethinking and countering neoliberal hegemony can become more important than ever. As Cedric Robinson reminds us, "We are not the subjects or the subject formations of the capitalist world-system. It is merely one condition of our being" (1996, 122). Enabling scholars to see that neoliberal thinking is merely one condition of our existence may require transforming the terms of reading and writing in our fields to counter unacknowledged neoliberal assumptions about argument that influence our debates (see Tomlinson 2010, 2019). To transform the terms of reading and writing requires, most urgently, a position of dramatically critical self-reflection about methods of scholarly argumentation—an unrelenting interrogation of how neoliberal assumptions of argument can inadvertently undermine the possibilities of our scholarship. Debates about particularity and universality, sameness and difference, identification and disidentification, rupture and continuity in the discourse of our fields may appear to represent resistant political positions while in fact reflecting and reinforcing the binary distinctions at the heart of neoliberal thinking, especially its privileging of the *either/or* over the *both/and*. In a neoliberal society, *even resistance is structured in dominance.* Claiming to transcend received categories is not to do so. Being in opposition to other scholars—finding them not resistant enough, or in the right ways—is not the same as being in opposition to hegemonic power. Staking out positions is not the same as waging the war of position. What is presented as an oppositional identity can become just another "brand," totally congruent with the market niches promoted by neoliberalism.

How Does the Work You Do Speak for You—and for Others?

At every stage, scholarship in fields concerned with social justice has been shaped by both residual and emergent elements—by the ways in which crises connect constituencies who have long memories of unresolved past grievances with emergent polities thrown forth by shake-ups in social relations and social identities. No part of the past ever disappears completely, yet remnants of the past never suffice to solve the problems of the present.

Nearly every approach that enables something inhibits something else. Desires to connect scholarship in the academy to the experiences of people outside can be particularly nettling sources of disagreement. Connecting teaching and research to the work of large social movement organizations can do important work in deepening the capacity for democratic deliberation and decision-making in society at large while infusing scholarly work with insights and ideas relevant to the urgent problems that large numbers of people face. These connections, however, can also lead scholars to absorb and accept the hegemonic and heteronormative models of identity, association, and affiliation that so often pervade social movement groups. Miranda Joseph (2002) has wisely warned against the romance of community that can easily morph into communitarian and even totalitarian constraints on individual and collective praxis. The trope of community can enable opportunists to disguise self-interest as service and solidarity. It can lead the more powerful and privileged members of a group to stand in for the totality, disavow the needs and interests of those of whom they disapprove, and still purport to represent the entire group. This can privilege heteronormative forms of identification, association, and affiliation at the expense of what Nayan Shah (2011) describes as queer sociality and "stranger intimacy."

Yet disidentification and disavowal of collectivities entail problems of their own. It may become tempting to savor the counterhegemonic possibilities of involvement with small groups of like-minded individuals who share the same identities, experiences, and values. These sites can be powerful sources of solidarity and support, places where working together builds reciprocal relations of care and concern. Yet the solidarities of sameness on which small groups depend also make them susceptible to becoming cliques made up of insiders who bond together mainly through shared aversion to those they exclude. They run the risk of replicating neoliberalism's privileging of private solutions to public problems. Friendship can serve as one valuable model of accompaniment. In her research on social movements of the 1960s, however, Francesca Polletta (2002) shows that groups based primarily on the friendship model find it difficult to expand beyond their original members, and their aversion to formal rules allows informal and status hierarchies to persist and remain beyond criticism and impregnable to challenge.

Balans as a Way of Knowing

Just as paradigms of generational succession turn potentially productive conversations into destructive oppositions, frameworks of unbridled optimism versus paralyzing pessimism impose a Manichaean binary on dialectical relationships. In an age of displacement, dispossession, and disciplinary subordination, any acknowledgment of popular agency can seem to some like dangerously uncritical celebration of—and ultimately collaboration with—neoliberal regimes of racialized security and austerity. This sensibility—rooted in a legitimate desire to avoid *underestimating* centralized power and state violence—can, however, also *overestimate* it, unwittingly confusing power's most grandiose stories about itself with the actual social relations of society. Such a position can discourage and disarm the very populations that most need to fight back. Yet unwarranted pessimism cannot be countered effectively by an equally unwarranted optimism. Decades of defeat and the paucity of short-term victories may lead some scholars to see any sign of agency as evidence of effective political resistance and transformation and to refuse to be critical of social movements because they seem to be the only visible marker on which hopes for change might rest.

At a time when scholarship in fields concerned with social justice is certain to come under attack, these tensions can be either productive provocations for new and better work or sources of destructive internal divisions that poison the well from which we all have to drink. Through acts of accompaniment, improvisation, and engagement, however, social justice scholarship can situate itself among the many sites in U.S. society where a collective capacity for democratic deliberation and decision-making can be nurtured and sustained. In the process of attempting to build a better society, this work can also lead to better scholarship because its research objects and research questions emerge out of the actual contradictions of social life. Social accompaniment and engagement require scholars to vet their ideas widely among large groups of people with very different experiences who can then appraise, verify, or contest their accuracy, authenticity, and validity. They offer an opportunity to connect work inside class bound, monolingual, and nationalist educational institutions to more cosmopolitan and critical conversations with people who feel compelled to develop new ways of knowing and new ways of being in order to resist the unlivable destinies that neoliberal society parcels out to them. In an era when the hegemony of market space and market time threatens to engulf all activities, it keeps the door open for new and better forms of association, affiliation, and understanding.

The future of scholarship concerned with social justice requires scholars to know *the work we want our work to do*; to frame scholarly relations not as *competition* but as *accompaniment*; to insist that our ideas and activism be infused with ethical judgment and wisdom; to clarify the significance of different aspects of our scholarly lives; to acknowledge that our work speaks for us but also for others; and to recognize the dialogic and dialectical nature of our views of society. Honing the critical edge of scholarship concerned with social justice depends not only on *what* scholars know but also on *how we go about knowing*.

In the introduction (2008b) to *Engaging Contradictions* (2008a), a landmark anthology on engaged scholarship, Charles Hale argues on behalf of research that emerges out of humble, friendly, and respectful conversations and collaborations between researchers and aggrieved communities of color. Drawing on the work of Davydd Greenwood (2008), Hale advances Aristotle's concept of *phrónêsis*. Unlike the scientific search for theoretical knowledge and the practical knowledge of craft making, *phrónêsis* refers to the wisdom that comes from practical concerns about ethics, deliberations about values, and action to imbue the world with more just social conditions. Hale argues that *phrónêsis* can be an overarching term that encompasses different ways of formulating research questions in response to the needs of oppressed people. It can produce analyses that are comprehensible and useful to the groups being studied. It can identify and build on the profound knowledge generated from communities in struggle, placing that knowledge in egalitarian dialogue with the perspectives of scholars, and utilizing the inevitable tensions and contradictions between academic and activist viewpoints to produce an experienced-based challenge to prevailing academic wisdom (Hale 2008b, 22). *Phrónêsis* does not ask researchers to aspire to be neutral, detached, or disinterested observers, but instead to embrace roles as active, engaged, and committed participants in social justice struggles. In the terms formulated by João Costa Vargas, scholars need to be observant participants not participant observers (Vargas 2006).

Engaged scholars grounded in principles of *phrónêsis* seek to study *with* aggrieved communities of color rather than *on* them. They formulate research questions through horizontal dialogue with people who are not credentialed as academic experts; they view social movement struggles as generators of new knowledge. This means their work is often misunderstood and mischaracterized as a departure from traditional scholarly allegiance to objectivity. Yet all knowledge is partial, perspectival, and interested. Objectivity does not require neutrality. Fidelity to evidence should not be confused with servility to the assumptions and interests of dominant groups. Hale explains that "all knowledge claims are produced in a political context; notions of objectivity that ignore or deny these facilitating conditions take on a de facto political positioning of their own, made more blatant by the very disavowal" (Hale 2008b, 2).

In the research projects that we explore in the next chapter, the ideas and actions of communities in struggle generate new knowledge. They open a door to an augmented awareness of the research process, of its occluded power dynamics and vexing ethical and political challenges. Focus on the perspectives of aggrieved groups reveals dimensions of social structures and social relations that would otherwise be invisible. Following Hale, we contend that equity oriented collaborative community based research can in fact *reclaim* objectivity. It expands and deepens the sources of data from which evidence is derived and from which research questions are formulated. Engaged scholarship conducted with awareness of *phrónêsis* can be objective in the sense that its authors are obligated to present accurate depictions of research objects. Yet it does not entail poses of distance and detachment that confuse objectivity with neutrality, impeding scholarly recognition of unjust power relations in society and in the research process itself. We argue that engaging in acts of accompaniment with aggrieved social movement groups are not departures from the responsibility of researchers to identify new knowledge, but are rather generative sources of it (Tomlinson and Lipsitz 2013; Hale 2008b, 23). In the next chapter we explore how the conditions of the neoliberal university can both inhibit and enable equity oriented collaborative community based research.

7 / Accompaniment and the Neoliberal University

To the free market fundamentalists who champion neoliberal values, college and K–12 classrooms seem like insubordinate spaces. They view these places as sites that are insufficiently integrated into the apparatuses that generate immediate profitable returns on investments. Although schools are essentially conservative institutions that seek to prepare students for future market activity, they are not conservative *enough* for today's investors and owners who now see schools as subversive to profit making in the present. If neoliberals were the conservatives they often claim to be, they would honor and emphasize study of the intellectual and artistic traditions of the past and encourage recognition of their relevance to the present. But the free market fundamentalists are not conservatives; they are revolutionary plutocrats who view university classrooms as vestigial remnants of a previous era of capitalism when it was still considered useful to nurture and sustain the critical distance that academic inquiry promoted as a way of training managers and professionals. The attack on the university is "ideological" in the largest sense: rather than merely a political attack on "dissenting ideas," it is an attempt to eradicate discourses and disciplines that might be concerned with "public or community good," that do not automatically place market practices at the center of the social world, and that offer alternatives to the subjectivity of the market actor fixated on material gain. In recent years it has become evident that the logic of neoliberalism is not confined to delegitimation of the humanities and the social sciences. It now calls into question the existence of all parts of the university—including the sciences—for similar reasons: not merely because university expenditures are "costly" in a time of artificially created financial limitations, and not merely because universities provide a "public good" offensive to ideologies of privatization, but explicitly because the university potentially refuses to allow the time and space of the market to occlude all other historical, social, and cultural times and spaces. Because neoliberalism works to delegitimize and eradicate *any* alternatives to market time and market space, it seeks to create the "entrepreneurial" university: a place of market competition where scholars study what the people who pay them tell them to study.

Audit and surveillance systems are central to this project. They operate as an apparatus of enforcement as well as a technology for production of neoliberal educational selves. As Davies and Saltmarsh argue, audit systems are framed as necessary exactly because neoliberalism frames individuals as wholly self-interested and, therefore, untrustworthy: "Within this competitive, consumer-oriented system individuals in pursuit of their own freedom must also be persuaded to freely accept responsibility both for themselves as individuals and for the success of their workplace. To this end an extensive audit system is needed since, in a neoliberal philosophy, trust and commitment to the collective well-being have been made redundant" (2007, 3).

Davies and Saltmarsh argue that the audit systems, built on distrust, increasingly reproduce it (see also Rose 1999, 155). Davies and Peter Bansel argue that audit systems not only "govern," but serve as "technologies of the self" to create faculty as neoliberal subjects:

> The operation of these technologies on and in the subject simultaneously secures the subject's viability and subjection. It secures their individuality and their regulation as responsibilised and accountable subjects who support an expanding industrialisation of the university: that is, capture by the market, market forces and practices. In this take up of the institutional ambitions as one's own and one's willing work on oneself to become the appropriate and appropriated subject of the new university, there is a slippage . . . toward the neoliberal subject whose morality is intimately muddled with that of the entrepreneurial institution whose project is a pragmatic one of survival within the terms of government. (2010, 9)

When school districts across the country succumbed to political and economic pressure and allowed for-profit educational entrepreneurs to set up charter schools subsidized by state funds in inner cities in Milwaukee, Baltimore, and San Francisco, most faculty members and students at Research 1 universities did not view those decisions as a threat to them. When charter schools failed to outperform their counterparts in the public system despite being able to choose their students and their teachers—yet were rewarded with more contracts and control over more schools—university faculty members and students did not generally perceive a threat to their own endeavors. When in the wake of the flooding that followed Hurricane Katrina in 2005 reconstruction of the city of New Orleans provided an excuse for the dissolution of the public school system, the firing of more than seven thousand school employees—union members and the backbone of the local Black middle class—and the provision of new state and federal subsidies for private for-profit charter schools, these actions were not perceived to be a threat to top-tier colleges and universities. But now, as privatization has come to the university with fuller force, faculty and students see that what was allowed to happen to inner-city students and teachers yesterday is happening to colleges and universities today.

What confronts higher education now is what has already been confronting people all across the nation and all around the world: what Naomi Klein calls "predatory disaster capitalism" (2007). Although it impacts different populations in different ways, predatory disaster capitalism always entails a fragmented, delinked, privatized, and devolved state unable to meet human needs but perfectly suited to assist investors in reaping the gains that flow from accumulation by dispossession (see Harvey 2003, 67; Klein 2007; Woods 2005, 1012). The ascendency of neoliberalism, its denigration of the notion of the common good, and the consequences of its shifting deployments of race, time, and space have long been at issue to those concerned with the future of the university. Bill Readings (1997), Masao Miyoshi (2000), Jennifer Washburn (2006), Christopher Newfield (2008, 2017), and Frank O'Donoghue (2008), for example, exposed the causes and consequences of the impending privatization of education in its early stages. With the exception of the education of the elite, neoliberalism positions the university according to market logic, as a site where consumers can buy the credentialing they believe they need to obtain jobs in the future.

Although there are parts of this credentialing that emphasize competition, in many cases students are encouraged to view themselves as entitled consumers who deserve a path of least resistance to the credentials they desire. College teachers will feel these changes deeply in their everyday lives. Rather than promoting a competitive culture of work and achievement, the end result of this corporate fiscalized, virtualized, and vocationalized higher education will be a "race to the bottom," a scramble by students to acquire the greatest amount of reward for the least amount of work. This climate will produce large amounts of cheating and vehement demands for the least strenuous kinds of assessment possible. The debts students incur from loans constrain their career choices and impede their chances of acquiring future assets. Students encounter increasingly limited vocationally oriented curricula and demoralizing pedagogies designed to accustom them to rote learning and following orders. The multiple-choice tests emphasized in high-stakes testing regimes already teach students that education entails providing short literal answers to short literal questions and that gratification comes instantly in the form of checking the correct box, a process that closes down rather than opens up intellectual inquiry. Students accustomed to the tasks mandated by high-stakes testing therefore look for simple and direct tasks in their college work. Teachers are urged to credential students but not to teach them—to ignore how the proliferation of commercially prepared research modules and high-stakes tests in K–12 education is producing generations of students who lack the ability to read carefully, write clearly, or think logically. A painful literalism leads them to look for the phrases they think they will need to reproduce when asked to write. Without self-actualizing reading strategies, they often mistake the views that authors criticize as the views that the authors espouse. They reduce complex arguments to simple propositions. Their responses to assigned readings foreground their satisfaction or dissatisfaction as consumers based on the accessibility of texts but display little engagement with the evidence, ideas, and arguments of the authors. They can make literal connections between questions and answers, but they cannot develop their ability to read carefully, write clearly, or think logically. They solve puzzles but are baffled by problems.

The neoliberal university values some of the knowledge considered to contribute directly to employment, but all other forms of knowledge are seen as hurdles requiring minimal rote learning rather than the skill building necessary to become a critical thinker, creative problem solver, and lifelong learner. Following the failed model of "teacher proof" education in K–12 schooling, university students will be rushed through their undergraduate years taking large classes taught by part-time adjuncts who give them standardized tests that can be graded by machines. The small areas of research and intellectual excellence that remain will not be valued in themselves. Instead, as top administrators in the University of California system have explained recently in reference to an expensive project they have already under way, universities' reputations for research excellence will be valuable mainly as a source of status useful for building the brand equity of online education modeled after for-profit MBA diploma mills but graced by the imprimatur of an elite university (Council of UC Faculty Associations 2010).

The cumulative consequences of school segregation, academic tracking, and two-tiered public school systems, coupled with dramatic increases in tuitions and fees, will undermine the cosmopolitanism of college conversations. The social base of the university will become narrower and narrower under these conditions. The diverse class, racial, and linguistic backgrounds of students that give academic inquiries enormous vitality and that make them different from the conversations that prevail in segregated suburban high schools will no longer inform college work. Instead, universities will increasingly be populated only by the children of investors, owners, managers, and professionals who will expect the university to provide them with the uniformity they have come to experience in the limited circles in which they travel. These changes pose daunting challenges to students and scholars concerned with the quality and integrity of academic inquiry. They will have to work within institutions inimical to their ideals and interests, yet create insubordinate spaces inside them. This can be difficult and debilitating work. As Albert Memmi argued in another context, "It is not easy to escape mentally from a concrete situation, to refuse its ideology while continuing to live with its actual relationships" (1991, 20).

Injury, Indignation, and Insubordinate Academic Spaces

Universities can and should be atypical and anomalous places in society—sites that counter the pedagogies of neoliberalism. They should be locales where evidence and argument matter more than influence, where original and generative thinking is more highly valued than entertainment, where independent researchers ask and answer important questions without interference from funders. Because the entertainment, advertising, and public relations industries generally teach people to seek easy, accessible, and simple solutions to complex problems, there is greater need now than ever before to have places where mental work that is necessarily difficult can be conducted. Under these circumstances, institutions of higher learning can serve important functions by preserving and protecting academic freedom, pursuing pure research, permitting unfettered inquiry, empowering students and scholars to ask and answer difficult questions, and promoting informed public discussions about vital issues. Particularly promising are what James Lee calls "the provisional spaces that institutions tolerate but do not fully sanction, and the conversations that compel us to read all kinds of different books and nudge us, at times, to put our books down" (2004, xxx). Yet negotiating the challenges of the neoliberal university requires full presence of mind and honest evaluation of the many social, cultural, economic, political, and psychological forces that impede the development of the high degree of clarity, courage, and conviction needed for meaningful social change.

Insubordinate spaces cannot be safe spaces. By nature, they are sites of struggle that entail conflict and contestation at the scene of argument. Acts of accompaniment and improvisation raise challenges to the practices, policies, and programs that prop up powerful interests, and as a result they are certain to come under attack. College campuses are derided by the enemies of free inquiry as bastions of political correctness, of reverse racism against whites, and of male bashing. The reality is that 84 percent of full professors are white and 60 percent are male, 89 percent of college presidents are white and 81 percent are male, and Black enrollment on predominantly white campuses has been decreasing rather than increasing (Hamer and Lang 2015). Commitments to diversity are frequently proclaimed but rarely practiced. They are invoked but not implemented. Prominent in press releases and publicity, they remain marginal in practice.

In diversity and all other matters, colleges and universities are structured in dominance. They are set up to conduct research and provide trained workers for business, the police, and the military. The neoliberal emphasis on forcing each unit in a university to pay for itself by teaching larger classes, competing for majors, and securing outside gifts and grants damages student learning, misallocates resources, and skews research agendas. Turning scientists and public health researchers into corporate product development specialists diverts energy and attention away from pressing public needs and problems. Researchers pick safe projects that will not offend potential funders. Universities seeking gifts from wealthy donors become reluctant to support research that questions the priorities that bring the highest profits. Regulatory agencies and political bodies are reluctant to implement recommendations based on research findings if they risk the wrath of powerful contributors to political campaigns.

Civil engineering researcher Marc Edwards offers an example of the harm enacted by the neoliberal capture of research. A privatization scheme in Flint, Michigan, changed the source of the city's water supply from the Detroit system to the Flint River. The owners and investors in the water privatization scheme saw an opportunity to cut costs by changing the source of the water without checking adequately how it would react to the available pipes. As a result, thousands of children and adults in Flint ingested toxic levels of lead, a condition that could lead to disastrous illnesses and developmental disabilities in the future. Fearful of being poisoned, residents had to purchase large amounts of bottled water. The illnesses emanating from that incident will plague the people of Flint far into the future. Yet city and state officials dawdled in response to residents' complaints. Despite a large body of easily available data about the high levels of lead in the water provided to denizens of Flint, officials belittled citizens who complained. One Flint resident contacted Edwards, a renowned specialist on issues related to lead. The researcher found that the levels of lead in Flint water were the highest he had ever seen. Edwards blames the privatization and fiscalization of research for the crisis in Flint because it drove researchers away from studies that serve public rather than corporate interests (Hiltzik 2016).

Colleges and universities are part of the neoliberal establishment, yet their residual commitments to free inquiry and democratic education enable some forms of counterpedagogy and accompaniment to exist, however tenuously. These activities emerge in insubordinate spaces when students and teachers campaign for diversity and inclusion in order to fulfill the obligation of education to be cosmopolitan and to draw its pool of interlocutors from the broadest possible range of social experiences and positions. These efforts to counter the artificial, arbitrary, and irrational exclusions perpetrated by racism, sexism, nativism, ableism, and homophobia seem like political correctness to opponents accustomed to enjoying the benefits of unearned privilege and permanent overrepresentation. As their perpetual complaints indicate, the cruelty, callousness, and contempt that neoliberal pedagogies inculcate in people do not disappear when they set foot on campus. Just as *off campus* the vituperation and violence that is directed against women, immigrants, Muslims, nonwhite racial groups, and lesbian, gay, bisexual, trans, and queer individuals promotes an orgy of bonding around an imaginary besieged white masculine propertied normativity, hate crimes and hate speech directed at scapegoats *on campus* become the modality through which a certain number of students, staff, and faculty constitute their identities. As a result, students from aggrieved groups have to contend with assaults, threats, and ridicule scrawled on walls and sidewalks and posted online and with lectures, assigned readings, and classroom discussions that portray them and their entire group as immoral, unfit, and intellectually deficient.

These are expressly *political* problems. In a neoliberal society, however, people are trained to perceive political problems through a language of personal insult, injury, and even trauma. That language is not entirely inappropriate when applied to the experiences of students from scapegoated groups on college and university campuses. They carry an enormous emotional and psychological burden because of the treatment meted out to them. Yet as Robin Kelley astutely argues, interpreting these experiences solely as personal *trauma* can lead people to see themselves as victims and objects rather than as agents (Kelley 2016, 6). They can become so invested in this discourse that they come to recognize themselves mainly through their injuries. Toni Cade Bambara warned against this self-destructive practice in her novel *The Salt Eaters*. At an early moment in the book, the narrator describes how people can become attached to the things that impair them. According to this depiction of patients in an infirmary,

> they wore their crippleness or blindness like a badge of honor, as though it meant they'd been singled out for some special punishment, were special. Or as though it meant they'd paid some heavy dues and knew, then, what there was to know, and therefore had a right to certain privileges, or were exempt from certain charges, or ought to be listened to at meetings. But way down under the knowing "special" was a lie, knowing better all along and feeling the cost of the lie, of the self-betrayal in the joints, in the lungs, in the eyes. (Bambara 1992, 108)

Recognizing that the injuries are real but viewing the response as self-sabotage, inconsistent with the survival strategies of oppressed people, Bambara has her narrator observe, "Sometimes a person held on to sickness with a fiercesomeness . . . So used to being unwhole and unwell . . . For people sometimes believed that it was safer to live with complaints, was necessary to cooperate with grief, was all right to become an accomplice in self-ambush" (Bambara 1992, 107).

Both on campus and off campus there are people who experience symptoms of trauma: loss of ego functions; numbness of spirit; susceptibility to depression, anxiety, and rage; loss of motor skills; inability to concentrate; preoccupation with death; retreat into dependency; and constant apprehension about the social and physical environment. For these individuals, both personal therapeutic treatment and changes to the conditions that cause and perpetuate trauma are necessary. An imprecise use of the word "trauma," however, along with an overemphasis on individual experiences, can lead to underemphasis on the harm perpetuated by normalized social structures, power relations, and actions that accentuate and augment collective social mistreatment.

Under these circumstances, injury, one of many conditions of individual and collective existence, can assume a psychic centrality, a position at the core of an innate and immutable identity. A discourse of trauma can elevate private therapeutic remedies over public political solutions. Fully in keeping with the logic of neoliberalism, this discourse makes the political concepts of oppression, suppression, and subjugation give way to the interior psychological concepts of trauma, post-traumatic stress, microaggressions, and triggers. Demands for help managing the effects of trauma replace demands for ending the social and structural forces that cause it (Kelley 2016, 6–7). Well aware of how they have been hurt, the people who have been injured do not notice who they can help, such as the low-wage workers who clean their classrooms and dorm rooms, the mothers on and off campus who cannot afford day care, the disabled who are locked out of opportunity by buildings without ramps and sidewalks lacking curb cuts, the queer and trans people criminalized for their sexual and gender identities, and all the houseless, hungry, shunned, sequestered, and silenced people that neoliberal austerity produces.

Psychological services are important and should be available and affordable for those who need them. Yet the prevailing terms of psychological diagnosis and treatment need interrogation. Influenced by the liberation psychology conceived by Ignacio Martín-Baró in El Salvador during the 1980s, researchers Nia Phillips, Glenn Adams, and Phia Salter argue that dominant approaches in social psychology wrongly address the injuries of racial oppression by promoting strategies of emotional management and self-efficacy training. The researchers recommend instead a decolonial approach organized around critical consciousness and collective action (N. Phillips, Adams, and Salter 2015). The same deadly conjuncture that led Archbishop Romero to explore the concept of accompaniment impelled Martín-Baró to challenge the universalist and ahistorical premises dominant in psychological research and practice. A member of the Catholic priesthood born in Spain and educated at the University of Chicago, Martín-Baró served as academic vice-rector and chair of the Psychology Department at the University of Central America in San Salvador. Working as a parish priest in the pueblo of Jayaque, he witnessed the psychological consequences among the peasants caused by the hunger, repression, and terror imposed on them by the ruling class and the army. Yet he also observed how brutally oppressed people continued the struggle for social justice despite a civil war that took eighty thousand lives and displaced 40 percent of the population. These experiences convinced Martín-Baró of the inadequacy of approaches to psychology that placed at the center of its inquiries and practices an autonomous individual outside of history and social contexts, seeking only individual happiness and satisfaction. He viewed the construction of more just societies as a mental health issue that required psychological practices grounded in the cultivation of interdependence and collective attachments (Adams and Salter 2011, 1368; Watkins and Shulman 2008, 23–28).

The ideas about perceiving injury and recovery as collective rather than purely individual matters that Phillips, Adams, and Salter derive from Martín-Baró open a door to thinking about the value of public practices of accompaniment and improvisation as events that enable members of aggrieved groups to recognize that their suffering is shared and needs to be addressed collectively. As performance theorist Diana Taylor explains with characteristic insight, performances that also function as protests can enable participants to recognize personal pain as an impetus for social change because they situate the repercussions of traumatic violence and loss as public rather than merely private (Taylor 2002, 154). Acts of accompaniment and improvisation can bring a new world into being, one based on what Watkins and Shulman describe as "the psychological capacity to bear a dialogue with difference, to tolerate conflicting experiences and points of view, while still finding common ground and constructing a shared future" (Watkins and Shulman 2008, 20).

Accompaniment can thus be therapeutic. Throughout history, the restorative and resilient practices of collective caring by oppressed people have been more responsible for their survival, sustenance, and shared well-being than recourse to personal and individual therapy. Robin Kelley identifies political resistance as an important form of healing. He argues that in the course of collective struggle, "we alter our circumstances; contain, escape, or possibly eviscerate the *source* of trauma; recover our bodies; reclaim and redeem our dead; and make ourselves whole" (Kelley 2016, 6). Struggle requires public political projects, tactics, and strategies, but it is also aided immeasurably by interior commitments, by what Toni Cade Bambara describes as the need to "walk upright and see clearly, breath easily, think better than was taught, be better than one was programmed to believe . . . to help a neighbor experience the best of herself or himself" (Bambara 1992, 107).

Students able to move beyond discourses of personal injury sometimes proceed to discourses saturated with politics, yet too often they do so solely through political indignation. They protest fraternity and sorority parties that revolve around degrading racist themes; challenge racist, sexist and homophobic graffiti and posts on social media; and oppose expenditures of university funds to bring to campus speakers who incite religious, racial, gender, and sexual hatred. They respond to provocations to "debate" whether their Muslim religion makes them terrorists, whether affirmative action is reverse racism against whites, or whether courses in feminist studies and queer studies should be allowed. These forums are not serious or substantive discussions but rather spectacles staged as a form of recreational hate by "haves" who feel entitled to make the "have nots" squirm. Students committed to antisubordination are always put on the defensive, always challenged to defend their right to exist, always prodded to justify their worthiness for inclusion before their enemies, positioned as antagonists who have already had their testimony ruled inadmissible even before they begin to speak. These students would, of course, be reviled as savage and monstrous if they turned the tables and presumed to put others on the defensive, for example, by inviting white propertied heteronormatively gendered males to "debate" whether they are the recipients of unearned advantages, whether Christianity's history of association with warfare endangers its status as a legitimate religion, or whether the prevalence of white males among the ranks of mass shooters makes them a danger to others and therefore legitimate targets of surveillance and suppression. Scapegoated students have a right to defend themselves—and it is understandable that they wish to do so—but by responding constantly to these provocations, they trap themselves in what New Orleans spoken word artist Sunni Patterson (2016) describes as "enemy-centered spaces." These students expend so much effort combating what they are *against*, they have little energy left to develop a full understanding of what they are *for*. Like the discourses of injury, the discourse of indignation constantly appeals for institutions of higher education to become safe supportive places where students can feel respected and loved. This is an understandable but unrealistic aspiration. It directly contradicts the neoliberal presumptions, premises, and practices by which the university is governed. If the students are to have a different kind of educational and social experience, it will not be given to them by those in power. They must help create it themselves by working with faculty, staff, and community members to create insubordinate spaces on campus and off.

The university is not an innocent victim of neoliberalism. Rather, higher education is one of the key sites where neoliberalism has been invented, learned, and legitimated. The university is an important institution in society. It is filled with what Gramsci called "experts in legitimation" whose ideas, evidence, and arguments support the organized abandonment of aggrieved groups. Expert academic knowledge commissioned by powerful interests and institutions has been consistently used to thwart the goals of antiracist advocates for environmental justice, for fair housing, and for augmented funding for AIDS research. It is deployed against antiracist opponents of massive prison-building projects, urban redevelopment schemes, and neoliberal economic austerity policies. Community activists constantly find themselves forced to challenge the expert knowledge of scientists, physicians, criminologists, bankers, urban planners, and economists. They should expect to find allies on campuses. Students and scholars refuting dominant neoliberal formulations can provide useful tools for their struggles. Scholars do not do enough simply by adding on new evidence to existing paradigms. Instead, the fight against the logic of neoliberalism requires exposing and challenging the epistemological and ideological underpinnings of contemporary science, law, medicine, urban planning, and business, while working together with the masses of people who are never allowed to set foot on a college campus to develop generative new ways of being and thinking.

We argue that scholars and students can develop a collective capacity for accompaniment inside the structures of academic life by deploying the concepts of *konesans* and *balans* in a way that combines critique and affirmation, blends generative ideas with generosity, and uses ego, energy, and ambition not primarily for personal gain but to help and serve others. Inside Research 1 institutions, *konesans* and *balans* can be especially valuable in helping negotiate the contradictions embedded in some of the key institutional entities that shape faculty lives, institutions that we encapsulate here as the *CV*, the *simulacrum*, and the *struggle*. In our discussion of these institutions, we raise some criticisms and make some recommendations about personal conduct and behavior. Yet while we believe that the choices people make do matter, we insist that these choices are not made in a vacuum. Practices and processes saturated with power pressure people to act within the logic of the dominant system. Ethical conviction and personal courage are not sufficient tools for challenging or even resisting an entire system structured in dominance. The potential for misjudgments, mistakes, and wrong choices that we explore below should not be seen as a critique of the personal failings of individuals but should instead be seen as evidence of the implied and inscribed logic of neoliberal society. Even if we were somehow capable of becoming radically different kinds of people on our own, we would still need to make systemic changes in society to create room for these new personalities, dispositions, and character structures to survive and thrive. Yet relentless exposure to neoliberal pedagogies is designed to prevent us from becoming thinking subjects who can even envision and enact meaningful social change. We cannot become different kinds of people unless society changes, but society will not change unless we become different kinds of people. This might seem like an unsolvable conundrum, yet a blend of *konesans* and *balans* can address each half of the problem to help solve the other half. Changing academic institutions and their practices is an important step toward changing ourselves, and changing ourselves is a necessary part of changing society.

The CV

The hierarchies, reward structures, and pressures of academic life make it easy to lose perspective. Individual professional histories and achievements are recorded on curriculum vitae that establish a public record that looms large in the lives of scholars. Because of the publications, presentations, positions, honors, and awards enumerated on it, the CV circulates out in the world as a strange surrogate for the person whose work it describes. As an "other directed" document designed to be examined by strangers, the CV functions as a professional passport that can open doors or leave them closed. It takes center stage every time scholars are reviewed, every time they apply for jobs, grants, and fellowships, and every time their departments are evaluated. Because past accomplishments augur well for future achievement, an impressive CV can make everything scholars do easier, while a weak CV can make everything more difficult. In academic life, moreover, no level of achievement is ever enough; every CV can be made to look small in some way. The importance of the CV can spur people to take on tasks they should pass up. It can lead them to disregard being tired, depressed, or ill because they want their CV to be healthy even if they are not. The CV can be a haunting presence, constantly rebuking its namesake for not containing enough entries or not enough of the right kinds of entries.

Differences across institutions can give the CV more or less weight. At some teaching colleges where pay is determined by rank rather than individual merit reviews, the CV may matter less than at Research 1 universities. Expectations about the quantity or quality of work recorded on the CV are not the same at state universities with comparatively lower tuitions and fees than at tuition-driven elite private colleges. Very few scholars, however, are completely unconcerned with the CV, since its presence looms so large as a symbol of and surrogate for the self.

The CV can promote preoccupation with personal prestige and success. It impedes accompaniment by separating the self from others, by positioning colleagues as competitors to be outdone, as people whose denigration is necessary for our elevation. Moreover, pinning hopes for affirmation on approval from others almost always leads to disappointment. Desires for external affirmation and admiration often become so grandiose that no amount of praise is enough, and the pursuit of praise and the neurosis of constant comparison inhibits the development of the mutual respect and recognition that makes praise meaningful. For that reason, as Watkins and Shulman astutely observe, "the severed self recreates its own abandonment again and again" as "intense needs for affirmation stand in where mutual relationships are absent" (Watkins and Shulman 2008, 68).

While too much emphasis on the CV can be a problem, so can too little. Winning peer validation of original and generative contributions to scholarship is an important part of the work scholars *need* to do in the world. From this perspective, writing is not something scholars *have* to do but something they *get* to do, a rare privilege in a world where most people do not get any public opportunity to express what they know or believe. As a record of peer-validated successes, the CV testifies affirmatively to the existence of impact, influence, and important achievement in the world—achievement that cannot be undone.

Balans is needed here. The CV represents scholarly achievement as if it is an individual activity capable of being measured in quantitative terms, yet the work scholars actually do is innately collective and qualitative. It entails accompaniment. Recognition and reward may flow to individuals, but scholarly conversations are consummately cooperative creations, the product of intersubjective collaborations in which all participants play a part. The CV will always be an inadequate and even inaccurate reflection of scholarly work. The full range of roles that scholars take on often take place behind the scenes. The work scholars do as researchers, writers, reviewers, editors, interlocutors, teachers, mentors, and colleagues will never be registered fully on a CV. Senior scholars with impressive CVs have more freedom to devote their time to these behind-the-scenes endeavors, while junior scholars can lose their jobs for doing so. Yet absolute capitulation to the logic of the CV is a mistake at any stage. Choices that appear merely tactical at the beginning can become thoroughly internalized after a while. No change can occur without some risk. Yet knuckling under and expecting to be rewarded for docility is also a risk. It is risky to bite the hand that feeds you, but it is somewhat easier to bite the hand that is no longer feeding you and never intends to feed you again. It all depends on the work you want your work to do.

The same CV that can earn a scholar the right to be heard and taken seriously can also become a paralyzing presence. The persistence and peculiarities of peer review coupled with the significant degree of personal exposure that comes from the public dimensions of teaching and writing can easily undermine confidence and self-esteem. People cannot produce scholarly books and articles unless they possess a measure of self-confidence— even arrogance—that makes them think that their ideas, arguments, and opinions matter. Yet they cannot produce good work unless they also have the requisite degree of humility needed to accept criticism graciously and learn from it. This *balans* is difficult to acquire and maintain. It is possible to become self-impressed to the point of clinical narcissism and to become self-doubting to the point of paranoia.[1] Scholars need to take the CV seriously but not so seriously that it distorts understanding. Its panoptical presence can take over academic lives unless scholars create a counterculture of serious shared work and mutual support. Yet they are often hindered from doing so because of the pervasive power of another panoptic force in our lives, one we describe here as the simulacrum.

The Simulacrum

The vagaries of the CV, the difficulty of knowing how much our scholarly work matters and to whom, the brutal anonymity of life in a society always seeking to separate the exceptional from the disposable, and the psychic injuries endured in a profession where most of what researchers and teachers read and hear about themselves is likely to be negative, all can lead scholars to seek success and respect in the realm of reputation and prestige, the arena in which public praise and admiration seem to serve as reparations for the indignities and humiliations of systematic surveillance by colleagues, administrators, students, and sometimes a broader public. Jean Baudrillard's term "the simulacrum" is appropriate here because this realm is a phantasm, an apparition with no real presence, yet it produces destructive real-world consequences (Baudrillard 1994). Scholars sometimes learn that injuring targets with outbursts of contempt and disdain can provide pleasurable amusement to many onlookers. They may try delivering injury in hopes of not receiving it. Much harm can emanate from this understandable desire. It can lead to familiar behaviors that take many different forms: aiming arguments at individuals rather than ideas, treating legitimate political and scholarly differences as moral hierarchies, or retreating to ever narrower circles of agreement and avoiding engagement with people who disagree. These practices set in motion a machine that runs by itself. It can become more satisfying to see the work of other scholars belittled than to help that work be developed, augmented, improved, and acknowledged. Hard-won intellectual assets and institutions necessary for anti-subordination practices can be squandered in the service of insatiable emotions, ambitions, and egos. Like many dynamics of life in neoliberal societies, the simulacrum recruits largely powerless people into an unbreakable circle of reciprocal recrimination and envy. The simulacrum works to make people produce *less* work rather than *more*. Fear of criticism keeps some people silent. Some of them promise work that is never produced, because a promise cannot be criticized in the way that actually produced work can be. They see praise for their past works not as incentive to contribute more to the conversation but as a kind of cultural capital that could only be diminished by a new vulnerable round of exposure. The resulting absence of their research limits the available tools for social justice struggles.

In his sermon "The Drum Major Instinct," Martin Luther King, Jr. described reputation, renown, and acclaim as a kind of vitamin A for the ego. Yet recognition never fully satisfies. It only stokes the desire for additional rewards (King 1991). The simulacrum is a trap because its pleasures are both unreal and superficial. Like the CV, the simulacrum is other-directed, but even more so. It revolves around the *image that people imagine that others have of them.* It is understandable that scholars want to be noticed, respected, and admired. When used in the right ways, as Dr. King maintained, this desire can lead people to cultivate their capacities and achieve a reputation for honesty, integrity, and loyalty. A reputation can be recognition of outstanding achievement and merit. Yet as Angela Glover Blackwell astutely observes, the only reason to have a reputation is to risk it (Blackwell 2017). Dr. King risked his reputation by leveraging it as a credential to take moral but unpopular positions—in favor of fair housing, against the Vietnam War, in support of antipoverty measures, against the suppression of union organizing. Academics with reputations can hoard them for their own benefit, or risk them in order to help others. Yet in a neoliberal society that entices every individual to fabricate his or her own "brand," the simulacrum opens the door to regrettable forms of self-promotion and puffery, bluster and bullying.[2] The central discursive form of the simulacrum is the shortcut, the casual move that attracts attention through its sensationalism rather than its substance. Shortcuts include branding one's own work as newer, hipper, and deeper than work done by others, coasting on the imagined pedigree that comes from knowing famous people or attending prestigious schools, speaking *for* aggrieved groups rather than speaking *from* their experiences and struggles, dismissing entire schools of thought because of minor quibbles with them. Familiar shortcut formulations that appear at the beginnings of books and articles include claims such as "no one has ever studied x," or that "many people have studied x but all of them have been inadequate," or that "the work in field x is deficient because it has not anticipated something else that I am more interested in." Similarly, as historian and cultural studies scholar Rachel Buff counsels her colleagues, a reader's report that declares "I know something you don't" is a destructive shortcut, while one that states "Let me help you make this work better" is a productive intervention.

Inside the simulacrum, some seek attention by dismissing all previous scholarship as inadequate and outdated, while others assess research conducted by others as valid or invalid on the basis of the identities of its authors, their discipline, their age, their race, their gender, their sexuality, or their politics. Moral posturing often substitutes for analysis inside the simulacrum. Serious intellectual disagreements become trivialized into charges about the moral failings of antagonists rather than evidence of problems unsolved and perspectives that need to be reconciled. In a neoliberal society where envy and contempt dominate social media, the easiest shortcut of all is what we call "attack mode," a form of argument based on belittling and denigrating others. Very different from the kinds of substantive critiques needed to take ideas seriously, attack mode engages in what Herbert Garfinkel (1956) describes as "degradation ceremonies," public performances of moral indignation designed to denounce and humiliate the victim before witnesses. As a key trope routinely used by others *against* scholars who champion social justice, attack mode can perversely be especially appealing *to* these scholars precisely because it offers a way to inhabit the superior position so often used against them, to imagine that they can rise up by lowering others and making them the objects of derision and scorn.[3] These ways of seeking a place in the sun in the simulacrum require always having someone to look down on, someone who is not radical enough, not transgressive enough, not virtuous enough, or not smart enough. They are forms of *neoliberal collaboration masquerading as critique.* They provide temporary satisfactions grounded in the smugness of cynicism and the satisfactions of sadism, but they undermine the causes they purport to promote. Just as popular teaching is not necessarily good teaching, being acknowledged as a person of notice in the simulacrum is not the same as doing something upright or helpful. No one should need to look down on others to raise themselves up. As the character Esperanza Quintero explains in a crucial scene in the film *Salt of the Earth*: "I don't want anything lower than I am. I'm low enough already. I want to rise. And push everything up with me as I go" (Rosenfelt 1993, 82).

The same simulacrum that leads scholars to dismissive negativity can also, on the other hand, lead people to be reluctant to make needed critical judgments. Every piece of scholarship has flaws. Every scholar has room for development and growth. The principles of peer review depend on open and honest exchanges of ideas. Everyone's work benefits from serious scrutiny by readers who think of themselves as custodians of a collective conversation, as accountable to the profession and to society at large. Yet when they imagine how they might be seen in the simulacrum, many scholars take the path of least resistance. They may refrain from delivering news that might be hard to hear. They place more importance on their personal popularity and friendships than on their responsibilities as scholars. They may seek to preserve the comity of a department rather than its quality or seek succor in the solidarity of insider networks from which they benefit. Their lack of *konesans*, however, often hurts the very people they imagine they are helping—because their actions deprive colleagues, students, and themselves of criticisms all need in order to improve. Every time they let things "slide"—when they sign off on an inadequate MA or Ph.D. thesis, when they make a faulty faculty hire, when they approve a deficient tenure and promotion file, or when they recommend acceptance of a manuscript that should be rejected—they strip their own side of the assets needed for the third major institutional frame in scholar's lives: the *struggle.* Through these failures to uphold high standards, each generation learns how to teach the next generation *how not to do the job.*[4] Teachers pretend to teach and students pretend to learn. But literally as well as figuratively, no one is any the wiser. In such conditions, scholars lose sight of the work they want their work to do.

The Struggle

There is worthy and honorable work to be done in every institution in our society in resisting the efforts of neoliberal pedagogies and in defending all the social, historical, aesthetic, and moral activities that proceed from principles outside of or in opposition to the mystifications of the market. These efforts will become most productive in countering neoliberal pedagogies, in developing strategies for the middle run, when they create networks of interracial counterpublics and polities that draw on the emerging archives, imaginaries, epistemologies, and ontologies of people and groups fighting for their lives because of the crises that neoliberalism has caused.

Everybody thinks, but not everybody is designated by society as a thinker. Individuals and groups outside of academia have experiences and understandings that are usually repressed, hidden or denied because of the systemic and structural segregation that pervades dominant institutions. The late composer Pauline Olivieros discovered and remedied one manifestation of that segregation through her development of the Adaptive Use Musical Instrument (AUMI) software. Standard musical instruments presume able bodies with arms and fingers capable of holding drumsticks and covering keys or players with mouths and lungs capable of blowing on reeds and metal mouthpieces. Olivieros realized that the historical technologies used to craft musical instruments excluded people with disabilities for reasons that are arbitrary, artificial, and irrational. She worked with Leaf Miller, a musician and occupational therapist, to design a motion-sensitive software interface that produced a wide range of sounds in response to a wide range of body movements.

Starting with a drum workshop for children with disabilities attending school in Poughkeepsie, New York, Olivieros collaborated with the IICSI to produce software tools that enable people with little voluntary movement to compose and play music. Musicologists and music therapists Mark Finch, Susan LeMessurier Quinn, and Ellen Waterman at Memorial University in Newfoundland, Canada, and American Studies scholar Sherrie Tucker at Kansas University utilized AUMI technology in therapeutic and performance contexts. The tool that functioned productively as therapy for children and adults with cerebral palsy also served as the medium for jam sessions involving a range of people with and without disabilities to make music together. Speaking of the musical events she staged using the AUMI technology, Tucker invoked Olivieros's commitments to expanding the entire sphere of musical activity "so that we could all learn from each other and hear from each other." Tucker remembers Oliveros saying "a true virtuoso is somebody who can play with anybody and have a meaningful experience" (Sanchez 2017, 4).

Like other initiatives related to dis/ability, the AUMI project should not be seen as a generous attempt by the able bodied to bring the joy of music to people previously excluded from it. Rather it is a provocation that reveals how accepted notions of normativity injure everyone. The AUMI project reveals the harm done to music and the musical imagination by uninterrogated assumptions and outmoded technologies that needlessly constrain both the range of people who play music and the range of music that can be played. The project opens a door to greater understanding of how all other forms of ableist exclusion similarly squander abilities and suppress creativities for artificial, arbitrary, and irrational reasons (Finch, LeMessurier Quinn, and Waterman 2016; Siddall and Waterman 2016). The AUMI project expanded the content, reach, and scope of music by expanding the constituency involved in creating and performing it. Its premises can provide new ways of thinking about improving scholarship by expanding the range of voices involved in research, creating new social relations of research, and recognizing and removing unnecessary and outmoded impediments to full participation.

Engagement with the experiences, actions, and ideas of large groups of people active in social movement struggles for social change can be a generative way of moving beyond market time and market space, of engaging with and learning from the particularities of historical and social times and places. Aggrieved racial groups are formed by the processes of history. Their political and cultural mobilizations for justice tap into repositories of collective memory that serve as sites for moral instruction and ways of calling communities into being through performances and practices that register their linked fate. Scholarly accompaniment of social movement activist groups in a spirit of respect, humility, and friendliness has enabled researchers across the disciplines to draw on previously occluded archives and analyses, to make original and generative contributions to the democratization of both knowledge and society. For example, sustained engagement with the organizing efforts of mothers in Los Angeles seeking justice for their incarcerated children enabled Ruth Wilson Gilmore to write *Golden Gulag*, the single best study of the causes and consequences of the prison-building boom of the 1980s (Gilmore 2007). Immersion in a hemispheric movement contesting violence against women provided Rosa-Linda Fregoso and Cynthia Bejarano with the contacts and knowledge base to organize their extraordinary edited collection *Terrorizing Women*, exposing feminicide and revealing the movements mobilized to challenge it across the Americas (2010a). Angela Stuesse's work in the immigrant rights movement helped frame the research questions she asked and answered in *Scratching Out a Living*, her brilliant prize-winning analysis of how recruitment of Latinx labor by the poultry industry in Mississippi changed the local racial order (2016). Many years of activism with the Committee Against Anti-Asian Violence in New York led Eric Tang to discover the compelling story of Cambodian refugee life in the North Bronx that he explained and analyzed in his splendid book *Unsettled* (2015). João Costa Vargas formulated his sophisticated critique of race, place, and power in Los Angeles in part through his active "observant participation" with the Coalition against Police Abuse (Vargas 2006). The peril, yet promise, of engaged scholarship is delineated brilliantly by Shannon Speed (2008) in her subtle, sophisticated, and discerning analysis of participating in the struggle for legal rights and recognition by the Indigenous Nicholas Ruiz community in Chiapas, Mexico, which enabled an augmented understanding of social dynamics while simultaneously advancing the concrete political objectives of a community in struggle. Susan Phillips drew on sustained and principled engagement with graffiti writers and gang members in her books *Wallbangin'* and *Operation Fly Trap*; she also remains involved in the struggles of the people she studied by serving as an expert witness about the criminalization of graffiti and tattoo images by immigration authorities (S. Phillips 1999, 2012, 2015).

Practices of accompaniment have been especially useful in collaborations between race-based but not race-bound social movements and academic experts. The Center for Collaborative Research for an Equitable California enabled academic researchers to accompany the efforts of two major community projects: Growing Equity from the Ground Up—an urban farming and food security initiative in Oakland—as well as the Young Adult Civic Engagement initiative in California's Central Valley that brought together representatives of twenty community organizations and academic research units to promote the long-term capacity for leadership among young people (ages 18–30) from low income and racially, culturally, and linguistically diverse communities (Center for Collaborative Research for an Equitable California 2017; Oaxacalifornian Reporting Team 2013). Houseless activists and advocates in Los Angeles joined forces with academics and artists to produce two remarkable books: *Downtown Blues: A Skid Row Reader* (Heatherton 2011) and *Freedom Now! Struggles for the Human Right to Housing in LA and Beyond* (Camp and Heatherton 2012). Produced in collaboration with the Los Angeles Community Action Network (LACAN) and the Southern California Library for Social Studies and Research with additional funding from an American Studies Association Community Partnership Grant, these books feature first-person narrative life histories of houseless people, interviews with activists and advocates, transcriptions of observations during walking tours of Skid Row by performers LisaGay Hamilton and Chuck D, and analytic articles by activist scholars. The books' editors, Jordan T. Camp and Christina Heatherton, created these volumes about segregated places as insubordinate discursive spaces, as sites for staging unexpected conversations across place, race, and class lines to generate new knowledge about the causes and consequences of race and class oppression (Camp and Heatherton 2012; Heatherton 2011, 6).

Countering the knowledge project of neoliberalism entails work inside and outside the university. Some of that labor will be in harmony with the traditions of the academy and some in counterpoint to them. In addition to the mastery of the empirical knowledge and difficult methods prized in the academy, this work also calls for social intervention. It tries to change the world it studies. The emphasis on intervention, however, does not lessen the demands on scholars to be accurate, fair, rigorous, and self-critical. On the contrary, asking and answering questions important to people whose struggles scholars accompany should compel them to do their work even better. They need to expose their ideas to large groups of people with firsthand knowledge about the conditions they study, to confront the multiple standpoints and perspectives that emanate from neoliberalism's proclivity for creating seemingly endless new forms of differentiation, and to learn to address issues that are important to the everyday life experiences of people who will most likely not be among the ranks of those studying or teaching in the university. This kind of research promotes an honest reckoning with the narrow range of experiences generally represented in academic conversations, and it requires scholars to take sides, to produce work worthy of contributing to social change. As radical sociologist George Rawick argued decades ago, this is significant work, because in order to do it "we must overcome our own pessimism, our own social isolation, our own fear of competing with mainstream sociology, our own fear of error. We must be willing to give intellectual blows when needed and to take and overcome them when they are aimed at us. The matters we deal with are not trivial, they will release human passion and energy, and we must not retreat behind our desire for peace in order to avoid these realities" (2010, 71).

8 / CONCLUSION

"Carry the Struggle, Live the Victory"

This book started its explorations into improvisation, accompaniment, insubordinate spaces, and social justice with an account in Chapter 1 of James Baldwin's 1963 conversation with Kenneth Clark. The doubts that Baldwin expressed a half century ago—worrying about his role in his country and his future in it—have a chilling relevance for our present predicament. The problems of today cannot be wished away. In the United States and all over the world, unprecedented prosperity for the upper classes comes at the cost of austerity for the masses. Privatization schemes enable elites to loot public resources for private gain. Corporate-controlled media outlets promote a pervasive culture of cruelty, callousness, and contempt. Warfare is now embraced enthusiastically as a permanent condition rather than tolerated reluctantly and regretfully as a temporary emergency. Attempts by Western powers to reshape governments in the Middle East have produced endless wars creating mass displacement and death. The war on terror has meant the abandonment of long-standing legal and moral commitments to due process, habeas corpus, and equal protection. A revanchist racism in the United States has led to relentless regimes of race-based surveillance, mass incarceration, and targeted voter suppression that systematically undermine the capacity of aggrieved communities of color to defend themselves. The criminal justice system routinely degrades and punishes poor people but refuses to hold employers, investors, and owners accountable for continuously violating laws that prohibit housing and hiring discrimination, protect the environment, require payment of minimum wages, and guarantee decent working conditions. In politics, fear-laden fantasies about immigrants and refugees, about allegedly nonnormative sexual practices and gender identities, and about the diminished overrepresentation of whites in positions of power and influence combine to fuel waves of punitive moral panic. The political process has less popular legitimacy than ever before. Electoral politics has become the domain of small cadre of affluent individuals. The well-financed and carefully coordinated corporate attack on democracy is no longer content with fomenting recreational hate against the usual targets: people of color, immigrants, religious and sexual minorities, and the poor. Now rage is directed even against groups that used to be considered middle class and normative, such as public employees with pensions, student loan seekers, workers unemployed during economic downturns, and even women who use contraceptive devices.

The public spheres of government and popular culture are rife with corruption and replete with open displays of crude and vulgar behavior. This does not represent a failure for neoliberalism, but rather its fulfillment. Defiling the public sphere is designed to force people to retreat into small spheres of private self-interest. As Claudia Bernardi noted about the ways in which the dictatorships in Chile and Argentina functioned in the 1970s and 1980s, "What they wanted was not to kill so many thousand people. . . . It was to create an atmosphere to last into the future, an atmosphere of bleak individuality, of hopelessness, of ugliness, even a lack of remembering what integrity is about. And they almost succeeded" (quoted in Watkins and Shulman 2008, 122).

The election of Donald Trump as president of the United States in 2016 was not widely expected, yet Trumpism should come as no surprise. His campaign and presidency simply brought to the surface many of the vile and violent impulses that have been there all along. Trump is a symptom, not the cause. His success is a continuation and consequence of the ongoing historical processes of Indigenous dispossession, slavery unwilling to die, coloniality, and heterosexism. The current crisis, however, does not represent simply one more episode in the long history of intermittent social ruptures and periodic economic downturns and upticks. What the world faces today is the chaotic breakdown and systemic disintegration of key social institutions. The people who control corporations and countries cannot fix the things they have broken. They cannot repair the damage they have done to the planet and its people. Yet this makes them more dangerous than ever.

More than a half century ago, Aimé Césaire asserted, "A civilization that proves incapable of solving the problems it creates is a decadent civilization. A civilization that chooses to close its eyes to its most crucial problems is a stricken civilization. A civilization that uses its principles for trickery and deceit is a dying civilization" (Césaire 2001, 31). This decadent, stricken, and dying civilization is unraveling. It has reached a turning point from which there will be no turning back. It is no longer a question of *whether* there will be radical changes but of *which* changes will be made and *whose* interests they will serve.

Individual chapters in this book have presented case studies of improvisation and accompaniment by Idle No More, Chicanx artists and musicians, and the Ferguson movement. These repositories of *konesans* and *balans* are important, not simply because they come from places where people are exploited and suffer, where people have been largely abandoned by the reward structures of the dominant culture, and where people's marginality limits their ability to embrace fully the vices of their oppressors. It is rather that the suffering, exploitation, and abandonment evident in these places are not marginal at all but necessary for the maintenance of dominant social, economic, political, and cultural structures and institutions. Because the people in these spaces often have no margin for error, because they have to endure coloniality, white supremacy, and racial capitalism without the "sugar" of optimism about the future, and because they are forced to fight for survival and dignity, the insubordinate spaces they create function as key sites that reveal to everyone how power actually works, how the world is actually governed, and why modest reforms and gradual changes will no longer work. These people cannot afford the illusions to which people in more privileged groups cling. They have already stared into the abyss. At this moment of systemic crisis, it makes sense to turn to the archives, imaginaries, epistemologies, and ontologies—the *konesans*—of aggrieved communities of color to recognize them as rich repositories of tools for resistance and persistence in the face of seemingly insurmountable odds. The principle of *balans* teaches that there are dangers in this move: the danger of instrumental and manipulative appropriation, the danger of misunderstanding and misrepresentation, the danger of compelling raced "others" to serve as what Elizabeth V. Spelman calls "spiritual bellhops," carrying the cares and tending to the psychic wounds of their oppressors (Spelman 1997, 1, 8, 119). Yet allowing fear of error to occlude the power and significance of the acts of improvisation and accompaniment that emerge from struggles by aggrieved groups would be the most dangerous move of all.

Accompaniment and Improvisation in
Theory and Practice

Like many things worth doing in life, accompaniment is easier to profess than to practice. It is extremely difficult for differently situated people to communicate, to work together, and to build mutual respect and trust. Moreover, past social movements have bequeathed to the present a mixed legacy of theory and practice, a legacy that both helps and hinders accompaniment in the present.

For example, the labor movement of the 1930s emerged out of a broad coalition of competing ideas and ideals. Its practical activities, however, coalesced around a model of vanguard leadership. The vanguard approach presumes that most members of aggrieved groups will not be willing or able to take on the risks and burdens of struggle. It proceeds from the premise that the people who control the government and the economy also control the educational system, journalistic venues, and commercial entertainment. In response, the vanguard model cultivates a core cadre of activists who commit themselves completely to the struggle, cultivate critical and oppositional understandings of social relations, and create hierarchical organizations with centralized leadership of the struggle. The vanguard is out in front, ahead of the people. The movement is like a spear and the vanguard is the tip. The vanguard wins the struggle *for* the people, and then—at least in theory—hands over to them the fruits of victory (George 1973; Schneider 1972; Weir 2004).

There is an undeniable logic to the vanguard perspective. It is strategically resistant to repression and infiltration, connects actions to well-worked out ideas, and has a long history of successes. It won major victories during the labor organizing drives of the 1930s and 1940s. Yet too often, vanguard institutions presumed to know more than the people they purported to represent and to see the masses as deluded and in need of top-down orchestration and manipulation. In the vanguard model, activists and organizers speak *for* aggrieved groups rather than *from* them. Impatience and eagerness for action leads some vanguard thinkers to engage in "exemplary actions" that they imagine will stir the masses from their lethargy. Too often, these actions provoke repression and reduce social movements to little more than legal defense committees. Even at best, they have often created movements that were militarized and bureaucratized, functioning similarly to the oppressive and alienating institutions that they positioned themselves to oppose. The labor movement focused attention on the injustices of class subordination, created reforms that democratized previously closed-off spaces of social life, and produced respect for the dignity of labor as a counter to the glorification of the wealthy. Yet its permissions for some entailed prohibitions against others. The white working class gained a measure of upward mobility by agreeing to close the door behind them and police the boundaries of inclusion against the racialized poor. Moreover, the vanguard politics of the labor movement and the left lived on, even after their vanguard institutions disappeared or became incorporated into the dominant system. They impeded the development of practices, processes, and institutions geared toward deepening popular capacity for democratic deliberation and mobilization.

The organizing tradition of the civil rights movement developed as a critique of some of the shortcomings of vanguard thinking. Exemplified by Ella Baker's contention that "strong people don't need strong leaders," implemented successfully through her influence on the work of the Student Nonviolent Coordinating Committee (SNCC), the organizing tradition emphasized participatory democracy. In the civil rights struggle it featured small groups making decisions by consensus rather than majority vote. It envisioned leadership as something grounded in collective accountability rather than in individual charisma (Ransby 2005, 188). SNCC sent college-age youths into impoverished Southern communities to organize democratic mobilizations. Their mission was to develop the long-term capacity for ongoing self-activity and leadership among the people. The outsiders who came to communities to organize began their work with respect for who people already were, rather than with impatience about who they wished them to be. They respected local culture and addressed local problems. They believed that everyone had a contribution to make. While looking realistically at *what is*, an organizer also had to perceive *what can be*. In the apt words of historian Charles Payne, organizers found themselves compelled "to look at a sharecropper and see a potential teacher" and "to look at a conservative lawyer and see a potential crusader for justice" (Payne 2007, 89). SNCC organizers encouraged the people they met to see things for themselves, to solve their own problems, and to learn from experience. They proceeded from the premise that meaningful change could not be won *for* the people but instead had to be won *by* the people. SNCC organizer Bob Moses encapsulated the emphasis on activism from the bottom up. Years after the peak of the movement, when he had shifted his efforts to crafting an algebra curriculum for inner-city students, Moses remained committed to the organizing tradition's particular vision. "The main thing," he advised, "is not to set out with grand projects. Everything starts at your doorstep. Just get deeply involved in something. . . . . You throw a stone in one place and the ripples spread" (Payne 2007, 411).

Like the vanguard politics of the labor movement, the organizing tradition of the civil rights movement won important victories but also endured painful defeats. Tom Dent, one of the movement's most impassioned, eloquent, creative, and effective participants, delineated those failures in his moving book *Southern Journey* (Dent 2001). Dent traveled in the 1990s to many of the places where landmark civil rights struggles took place thirty years earlier. While noting some permanent gains, he discovered that much of what had been struggled for had been lost. Capital flight, economic restructuring, reductions in social welfare programs, refusals to enforce civil rights laws, and voter suppression left the region—and especially much of its Black population—mired in conditions marked by unemployment and underemployment, mass incarceration, low wages, job and housing insecurity, and environmentally caused illnesses. Rather than the fundamental revolution in values that the movement had sought, it succeeded primarily in placing a few more dark faces in high places, modestly desegregating the ranks of the pain inflictors of the world but unable to prevent the pain. The movement as a whole placed too much emphasis on reforming the state and prodding it to solve problems, and not enough emphasis on creating enduring structures of democratic participation and power. Some of the new opportunities for those designated as representatives of people of color depended upon their effectiveness in suppressing and repressing their own constituency. Although profoundly transformative in the lives of individuals and powerfully productive in generating new social imaginaries, identities, and public and private institutions, the organizing tradition did not build an enduring mass base capable of resisting the implementation of global neoliberal structures of deprivation. Aggrieved and oppressed people probably have less access to participation in making the important decisions that affect their lives today than similarly positioned people had fifty years ago.

The legacies of the vanguard and organizing models set the stage for the revival of anarchist ideas and actions focused on affinity and assembly starting in the 1990s. In the wake of globalization, the evisceration of the social wage, and the augmentation of the repressive power of the state, social movements motivated by neo-anarchist principles and priorities came to the fore. In the Nuclear Freeze, AIDS awareness, antiglobalization, Occupy, and Black Lives Matter movements, principles of affinity led to massive but seemingly spontaneous and nonhierarchical demonstrations and assemblies. The decentralized and nonideological qualities of these movements unleashed creativity, generating new ideas and identities, and resisting dogmatic conformity. The movements sought concessions from the state but not positions of influence inside it.

Yet as the concept of *balans* entails, everything that can enable can also inhibit. The ambiguity and open-ended nature of the Occupy movement's claim to represent the 99 percent rather than the wealthy 1 percent provided an important part of its appeal, but that very move evaded the necessity of coming to grips with the racial, gendered, linguistic, and legal status differences that divide the 99 percent. Eschewing ideology and organization made it easier to create mass assemblies of opposition, but the emphasis on congregating together in public did little to advance the development of organizations capable of raising transitional demands and putting in place structures that could not just critique power but actually contest it (Kelley 2015). Mass mobilizations galvanize a mass constituency and often change the parameters of public debate, but they lack an apparatus to sustain and advance the struggle in the middle run.

In this book, we are not presenting accompaniment and improvisation as new universal tools to supersede the vanguard, organizing, or anarchist models. Instead, we propose them as decolonial options, as part of a pluriversal struggle that envisions no single privileged origin, intention, or outcome. Moreover, no meaningful part of the past ever disappears completely. Elements of the vanguard, organizing, and anarchist traditions are all present in some form within the acts of improvisation and accompaniment around which this book coheres. In developing a midlevel theory for the middle run, however, we emphasize practices that enact the changes they envision—practices that open up possibilities rather than close them down. Those practices presume that big changes can come from small acts and that transformative politics also require cultural practices and knowledge projects. The long history of projects like these from the past can play a key role in deploying *konesans* and *balans* in the middle run.

It is important to remember, however, the ways in which effective forms of political and cultural struggle have emerged from insubordinate spaces. In the 1930s, at the height of success for vanguard politics in the labor movement, organizers recruited workers to join radical parties and trade unions. For the most part, they were invited to become the rank and file of top-down organizations. After the 1934 San Francisco waterfront strike, however, dockworkers improvised a form of accompaniment that enacted the solidarity that trade unions and radical parties had largely only envisioned. Before the strike, jobs loading and unloading ships were secured through the system known as the shape-up. Twice a day, job seekers would gather in front of a company foreman who determined who got to work that shift by giving out buttons to those he favored and assigning the recipients of the buttons to labor where he wanted them. Workers learned to stand in ways that communicated docility and servility. They could not look the boss in the eye, raise their voices, or refuse unfair demands. The shape-up system opened the door to bribery. Slipping the foreman a bottle of whisky might make it more likely to be hired the next day. Men whose work required this degradation came home filled with anger and resentment. All too often, they took out their frustrations on their wives and children, who learned to suffer in silence but then transfer their resentments onto others. The humiliating conditions of employment exacerbated the radical divisiveness in all areas of working-class life.

Once the 1934 waterfront strike ended, however, the workers improvised an imaginative form of accompaniment. When they returned to work they refused to appear at the shape-up, informing their employers that from then on, all jobs would be dispatched from the union hiring hall on the basis of what they called the low man out system. The company could still tell the union which jobs were open and how many workers were needed, but through the low man out system the workers themselves would determine how those slots were to be filled. The system mandated that the workers who had labored the fewest hours the previous week would get first choice for new positions that opened up. If a worker refused a posted job, it would be offered to the one with the next fewest hours. This system turned a competitive situation into a cooperative one. It enabled workers to share scarce jobs equally rather than compete with each other for them. It meant that they could select the kinds of work they wanted to do—choose to labor on the docks, on the decks, or in the holds of ships. They could turn down work they judged to be dangerous, and select the kinds of tasks they liked to do. Soon the low man out system led to an entire system of shared labor. Workers banded together in crews so they could do their jobs in accompaniment with people that they knew labored at a compatible pace or with those who told jokes that made the workday more enjoyable. The low man out system produced a culture of mutuality and solidarity that was relearned and reenacted every single day. It produced a different kind of dockworker and a different kind of person.

Stan Weir fondly recalls the colorful characters that he met as a long-shore worker, savoring how their diverse attributes and personalities made going to work into a pleasurable experience. Some were known by nicknames given to them by other workers because of their personal traits. There was Dress-Up Danny, who wore suits and ties to work yet remained "sartorially immaculate" despite the hard physical labor he performed. A passion for reading led to another laborer's nickname: Books Cartwright. A favored mode of transportation gave Bicycle Kovacs his nickname. For Weir, working on the docks meant enjoying the company of "wise men, clowns, shamans, and eccentrics" who became "conduits of expression for those around them" (Weir 2004, 95). The workers who enacted solidarity every day because of the low man out system became militant union members not because they followed charismatic leaders, but because going to work every day strengthened their confidence in themselves and others. In casting off the humiliating subordinations to which they had become accustomed, their lives got better. It became a pleasure to go to work. They withstood employer attacks for twenty-five years and maintained working conditions and pay levels that benefited them directly, while at the same time setting a standard of comparison that elevated the bargaining position of many other workers outside their industry. Unable to defeat workers made militant by the low man out system, to destroy the social world that the low man out system created employers eventually had to turn to automation subsidized by the government (Weir 2004).

Another example of improvisation and accompaniment producing democratic insubordinate spaces came from the organizing tradition at the height of the civil rights movement's mobilizations when Bob Moses entered Southern cities and towns to organize for the movement. Moses did not begin his work by giving a speech, posting a manifesto, or calling on the visible leaders of the Black community. Instead, he stood on a corner bouncing a ball on the pavement. "You stand on a street and bounce a ball," he explains. "Soon all the children come around. You keep on bouncing the ball. Before long, it runs under someone's porch and then you meet the adults" (Payne 2007, 243). Engaging in friendly, respectful, and patient interactions with the community no doubt hindered the pace of public mobilizations and demonstrations. Yet it also grounded participation in the movement in established friendly, humble, and respectful relations. It offered participants a way to achieve the recognition and respect denied them in the rest of their lives as workers and citizens. It built bonds that gave people a stake in the struggle as accompaniers, not merely as spectators or followers.

Similarly, the story circles of the Free Southern Theatre (FST) created insubordinate spaces for improvisation and accompaniment. Started in Mississippi in the 1960s by John O'Neal, Doris Derby, and Gilbert Moses, three civil rights activists who had been theater majors at Jackson State College, the FST attempted to stage theatrical pieces relevant to the movement, pieces they hoped would function as instruments of education, agitation, and moral elevation. The FST name emphasized two meanings of the word "free." It reflected the group's desire to stage performances with no admission charges so that poor people could attend them, but it also represented a desire to "free" the theater from the ways in which its traditional dependency on ticket sales and performing canonized works shaped the content of the plays produced. At the same time, the FST hoped to use the free theater to promote the emergence of free people capable of insisting on freedom in society. The FST founders and followers discovered that the insurrectionary character of their movement provoked repressive measures against it. They rarely had access to performance spaces in actual theaters. Moreover, plays that would be relevant to the experiences of the farmworkers, day laborers, and domestic workers that the FST wanted to reach had not yet been written. Yet they were able to use those very difficulties as the basis for rethinking what theatre could be. Through a long process of trial and error, the FST created a floating form of accompaniment: the story circle. The FST convened community members in fields, barns, churches, schools, and on rare occasions in actual theaters. Sitting in a circle that evoked the spatial and social relations of the traditional African American ring shout, participants would speak one at a time about something that happened to them or that concerned them. Once everyone had spoken in turn, the group would write a collective play based on the conversation and later perform it with a troupe made up of both trained actors and community residents. After the performance, a talk back would enable people to speak about the play, the process that produced it, and the political actions that might flow from it. Long after the FST ceased to exist as an institution, the story circle continued to produce places of accompaniment when it became adopted as the core pedagogy of Students at the Center in New Orleans high schools (Lipsitz 2015, 313–316).

The organizing tradition enabled the creation of insubordinate spaces for knowledge projects based on finding value in previously undervalued people. Citizenship schools for adults and freedom schools for children taught basic literacy through an ambitious curriculum and pedagogy that asked participants to answer big questions about human rights and human dignity. Rather than simply teaching the students the alphabet or asking them to memorize and write down things they had read or heard, the citizenship curriculum of SNCC was a knowledge project that revolved around three important questions that asked people to think about their place in the world and their future in it: "What does the majority culture have that we want? What does the majority culture have that we don't want? What do we have that we want to keep?" (Payne 2007, 303).

During the 1990s, when the mobility of capital, the demise of the welfare state, and the creation of new transnational regimes of security protecting capital accumulation seemed to render obsolete important parts of the vanguard and organizing traditions, activists revived the long and honorable tradition of anarchist mass mobilization. Demands to address the AIDS epidemic by ACT UP, to change national security policy by the Nuclear Freeze movement, and to challenge the destructive economic and environmental aspects of globalization in protests like the ones against the World Trade Organization in Seattle in 1999 gave new visibility to the politics of affinity and assembly (D. Gould 2009; Meyer 1990; Yuen, Burton-Rose, and Katsiaficas 2004). In the midst of that ferment, the Okinawan Women Act against Military Violence (OWAAMV) came up with the tactic of "A Minute on the Mic," which, like the low man out system, the story circle, and the SNCC citizenship curriculum enacted in embodied form new social relations based on recognition of a linked fate (Fukumura and Matsuoka 2002).

Peace activism had long occupied a prominent place in Okinawa. Residents of the island had been made keenly aware of the costs of militarism by living in a place serially colonized by Japan and the United States, a place which served as the locus of a battle that saw one hundred thirty thousand people killed in one month alone in 1945 and as a key launching site for U.S. military actions in Asia during the Korean and Vietnam Wars. Living far from—but firmly under the grip of—governments in both Tokyo and Washington, DC, that had no intention of listening to their concerns, the OWAAMV struggled to assert their views. The OWAAMV called for an end to the military occupation of Okinawa that made women vulnerable to sexual assaults and made employment in sex work more lucrative than other jobs. They pointed to the environmental destruction caused to land, air, and water by the military presence in Okinawa. These principles guided a clear set of demands for the reduction, realignment, and eventual removal of military bases from Okinawa, for full disclosure of environmental contamination and mandatory toxic cleanups, and for rape crisis intervention programs and job training initiatives. Yet these concrete immediate demands coalesced around a more abstract middle-run knowledge project: attempting to change the popular understanding of the word "security." The OWAAMV contended that prevailing understanding of security deployed by those in power sought security only for nations and corporations, which in turn produced only insecurity for women, children, the elderly, and the environment (Fukumura and Matsuoka 2002).

This new goal of redefining security led to a new tactical formulation when women active in OWAAMV attended the World Conference on Women in Beijing, China, in September 1995. While they were away, three men serving in the U.S. military raped a twelve-year-old Okinawan girl. The victim displayed courage in reporting the attack, but U.S. military officials responded to it dismissively. They did not turn over the accused to local authorities until four weeks after the assault. They insisted on putting the men on trial in U.S. military courts rather than the Okinawan judicial system. Admiral Richard Macke joked that the perpetrators of the crime were foolish to have rented a car the night of the attack because "for the price they paid to rent the car, they could have had a girl" (Keyso 2000, 139). Like the killing of Michael Brown in Ferguson in 2014, the incident in Okinawa in 1995 became important not because it was so unusual, but because its ordinariness and seeming inevitability crystallized and distilled lessons learned from a long history of abuse and humiliation.

To protest the rape, the U.S. military's response to it, and the broader conditions that it emanated from, the OWAAMV called for a mass demonstration just three weeks after the rape took place. They improvised a novel practice of accompaniment. Instead of inviting particularly prominent or unusually eloquent speakers to address the assembly, they shared the burden by inviting women in the audience to step up and speak for "one minute on the mic." The format called for sixty women to speak for sixty seconds each. Conventional understandings of social movement mobilization might see this strategy as a recipe for disaster. Untrained speakers unaccustomed to addressing large audiences might not even be heard much less understood. Confining remarks to only sixty seconds precluded any detailed or sustained analysis. Without prior planning or orchestration, each woman might repeat what others have said before, depriving the event of any momentum or drama. Yet like the low man out system and the story circle, the minute on the mic tactic succeeded splendidly. The steady accumulation of testimony uttered in different voices revealed clearly how differently positioned women all suffered from the military presence on their island. Previously private and personal injuries and anxieties became public issues. Several speakers indicated that the event provoked them to reveal for the first time that they had been raped by U.S. military personnel. Each sixty-second segment contributed to a collective eloquence that established the event as a turning point, as a declaration of determination to work together to stop the dehumanization of women and militarism's impact on their worlds. One month later, some eight thousand Okinawans came together to rally against the continuing presence of U.S. troops (Fukumura and Matsuoka 2002, 251).

The low man out system, the story circle, and the minute on the mic format came into being through practice and out of necessity. West Coast longshore workers, Black activists in the rural South, and Okinawan feminists and pacifists forged accompaniment appropriate to their everyday circumstances. They used the tools available to them to achieve the ends they desired. In similar fashion, between 2011 and 2013 prisoners confined to the California Department of Corrections and Rehabilitation's Security Housing Unit in Pelican Bay used hunger strikes as instruments of accompaniment. Locked in isolation cells in solitary confinement, the caged men's bodies were virtually the only things they could use to advance their aims. By refusing food and demonstrating a willingness to die, they established clearly what was at stake in their struggle. In addition, they used overt and covert means to communicate to others the reason for the hunger strikes that lasted as long as six weeks. They did so effectively. Eventually thirty thousand inmates joined in, staging their own support strikes in institutions throughout the state. The struggle required people of different races and rival social groups long accustomed to violent competition with each other to work together. It depended on the communicative abilities of individuals who had been locked up in solitary confinement twenty-three hours a day and seven days a week. Some of them had been in that circumstance for decades. The coordinated mobilization took place despite the repressive and punitive power of prison officials, lack of concern by legislators, and sustained silence in media outlets about prison conditions and responses to them.

The Pelican Bay State Prison is a concrete structure with no windows. It is designed so that prisoners can be isolated and cut off from any form of accompaniment or companionship. Purportedly intended as a punishment of last resort for only the most violent, dangerous, and incorrigible convicts, over time these "maximum" punishments became routine, meted out to people on the basis of administrative whim and malicious gossip. Assignment to maximum solitary units did not depend on actual crimes committed inside or outside the prison but was utilized by prison administrators routinely treating tattoos, drawings, letters, and particular books as evidence of dangerous gang affiliations. These administrators' decisions were never reviewed by judges or juries. More than five hundred of those incarcerated under those conditions had gone a decade without a handshake or a hug (Reiter 2016, 2, 7).

Coordinating a system-wide hunger strike seems impossible under these circumstances. Yet people find ways to survive what they must survive. Through legal filings and court proceedings, the prisoners learned about a previous hunger strike by an interracial group of inmates at the Ohio State Penitentiary that led to positive legal precedents that could be used to improve their conditions. Working with supporters outside the prison walls they discovered an online network of allies mobilized by sociologist and activist Denis O'Hearn, an Irish American and Native Alaskan (Aleut) who had written *Nothing but an Unfinished Song* (2006), a book about Bobby Sands, who fasted to death in a British jail in Ireland in the early 1980s. The California activists constructed an oppositional knowledge project out of the meager means at their disposal. Black, Latino, and white prisoners circulated copies of O'Hearn's book, as well as studies of Mayan cosmology and writings by historian Howard Zinn and colonial era pamphleteer Tom Paine. The hunger strikers formulated a description of their collective experience as "twenty-plus years of torture." They developed demands that called for an end to group punishment and to the relentless pressures they faced to incriminate other inmates. They insisted that solitary confinement should be a punishment of last resort with a limited duration. They demanded inmate access to sunlight, adequate health care and nutrition, an end to withholding food as a means of punishment, and expanded access to visits, phone calls, and letters along the lines routinely accepted in similar "supermax" prisons in other states (Lynd 2012, 132–138). As Staughton Lynd emphasizes, the strike constituted "a spectacularly large mass movement initiated and controlled wholly from below" (Lynd 2012, 142). The movement negotiated a settlement that won limited victories, entailing some compromises, as every short-term struggle does. But the process of accompaniment in struggle enabled the people who participated in it to develop a new understanding of their place in the world and their role in it. They refused to accept the prison system's understanding of them as "the worst of the worst," whose complex identities could be reduced to the crimes they were alleged to have committed. One participant concluded, "We've all collectively shattered 30–35 years of CDCR status quo in three months. We should be proud of that" (Lynd 2012, 144).

Academic Work as Accompaniment

The social movement struggles that enabled the development of activist knowledge projects in communities such as the low man out system, the story circle, the minute on the mic protest, and the prison hunger strike influenced and were influenced by academics and artists. The trade union–based culture of unity of the 1930s that gave rise to the low man out system attracted cinema scholar Kenneth MacGowan to teach night school classes for workers along with screenwriter John Howard Lawson and composer Earl Robinson (Denning 1996, 69–70). Performance studies scholar Richard Schechner worked with the FST (Dent and Schechner 1969). The OWAAMV formulated their critique of security through dialogues with peace studies scholar Betty Reardon. Attorney and historian Staughton Lynd represented and accompanied prison hunger strikers in Ohio, and he helped convey the story of their struggle to the Pelican Bay protestors (Lynd 2012).

In his splendid book *Accompanying: Pathways to Social Change*, Lynd presents a cogent and concise argument about the historical importance of accompaniment in the labor, civil rights, and antiwar movements, in the theology and political practice of Archbishop Oscar Romero in El Salvador, and in the struggles for dignity and decent treatment waged by people locked up in U.S. prisons. In Lynd's formulation, accompaniment requires physical proximity, not just vicarious identification. It demands that differently situated people share the work, equalize the risks, and change each other in the process (Lynd 2012). Like social movement mobilizations and performances of expressive culture, classroom instruction and academic argument can provide ample opportunities for these kinds of face-to-face interactions. They can also be endeavors that produce new research practices grounded in new social relations of research.

Scholarship conceived of as an insubordinate space for accompaniment and improvisation can generate new understandings of social structures and social relations. For example, historian Kelly Lytle Hernández set out to study the origins and evolution of the mass incarceration of African American and Latinx in Los Angeles. Conversations with contemporary activists fighting mass incarceration made her sensitive to the importance of spatial displacement and the logic of "eliminating" allegedly unfit people from the body politic. When Hernández examined evidence in archival holdings dating back to the eighteenth century, she made an unexpected finding. The practices and justifications used initially to clear the Los Angeles region of its Indigenous Tongva inhabitants in order to make room for white settlement corresponded closely to the ways in which subsequent racialized outsiders—including Chinese, Mexican, and Black migrants—were targeted for disappearance through arrests and imprisonment. It was the language of present activists discerning, critiquing, and resisting the logic of elimination facing

Black and Latinx targets of incarceration that enabled Hernández to see the links that connected them to previous regimes of Indigenous repression and Asian exclusion (Hernández 2017, 197). These findings led Hernández to argue that "disrupting the roots of mass incarceration in the United States will require addressing the structure of conquest, its eliminatory logic, and what it means for all of us, but especially for the Native peoples and racialized communities that are, in the words of Lorenzo Veracini, targeted 'to progressively disappear in a variety of ways'" (Hernández 2017, 197, quoting Veracini 2010, 16). Toward that end, Hernández surrenders the final 22 pages of her 220-page book to testimonies by activists about their ideas, analyses, and actions. Their writings complement the evidence that Hernández gathered from exhaustive research in official archives. She names this section of the book "The Rebel Archive" (199–220).

Experience as an activist helped Eric Tang make original and generative contributions to scholarship in his book *Unsettled* (Tang 2015). Working as a community organizer for the Southeast Asian Youth Leadership Project, Tang trained Cambodian refugee teenagers in New York City to address their community's concerns about inadequate housing and discriminatory welfare policies. Contacts made during his organizing efforts helped guide his research as a scholar. In his book Tang shows how spaces that generate bottom-up critiques of power can also serve as sites for new cognitive mappings and forms of creative place making. Tang relates many instances of how displaced and dispossessed people come to forge a new spatial imaginary. Relocated to a tenement building in an impoverished and crime ridden North Bronx neighborhood, the refugees were warned by social workers and police officers to stay in their apartments, purchase strong locks, and reinforce their doors. The refugees discovered, however, that this process made them *less* safe. It fragmented their community and made each family individually vulnerable to home invasions and abusive visits from landlords. The refugees responded by reconfiguring their space. They turned to the spatial arrangements already known to them from their experiences in village life and refugee camps. They kept their apartment doors wide open, moved back and forth freely inside each other's dwellings, and placed rugs and straw mats on stoops, lobbies, and hallways, turning passageways and thoroughfares into public common areas. Rejecting the normative model and improvising an alternative to it increased individual safety and augmented social cohesion and mutual aid (Tang 2015, 74–75).

Tang argues that the new spatial imaginary forged from necessity by Cambodian refugees displayed an advanced critical consciousness about their collective condition. The advice they received from social workers and police officers presumed that once they had been resettled in the Bronx, refuge had been found and exile was over. The assumption was that the refugees at that point could and should live as individual neoliberal subjects inside nuclear family households, as people with private property to defend and protect. Yet the refugees perceived this logic of hostile privatism and defensive localism as profoundly illogical for them. For the Cambodians, exile would never end and refuge would never be found. They saw the recommended arrangements as simply transferring them from one state of captivity to the next: from their embattled villages in Cambodia, to refugee camps in Thailand, and then to an overpoliced but underprotected urban sacrifice zone in the United States—a zone shared with Puerto Rican migrants grappling with the enduring consequences of their island's colonization and with displaced African Americans facing the cumulative effects of slavery unwilling to die. Unable to control or profit from the exchange value of the spaces they inhabited, the Cambodians improvised a form of accompaniment that augmented the use value of their dwelling places. By rejecting the premise that they needed to live in separate and autonomous private units, they forged a solution to common problems that recognized the collective nature of their linked fates and the utility of working together cooperatively rather than seeing each other as threatening competitors.

In addition to creating new common areas, the refugees also reconfigured spaces inside their dwellings to meet their needs. Tang reports that the key interlocutor in his study moved the family refrigerator from the kitchen into the living room, placed a sewing machine in the kitchen, and removed all furniture from the living room. What might seem like illogical moves were guided by an oppositional spatial imaginary with profoundly logical utilitarian aims. Placing the sewing machine where the refrigerator had been provided a vantage point where it was possible at one and the same time to make products for sale to support the family, to see food as it was cooking on top of the stove, to view the children playing in the living room, and to observe the front door. The empty living room provided a workspace for the older children who assembled and packaged the products sewn in the kitchen as well as a place for a baby to crawl and play around them. Yet the ephemerality and unexpectancy of refugee and immigrant life militated against thinking of this home as permanent. An absence of furniture, photographs, and decorations in the living room made it easy to pack up and leave: "I wanted to see everything in front of me," the woman explained to Tang, "because I never knew how long I was going to be in one place. I don't put anything away because you have to take everything with you when you leave" (Tang 2015, 124).

Displacement, dispossession, and deprivation compelled the refugees that Tang studied to develop alternative and oppositional understandings of space and time. The normative configurations of domestic space recommended to the refugees would not work for them. The police officers and social workers did not understand that the refugee homes had to be workspaces as well as dwellings. The contours of a standard apartment kitchen are not set up for child care. The conventions of home decor presume stability in place. Yet for refugees, home is a node in a network of constant fluid movement, a space of improvisation and adaptation, as place where dominant understandings of private domesticity do not make sense.

Seeing how Cambodian refugees challenged and countered the dominant imaginary of domestic space helped Tang discern other spatial realities in his research. The Cambodian refugees left a region of the world that was devastated in the 1960s and 1970s by U.S. counterinsurgency tactics in Southeast Asia, including bombing raids, herbicidal warfare, and dispersal of populations. Many of these tactics were formulated by credentialed scholars working for the RAND Corporation, a private research think tank established to bring "order and rationality" to military decisions. The refugees were relocated to the North Bronx, a largely Black and Puerto Rican neighborhood devastated by a policy of "planned shrinkage" that orchestrated public and private disinvestment in communities of color and the dispersal of their population through urban renewal projects. This too had a RAND Corporation connection. The idea of planned shrinkage originated in the writings of Anthony Downs, a researcher who had previously done work for RAND (Tang 2015, 59). Connections like these enabled Tang to advance an original and generative argument that the experiences of Cambodian refugees demonstrated the cumulative consequences of not just imperial war in Southeast Asia but also its links to the colonization of Puerto Rico, slavery unwilling to die, and the "war" against Black people, Puerto Ricans, and other communities of color created by racialized regimes of drug arrests and convictions, the evisceration of the social wage, and neoliberal privatization of public resources (Tang 2015, 13).

In similar fashion, work with environmental justice coalitions enabled Julie Sze to discern previously underexplored aspects of problems of public health. Medical researchers found that Black children suffering asthma were three times more likely to be hospitalized and four times more likely to die from the disease than similarly afflicted white children. The highest increase in asthma cases during the 1980s and 1990s occurred among children of color in low-income neighborhoods, a racial disparity that has grown significantly since 1980 (Sze 2007, 92, 95). Researchers trained in biomedical approaches to public health focused on individual pathways to the disease, on personal physiology, metabolism, and absorption. Community activists, however, viewed the increase in asthma cases differently. Concerned with the pervasive presence in their neighborhoods of incinerators, garbage dumps, and fumes from diesel truck engines, they advanced a politicized approach to illness that located illness within a larger social ecology. In dialogue with these community activists, Sze discovered that systemic structural shifts from a production-based economy to a service economy led to overproduction of wastepaper and other disposable waste. Increased consumption of fast foods, greater use of a variety of packaging materials, and an augmentation in the amounts of disposable cups, plates, and utensils generated a need for more incinerators and landfills. At the same time, the rise in urban producer services and luxury shopping and housing areas made significant sectors of the urban landscape too expensive to devote to garbage. This meant an increase in the nuisances and hazards pushed into neighborhoods occupied by impoverished people of color (Sze 2007, 117–118). Moreover, just as consumption of waste materials in wealthy neighborhoods in Manhattan led to increased environmental injustice in parts of Brooklyn and the Bronx, urban garbage from New York also found its way to rural areas inhabited by people of color in Virginia. In order to address and redress incidences of asthma, environmental justice activists and their academic allies had to develop a new cognitive mapping of relations inside cities and relations between cities. They discerned connections linking what appeared to be separate and autonomous social practices and processes.

Sze also made important discoveries about research methodologies by studying environmental justice activism. Polluters routinely evaded responsibility for increases in asthma and other diseases (particularly cancer), by defying their critics to provide scientific proof of their culpability. Such proof is often difficult because clusters where asthma or cancer is concentrated often reveal too few cases to meet the threshold of statistical significance. Sze explains that scientists respond to situations like this as they have been trained to do, rejecting environmental causation out of a fear of accepting a false positive. Yet preventing deadly diseases is a political and moral problem as well as a scientific issue. The scientific standard of proof creates a burden that is virtually meaningless outside of laboratory conditions. Rather than leaving the burden of proof to rest with the afflicted, environmental justice movements advocate a different research methodology—the precautionary principle—which places the burden on polluters to prove their projects are without risk and to fashion preemptive remedies (Sze 2007, 94, 182).

In another case of unexpected findings emerging from collaborations between community activists and campus researchers, feminist scholar-activists from Europe, the United States, Brazil, and Mexico discovered that their standing as credentialed experts made them useful to activists from the Women's Human Rights Center in Chihuahua, Mexico. These scholars were asked to serve as judges on a people's tribunal established to challenge state indifference to a flood of unprosecuted and even uninvestigated murders of women in their state and throughout Mexico. Along with a wide range of other groups in civil society, the human rights activists turned to the Permanent People's Tribunal established in Italy in 1979 to address state indifference to war crimes around the world. Under the aegis of an investigation authorized by this international organization independent of state authority, the women in Chihuahua organized a Tribunal of Conscience to investigate "Free Trade, Violence, Impunity and People's Rights in Mexico (2011–2014)." The women professionals who served as judges heard three days of testimony about twenty-seven cases of disappearances, killings, trafficking, domestic violence, forced exile, and sexual violence carried out with state complicity. The public testimony entailed accompaniment among differently situated families of victims, spectators, and human rights advocates. The tribunal's verdict—condemning the Mexican federal and state governments, transnational corporations, and the media—gave greatly needed visibility and legitimacy to local activists. A plaque declaring the verdict placed on a cross with nails left a lasting physical reminder in place of the crimes, the cover-ups, and the condemnatory verdict (Fregoso 2016).

The Tribunal of Conscience in Chihuahua drew on the collective wisdom forged from collaborative accompaniment among feminists across borders attempting to win recognition for the idea that violence against women is systemic and structural rather than purely private and personal. Many of the creators of that perspective contributed chapters to an unusual yet unusually generative example of scholarly activism and accompaniment, the book *Terrorizing Women: Feminicide in the Américas*, edited by Rosa-Linda Fregoso and Cynthia Bejarano (Fregoso and Bejarano 2010a). This compelling anthology authored by scholar activists from throughout the Western Hemisphere reveals how campaigns to counter violence against women constitute a distinct knowledge project forwarding ways of thinking that reveal the limits of existing paradigms in public policy and scholarly research.

FIGURE 8.1. Painting a pink cross to honor slain and disappeared women in Juarez. (*AFP / Stringer / Getty Images*)

Fregoso and Bejarano argue that understanding violence against women requires rejecting the idea that public and private spheres are mutually incommensurable realms (2010b). In a stunningly compelling and moving analysis, Rita Segato argues that the men who kill women and mutilate their bodies are not lonely antisocial hunters but rather exhibitionists who perform their sadistic acts for the direct and indirect pleasure of other men (2010, 74). The raped victim, she explains, functions as "the immolated sacrificial victim of a ritual of initiation" (76). The murderous rapist seeks entry into "a virile brotherhood." Like other protofascist and fascist formations, the killers are like a secret society that acts openly, with impunity, to divide the world between fanatical "blood bondage brothers" and "an indefinite and inarticulate mass of sworn enemies" who must be brutally beaten, defeated, and forced to accept the discretionary death power of masculine violence (86).

Yet while created and sustained by "the collective gender imaginary," feminicide has structural causes as well. Mexican scholar Mercedes Olivera connects violence against women and other forms of personal and family violence to the social ecology of the neoliberal conjuncture through which "men are driven to hypermasculinity, exaggerating the violent, authoritarian, aggressive aspects of male identity in an attempt to preserve that identity" (Olivera 2010, 51). U.S. legal scholar Deborah Weissman observes that the structural adjustment policies imposed during the 1980s on the global south (and later much of the north) produce misery in the present and pessimism about the future. Powerlessness and fear generate resentment and anger, while weakened states lose their authority and ability to contain corruption—the result encourages forms of private plunder and violence that constitute a shadow second state (Weissman 2010, 227–236).

The hemispheric wide campaign against antiwoman violence produces new knowledge. It reveals, for example, that it is false to portray the family as a safe space for women. Costa Rican scholars Montserrat Sagot and Ana Carcedo Cabanas point out that "for many, especially women and girls, the family has been the most violent social group, and the home, the most dangerous place" (Sagot and Cabanas 2010, 138). The campaigns against feminicide also expose the limits of international law. Feminist activists protesting against the use of rape as a tool of torture and warfare by government officials in El Salvador, Peru, and Haiti won a short-run victory when they succeeded in getting international law to define certain rapes as public crimes rather than private acts. Yet that victory also ran the risk of having other rapes framed as private acts considered to be less serious offenses (Fregoso and Bejarano 2010b, 9, 11). Shared struggle also helped feminists see how short-run victories can obscure knowledge needed for the middle and long run. Protests against the unprosecuted murders of women in Ciudad Juarez led to attacks on and denigration of both the protesters and the murdered women: they were labeled "public women" who were therefore indecent and unfit to be taken seriously. In order to protect themselves and to find interest convergence with leaders of the state and civil society, protestors chose to refer to the disappeared women as "daughters" mourned by grieving families. Effective in winning short-run support because of its appeal to normative family relations and expectations, this narrative at the same time obscured real truths about the family, perpetuating its image as a haven for women, when in fact studies show that most murdered women are killed by current or former husbands or lovers (Wright 2010, 314, 326). This tactic also ran the risk of making it seem that the deaths of women without families to mourn them or speak up for them were less worthy of investigation and prosecution.

Knowledge production in the streets can provoke changes in academic inquiries and arguments. The situated knowledge and grounded optic on power originally developed among aggrieved groups have become driving forces in ethnic studies, feminist studies, queer studies, and a multitude of disciplinary research endeavors. Forced to reckon with the nature of higher education as a managerially oriented apparatus strictly segregated by class, race, and national origin, scholars and students have come to recognize how the search for knowledge is hampered by injustice and inequality. Research, teaching, and learning are activities that must be innately cosmopolitan, but segregation and inequality constrain the knowledge base and range of available interlocutors. Arbitrary, artificial, and irrational exclusions based on race, class, language, disability/specialty, and sexuality narrow the circles from which scholarly conversations can proceed. This discovery has impelled scholars to develop research and social outreach initiatives to alternative academies in communities. These knowledge projects and acts of accompaniment include collaborative equity-oriented, community-based research projects about Black and Latinx anti-AIDS programs, Native American water rights, graffiti writing, educational equity, and struggles against gang curfews and for environmental justice and housing security (Aldern 2010; Austin 2001; Camp and Heatherton 2012; Chun, Lipsitz, and Shin 2010; Fregoso and Bejarano 2010a; Gilmore 2007; Hernández 2009; Moseby 2012; Phillips 1999, 2012; Rodríguez 2003, 37–83; Sze 2007; Woods 2009). The Community Partnership Grant Program of the American Studies Association has helped civic-minded scholars fashion programs offering language, literacy, and computer-training classes to new immigrants, to produce a theatrical and photographic exhibition about the work of women leaders in environmental justice campaigns in impoverished communities, and to connect scholars and community youths in the shared work of uncovering, preserving, and increasing knowledge about the diverse culture of inner-city neighborhoods. Research and teaching in higher education has thus been well positioned to promote democratic discussions and deliberations about the causes and consequences of the problems of the present and to serve as one of the sites where the capacity for democratic renewal can be developed and deepened (Woods 2009).

Although academic inquiry is and will remain an important site of knowledge production, it does not have a monopoly on inquiry, education, or pedagogy. Academics engaged in accompaniment with community groups can bring new and greatly needed knowledge to the academy, yet the struggle for social justice also requires recognition of accompaniment with educational endeavors that take place in insubordinate spaces far removed from formal educational institutions.

Insubordinate Spaces

Powerful forms of knowing and doing, accompaniment and improvisation, and *konesans* and *balans* have been invented by Asian Immigrant Women Advocates (AIWA) in Oakland in the form of the Community Transformational Organizing Strategy (CTOS). This is a collective and collaborative project that seeks to build the long-term capacity for agency and leadership among low-wage, limited-English speaking immigrant women workers. CTOS training offers women a space where they teach each other lessons in English and computer technologies, strategize together about workplace safety and grievance procedures, and learn about racism and language discrimination. In their work with AIWA, women experience a space where their identities as wives, mothers, daughters, and sisters are momentarily held in abeyance while they engage in deliberative talk, face-to-face decision-making, and workplace and community activism. The organization's membership includes immigrant women—from China, Korea, Vietnam, Thailand, Nepal, and other Asian nations—who work in garment and electronics manufacturing, nail care, home care, and cleaning. Its Youth Build Immigrant Power component mobilizes immigrant daughters to accompany their mothers' social justice struggles and to wage their own. Its public political campaigns to secure workplace health and safety, to compel employers to pay back wages, and to pressure the state legislature to recognize the rights of domestic workers entail alliances and affiliations with labor, environmental, feminist, and antiracist organizations and activists. In one especially significant campaign, AIWA and its supporters persuaded the city government in Oakland to fund an Ergonomic Chair Lending office that provided garment workers with workstations that protected their health, even when small shop employers refused to provide them on their own (Chun, Lipsitz, and Shin 2010).

Accompaniment has not been a painless process for AIWA. For five years in the 1990s, the organization mounted a campaign to secure unpaid back wages for workers employed by a subcontractor working for the Jessica McClintock Company. The garment workers also sought to have safety warning signs posted in languages other than English and to improve the state's system for receiving complaints about violations of labor laws in small shops. One strategy entailed calling on consumers to boycott clothing with the McClintock label. This move attracted allies from many different sectors of society. Support from high school students proved to be especially effective because prom dresses comprised one of the firm's key products. Feminist and antiracist activists publicized the boycott and labor groups helped recruit organizers with expertise in boycott tactics. These combined efforts during five years of struggle won significant victories—notably back wages for aggrieved workers, promises to post warning signs in the languages workers understood best, and establishment by the state government of a free telephone "hotline" for reporting wage theft, sexual harassment, and health and safety violations. To this day, the boycott is the victory for which AIWA is best known and celebrated. Yet inside the organization, the membership expressed regret that the boycott shifted too much of its strategic thinking and decision-making toward allies and away from the rank and file that initiated the struggle in the first place. Victory brought welcome concessions that improved working conditions but at the expense of the organization's core mission of developing the long-term capacity for collective leadership and agency among low-wage, limited-English-speaking immigrant women workers. AIWA still mounts campaigns guided by the principles of accompaniment, but the membership has made a collective commitment to keep the group's core mission its highest priority (Chun, Lipsitz, and Shin 2013a, 2013b). The *konesans* honed collectively in struggle produced a recognition of *balans*, of the ways in which victories and defeats are not immediately or easily recognized.

Social Movements as Knowledge Projects

Research projects, political struggles, and artistic interventions alike occur within contexts determined by conditions at different scenes of argument. They require communication and coordination. They encounter unexpected obstacles and opportunities. They require presence of mind and readiness to anticipate and make difficult choices. Their ability to remake the world depends upon how the struggle shapes up and on the moves made in response to it. People in struggle fight with the tools they have in the arenas that are open to them. The less they have, the more imaginative they have to be.

The knowledge projects of aggrieved groups often teach their lessons through middle-run decisions about design and representation. For example, when the prison abolition organization Critical Resistance felt it needed a logo to symbolize its opposition to the prison system and mass incarceration, the images that first came to mind were prison walls and bars and inmates locked up and chained together. These images, however, seemed to unwittingly reinforce the power of the state. They portrayed prisoners as helpless victims. They reaffirmed the distance and difference between those locked up on the inside and those on the outside. These designs ran counter to the aims and ideals of the organization. Critical Resistance then turned to the renowned artist Rupert Garcia for help. He designed a logo that featured a pupil inside an eye. This seemingly simple yet agency-laden image connoted an observant and watchful eye, the eye that people can use when looking for each other, and the eye they can use to keep watch on the prison system, an eye that can be an alternative to the punitive notion of justice that demands an eye for an eye. The symbol is flexible enough to show the other side of the equation as well, how the war on drugs and the war on terror produce massive surveillance, how the National Security Agency reads emails, and how eye-scan recognition technology can be used (and abused) for purposes of social control. Yet this too can be inverted at the scene of argument. While security apparatuses conduct their surveillance, people also watch each other, looking for good examples and allies. The victims of state and vigilante violence, the sexually abused and assaulted, the houseless and the poor are looking to see who sees them and who will accompany them.

For a similar development of symbolism, houseless residents of downtown Los Angeles focused on the shopping cart as an object to represent their condition. Over the years, people on the streets have used improvisation to transform abandoned shopping carts into mobile closets, conveyance devices, and sources of shelter. City planners, politicians, and police officers view the carts as stolen property that contributes to a dangerous and deviant lifestyle. Houseless people understand the prevalence of shopping carts in the areas where they live from a different perspective: as physical evidence of their resilience and creativity. Vehicles created to make shopping more convenient for people with money become abandoned in parking lots, alleys, and vacant lots. Houseless people with little or no money appropriate these abandoned devices and put them to use as closets and forms of shelter—tools for survival.

The Skid Row area in downtown Los Angeles where houseless people congregate is one of the most heavily policed areas in the world. A phalanx of city police officers and federal drug enforcement agents invade this one square mile area every day seeking to cite and arrest houseless people for the kinds of "quality of life" offenses discussed in relation to Ferguson in Chapter 5. People with low income, and in some cases no income, routinely find themselves fined and jailed for minor offenses such as sitting on the sidewalk, possessing an open container of liquid, or jaywalking. This use of "broken windows" policing has little to do with public safety. It is intended to drive poor people out of downtown areas so that the territory can be captured for development projects designed to make the city attractive to owners, investors, and high-end consumers. Houseless people do fear crime, but they are more afraid of being harassed by the police than they are of crimes by other residents of the area. Through the LACAN, they created their own community safety patrols because while they believed that while some disputes and behaviors required outside intervention, police officers generally escalated tensions—while community patrols defused them. City officials claim that Skid Row is a high-crime area, but most of the crimes they refer to are in fact created by police officers by the very act of citing and arresting people for actions that would be perfectly legal and draw no police intervention if they took place (as they do) in college fraternity houses, suburban cul-de-sacs, and yacht club grounds. These are crimes of condition, not crimes of conduct (Camp and Heatherton 2016).

One particularly cruel tactic of law enforcement on Skid Row has been to confiscate shopping carts of houseless people. To protest this hurtful policy, Steve Crawford (better known on the streets as General Dogon) customized a shopping cart. He painted it bright orange and black to attract attention. He decorated it with rearview mirrors. He installed a car battery to power stereo speakers so they could play his favorite music. General Dogon's creation demonstrated that the shopping cart served functions for houseless people equivalent to how automobiles worked for others. Crawford led his creation at the front of a caravan of carts followed by some three hundred demonstrators marching through the streets of downtown in a protest against the confiscations. This demonstration evidenced the determination of the poor to insist on their right to live in the city. The shopping cart parade took the very objects that law enforcement officers used to associate poor people with indolence and theft and displayed them in a way that demonstrated their resilience and resistance. This action transformed humiliating surveillance into defiant display and self-affirmation. It underscored how value can be found in undervalued objects and, by extension, in undervalued people.

Similar to the ways in which these activists inverted the meaning of the shopping cart, the group has also devised new and unexpected ways to deploy the plastic handcuffs that police officers use to restrain those they arrest. LACAN demonstrators placed the handcuffs on their own wrists and paraded through the streets behind a banner that read "House Keys Not Handcuffs." The slogan encapsulated the group's demands to divert the funds now wasted on stops, frisks, arrests, fines, and stints in jail to projects that would provide housing, sinks, toilets, health care, and treatment for substance abuse. The parade of handcuffed Black people through the city streets reenacted the slave coffle, the parade of bound Africans through the streets on the way to the auction block in eighteenth- and nineteenth-century U.S. cities. By walking in the footsteps of their enslaved ancestors, houseless Black people connected the concerns of the present to the patterns of the past. At the same time, demonstrators invited others to accompany them. The shopping cart and handcuffs demonstrations attracted supporters to their side. Some had credentials to serve as attorneys and represent houseless people in court. Academic researchers and their students created publications explaining and analyzing the causes of houselessness. People of many different races, religions, sexual identities, and class standings flocked to their side to lobby city government on behalf of a vision of urban planning from the bottom up, to support LACAN's wide-ranging proposals designed to build a democratic and inclusive city, not one solely oriented to the interests of investors, owners, and high-end consumers. These goals are aired through the newspaper published by houseless people working with LACAN, the website they and their supporters maintain, the hip-hop concerts they stage, and the wide array of events, activities, and clubs they organize to create a rich civil society and to promote a new cognitive and physical geography of accompaniment.

Carry the Fight, Live the Victory

When James Baldwin told Kenneth Clark in 1963 that he wondered about his place in his country and his future in it, Clark responded by asking Baldwin if he was essentially optimistic or pessimistic about the future. Responding in a manner that slightly reframed the question, Baldwin replied, "I can't be a pessimist because I'm alive. To be a pessimist means that you have agreed that human life is an academic matter, so I'm forced to be an optimist. I'm forced to believe that we can survive whatever we must survive" (American Experience 1963).

Baldwin's answer defines "an academic matter" as a detached and disinterested judgment made at a distance, as a rumination or speculation that will either confirm or disprove the speaker's judgment and prescience. This stance as a spectator and prognosticator does not interest him. He speaks instead as a participant in the processes he describes, as an actor whose agency will help determine the outcome of the question posed to him. This book has argued that the active and accountable disposition Baldwin evokes can and should be an "academic" matter of sorts, just as it can and should be an artistic matter and an activist matter. Choosing between pessimism and optimism as those words are generally understood is not the issue. When Baldwin says he cannot be a pessimist because he is alive, he is not speaking literally. Pessimists and optimists are equally alive in a physical sense: their hearts beat, they take breaths, their organs function. Being alive in

Baldwin's formulation means something else. It entails being ready to act and being responsible for one's actions. It means being fully in the moment, having presence of mind, and doing what needs to be done to make right things come to pass, even if there is no guarantee of success. Baldwin did not present himself as an optimist because he had a rosy view of the conditions that prevail in the world, but rather because he believed he had to act in a responsible manner at scenes shaped by conflict and struggle. The question to him was not about how he must *feel,* but about what he must *do.* Helping to create a just outcome was a responsibility he undertook. He embraced the stance of an optimist not as a handicapper or seer envisioning the future but as an improviser and accompanier compelled to explore how to make a better future possible, or at least how to prevent an even worse one from developing. "We can survive whatever we must survive" *does not* mean that we are invincible or immune to despair. It *does mean* that the ways we conduct ourselves and carry our burdens will influence others in ways that can arm them to develop the requisite degrees of clarity, courage, and conviction needed to play the hand that history has dealt to the world at this moment of danger.

As things fall apart, it will matter who tries to put them together again, and how. It will matter whose voices are heard and whose are silenced, which interests are represented and which are obscured. In our view, this is "an academic matter" in ways that are very different from Baldwin's deployment of the term. Institutions of higher education can play an important role in shaping society. They influence, and are influenced by, contention and contestation in every realm of life. Knowledge projects, however, are not confined to the academy. The deft blends of activism, art, and ideas that fuel the emergence of new social subjects and new social relations in Idle No More, Chicanx cultural production, and the Ferguson insurgency appear in a wide range of insubordinate spaces that are powerfully present inside aggrieved communities, but they are all but invisible to mainstream arts and education institutions. Rebuilding society in the wake of the devastation of the neoliberal conjuncture is activist, artistic, and "academic" work, a process that can be shaped in decisive ways by the knowledge projects that emerge from masses in motion, organized political struggles, art-based community making, and refusals of unlivable destinies.

Ils Sont Parti

When the bell rings to start horse races at the Evangeline Downs track in St. Landry Parish, Louisiana, the public address announcer always exclaims,

"Ils sont parti." Similar to the phrases voiced by track announcers speaking in English at other tracks—phrases such as "they're off" and "away they go"—the Cajun French expression connotes many additional meanings as well. It can describe heading out on a journey, bursting forth, starting a project, or going out to accomplish a task. One might argue that the many different meanings conveyed by the French phrase better describe what happens in a race than their Anglophone equivalents. Once the bell rings, everything depends upon how the race shapes up. Jockeys with horses positioned close to the inside rail, where the distance around the track is shorter, try to maintain that advantage. Horses in the outside post positions try to move toward the rail. Jockeys riding entries with strong closing kicks will stay back until they sense the time is right. In contrast, a horse that does not like to feel the turf kicked up in the face by horses ahead will be encouraged to take the lead and run in front. At every stage of the race, horses respond to jockeys, jockeys respond to horses, horses respond to other horses, and jockeys survey possible moves they can make without signaling their intentions to other riders who would then counter with moves of their own. The horse that starts closest to the rail does not necessarily win the race. The fastest horse does not necessarily win the race. The outcome hinges on the activity and interactivity that may be planned in advance but nonetheless needs to be improvised along the way.

Social justice struggles take shape in ways similar to the races at Evangeline Downs, but there is no one track and no shortage of participants. Configuring how the struggle will form is often the work of politicized cultural practices. For example, in her 2004 book *Speak It Louder* and in her forthcoming book *Louder and Faster: Taiko in Asian American California*, academic musicologist, musician, and antiracist activist Deborah Wong demonstrates how Asian Americans employ Japanese taiko drumming as an artistic practice, a knowledge project, and a political statement (2004, 2019). Wong's work reveals how the revival in the United States of a traditional Japanese cultural practice became a site where new identities and identifications were created. The revival emerged initially as a way of reconnecting with Japanese identity for young Japanese Americans who had been cut off from their heritage because of the ways in which the internment during World War II entailed confiscation and destruction of Japanese language books, music, and artifacts as well as attempts to dissolve Japanese cultural institutions. Taiko survived in some ways because it is visual rather than verbal and textual. It enabled Japanese Americans to embrace the national identity even if they did not speak or read Japanese. It then became

FIGURE 8.2. Taiko drummers in Little Tokyo, Los Angeles, August 16, 2015. (*Supranee Hickman/ Shutterstock.com*)

a surprising *ur* sign of a panethnic Asian American identity, a common ground and lingua franca for Asian Americans, even those who are not Japanese. Taiko offered a participatory way of affirming Asian identity in a way that was not reducible to any one national identity, language, religion, or immigration cohort. Its grounding in a culture rather than a color enabled taiko groups to attract participants from all races as well. Asian American women, especially, but also women of other races embraced taiko as a form of feminist glamor, a way to escape gendered stereotypes by performing an identity that is athletic, loud, and collaborative.

Wong's research delineating her experiences practicing and performing the genre reveals that taiko groups function as alternative academies teaching discipline, mastery, and strength through acts of improvisation and accompaniment. Taiko requires being together, breathing together, thinking together, moving together, and playing together. The different instruments in the ensemble sound different—and better—when layered together. Differentiated roles and different levels of skill offer plenty of room for individual improvisation and virtuosity, yet the group's success depends upon how all the pieces fit together. At obon festivals honoring departed ancestors, the participatory ethic of the taiko is in full effect. Like the Indigenous round dance in Idle No More discussed in Chapter 3 and the Fandango delineated in Chapter 4, there are no spectators at an obon observance: everyone must participate; everyone contributes; everyone counts.

Despite its many rituals, rules, and training regimens, taiko is first and foremost about self-activity. In *Louder and Faster* Wong presents a section of a Buddhist Temple newsletter in which Reverend Mas Kodani explains the core principles of taiko. The message is long and detailed. It presents fourteen points that delineate the proper practices, aims, and ethos of taiko. At the close of this detailed explication of how the art must and should be practiced, however, is a message in both English and Japanese that is more open ended and that captures perfectly the ways of thinking and being that inform all the chapters of *Insubordinate Spaces*. Beneath an aphorism that announces that to *not* dance is to lose, Reverend Kodani advises, "Without conditions, without calculating, without needing to be in control—just dance and become alive and connected" (Wong 2018, 158).

Surviving what we must survive will entail suffering, sacrifice, and struggle. Yet as New Orleans cultural visionary Sunni Patterson teaches us, it is not enough merely to carry on the struggle. It is necessary as well to live the victory.

Notes

CHAPTER 1

1. Robert Kennedy enlisted in the Navy on his eighteenth birthday during World War II and had one brother wounded and another killed in combat in that conflict. Beyond personal considerations, however, the attorney general was also aware of the deteriorating situation in South Vietnam where the U.S.-backed regime's corruption, incompetence, and repression of protests led by Buddhist clerics made it increasingly unpopular and in potential need of an augmented U.S. military presence. An anti-draft movement among Black people along the lines proposed (although never actually implemented) by A. Philip Randolph in the late 1940s would be devastating politically and militarily to U.S. prosecution of the global Cold War—an endeavor to which the Kennedy brothers were deeply and irretrievably committed.

2. In his sermon "Transformed Nonconformist," Martin Luther King, Jr. points to Romans 12:2 and its injunction to "Be not conformed to this world" to argue for the necessity for Christians to be nonconformists. Then, in a balancing turn, Dr. King argues that nonconformity is not a virtue by itself; it can be little more than a form of exhibitionism unless it is "controlled and directed by a transformed life" and "embraces a new mental outlook" (King 2010, 17–18).

3. George Lipsitz, notes, March 24, 2016.

4. For hysteresis, see Mindy Thompson Fullilove 2013, 3. For the things that can kill also being able to cure, see George Lipsitz and Russell Rodriguez 2012.

CHAPTER 2

1. We thank Alice Lynd and Staughton Lynd for introducing us to Oscar Romero's concept of accompaniment in their brilliantly generative and characteristically

principled discussion in their joint autobiography *Stepping Stones* (2009) and in Staughton's single-authored book *Accompanying: Pathways to Social Change* (2012).

2. We thank Daniel Fischlin, Ajay Heble, Susan McClary, and Rob Walser for rich dialogues over the years about music that inform this part of our argument.

3. The coauthors of this book recognize and acknowledge our many limitations in attempting to learn from the global south. Like other credentialed academic experts in the global north, we have been educated in largely monolingual schools that generally ignored the legacies of Indigenous dispossession and slavery, directed researchers toward archives structured in dominance, and countenanced no alternatives to colonial ways of knowing and being. Moreover, our embodied identities as whites in a settler colonialist country should raise genuine concerns about our capacity to speak about the insurgent knowledge of the global south and people of color in the global north. Yet the collective intelligence honed in struggle by aggrieved groups around the world compels us to engage with it, to risk the inevitable misunderstandings that might initially ensue from that engagement. Accompaniment as a praxis and a practice can be an important part of a process that can teach the people of the world how to move toward decolonizing knowledge, informing action, and helping people discern in all realms of life the work we want our work to do. It cannot be attempted without risk.

4. Although indebted to Archbishop Romero's formulation and deeply respectful of it, we do not presume that our projects are the same. We do believe that Romero's ideas can be transposed to a different setting with salutary results.

5. EZLN, "Fourth Declaration of the Lacandon Jungle," available at http://www.struggle.ws/mexico/ezln/jung4.html, accessed March 18, 2017.

6. Of course not everyone proclaiming "I am Mike Brown" in a street demonstration actually shares the precarious existence that haunted Brown's life and led to his premature death.

7. The IICSI has its headquarters at the University of Guelph. It is a consortium of fifty-eight researchers from twenty different institutions that has formal partnerships with more than thirty community organizations. A description of the project by its director, Ajay Heble, is available at http://improvisationinstitute.ca/about-iicsi/directors-welcome/.

8. Wallerstein argues that our choices in the short run always involve compromise: "In the short run, not only should we support the lesser evil, but there is no other choice available, ever. Every one, without exception, chooses the lesser evil. We just disagree about which choice is that of the lesser evil" (2008, 52–53).

9. According to Wallerstein, our ability to predict the "long run" is limited and does not depend on the quality of our plans. He argues: "Specifically, I do not think that we can define in advance the institutional structures that would result in a more democratic, more egalitarian world. We can draft whatever utopian models we wish. I don't think it matters, because I don't think that drafting such models will have too much impact on what actually emerges. *The most we can probably do is to push in certain directions that we think might be helpful*" (2008, 51, emphasis added).

10. See K. Brown 2006. We are grateful to Claudine Michel for all the guidance and instruction she has given us on the moral, spiritual, and epistemological significance of voudou. As with our use of accompaniment, however, we recognize that the situations facing the authors and most readers of this book are far different from those confronting peasants in Haiti or El Salvador, and in some ways we have the luxury of

exploring their ideas because their oppression creates privileges for us. But we engage with the concepts of *konesans* and *balans* as acts of accompaniment, moves that might help turn poison into medicine.

11. Paula Ioanide, "Introduction of Dr. George Lipsitz 'How Racism Takes Place' Lecture," Centering the Margins Discussion Series, Center for the Study of Culture, Race and Ethnicity, Ithaca College, April 11, 2011. Ithaca, New York. Authors' notes.

12. Jürgen Habermas deployed this chiasmus in "Ernst Bloch—a Marxist Romantic" (1969–1970).

13. This phrase generally attributed to Gramsci appeared on the masthead of the newspaper "L'Ordine Nuovo," which he edited.

CHAPTER 3

1. We are profoundly appreciative of and grateful to Deborah McGregor (Anishinaabe), Jodi Byrd (Chickasaw), Rick Kotowich, Ingrid Waldron, and Leela Viswanathan for comments and criticisms on an earlier draft of this chapter.

2. Once Chief Spence initiated her fast, Cross Lake First Nation activist Raymond Robinson followed suit. Shortly after, Elsipogtog First Nation activist Jean Sock launched a protest fast as well (Kino-nda-Niimi Collective 2014b, 391).

3. Deborah McGregor. Personal communication to authors. December 15, 2017.

4. We are indebted here to the deft formulation by the brilliant Dena'ina musicologist Jessica Bissett Perea who notes that in Native life nothing is more traditional than being contemporary. Authors' notes, University of California Humanities Research Institute Manuscript Seminar. April 14, 2017. Berkeley, California.

5. Idle No More, Courtenay, British Columbia, available at https://youtu.be/tH5 Er9y4A4U, accessed April 20, 2017.

CHAPTER 4

1. We thank Kurt Newman for introducing us to the artistry of Chingo Bling in 2007.

2. Representative Steven King of Iowa charged that large numbers of immigrants are drug mules while President Trump based much of his successful 2016 electoral campaign on raising fears about criminal immigrants from Mexico.

3. Much of the evidence in this section comes from the interview of Ramiro Gomez by George Lipsitz in Santa Barbara, California, February 27, 2012. Video of that interview is held in the California Ethnic and Multicultural Archives on that campus.

4. The *requinto* is a miniature guitar.

5. "Estoy Aqui—Quetzal—Youtube," available at https://www.youtube.com /watch?v=_PQ9QNV4U6g, accessed June 5, 2017.

6. A formulation made famous by Karl Marx.

CHAPTER 5

1. The authors thank Jamala Rogers, Percy Green, Tef Poe, Jodi Rios, Walter Johnson, Robin Kelley, and Brendan Roediger for conversations and communications about the Ferguson insurgency.

2. Poe is referring here to the state of Israel's contention that it can treat all Palestinians as terrorists because the Hamas Party won an election among them.

3. Available at http://www.city-data.com/city/St.-Peters-Missouri.html.

4. Arch City Defenders. Municipal Courts White Paper 2014, 27–34, available at http://03a5010.netsolhost.com/WordPress/wp-content/uploads/2014/11/ArchCity -Defenders-Municipal-Courts-Whitepaper.pdf.

CHAPTER 6

1. We are not asserting here that coloniality is solely a knowledge project. As Eve Tuck and Wayne Yang argue, decolonization is a specific political project grounded in battles for repatriation of Indigenous land and life. Yet the ways of knowing forged during Europe's internal and external colonizations as described by Anibal Quijano and Cedric Robinson undergird systems of exploitation and subordination around the world. Decoloniality as it came to be known during the era of Third World identification and mobilization fuels projects of accompaniment and improvisation. When it is complicit with the suppression of Indigenous repatriation they need to be named as such and opposed. Yet while we agree with Tuck and Yang that the use of decolonization as a metaphor "makes possible a set of evasions or 'settler moves to innocence,'" we do not believe it necessarily must do so (see Tuck and Yang 2012).

2. For more information on Okinawa see the website of the International Women's Network against Militarism, available at http://iwnam.org/.

3. All maps contain distortions and are guided by political choices. Many geographers defend the historical utility of the Mercator map for facilitating navigation and deride the Peters map created in Germany in 1974 for erring on the side of the global south in ways similar to the Mercator map's bias in favor of the north. The key question for us is not which map is technically most accurate or inaccurate but the way in which the map created the very world it purported to describe, similar to the histories of the census and the museum as explained by Benedict Anderson (2016).

4. The harm done by the racialized dimensions of psychological testing has been well chronicled by Stephen Jay Gould (1981). A seemingly trivial example illuminates the illogic of these policies. In 1958, psychologists working with the Brazilian national soccer team concluded that Pelé and other Black players lacked the emotional stability needed for successful performance. That advice convinced the team's coach not to play them in a decisive qualifying game against the Soviet Union. It was only a revolt by the other members of the team that got Pelé into the game, enabling Brazil to win the World Cup and launching what is widely considered the most distinguished career in the history of the sport. See João Costa Vargas 2013.

5. There are many useful analyses of neoliberal thinking and its effects. See, for example, W. Brown 2015, Hall 2011, Harvey 2005, and Peck 2010. Pierre Bourdieu called neoliberalism a program of methodically "destroying collective structures which may impede the pure market logic" (1998).

6. Tricia Rose reminds us that the lyrics of *One Nation under a Groove* by George Clinton describe an obstacle so wide you can't get around it, so high you can't get over it, and so low you can't get under it—so we need to find the chance to dance our way out of our constrictions.

CHAPTER 7

1. There are interesting parallels between the kinds of mood management and mental activity required of academics and the advice that thoughtful athletes offer about their endeavors. See, for example, Ken Dryden 1983 and Dirk Hayhurst 2010. Basketball player Kareem Abdul-Jabaar contended that the kinds of accompaniment that his college coach John Wooden demanded from the team depended on the "structured freedom" that Abdul-Jabaar discerned in jazz ensemble playing. Wooden did not expect his team to run set plays outlined on paper with diagrams and arrows, but instead taught the players to react to each other in the middle of the motion, to express individuality within the context of what the other athletes were doing. "We soloed or played backup for another player," Abdul-Jabaar observed, but we always played the same song, like a jazz band. We were playing in context" (Abdul-Jabaar 2017, 71).

2. For a thoughtful and insightful analysis of branding, see Sarah Banet-Weiser 2012.

3. For a particular kind of attack mode aimed at feminists, see the evidence, analysis, and arguments in Barbara Tomlinson 2010, esp. 87–113.

4. This line comes from the character Cedric Daniels played by Lance Reddick in the television series *The Wire*.

REFERENCES

Abdul-Jabaar, Kareem. *Coach Wooden and Me: Our 50-Year Friendship On and Off the Court*. New York: Grand Central Publishing, 2017.

Academics in Solidarity. "Open Letter to the Right Honorable Prime Minister of Canada Stephen Harper and the Right Honorable Governor General David Johnston." With Chief Spence and Idle No More. In *The Winter We Danced: Voices from the Past, the Future, and the Idle No More Movement*, edited by the Kino-nda-niimi Collective, 230–233. Winnipeg, MB: Arp Books, 2014.

Adams, Glenn, and Phia A. Salter. "A Critical Race Psychology Is Not Yet Born." *Connecticut Law Review* 43, no. 5 (2011): 1355–1377.

Adams, Paul C., Steven Hoelscher, and Karen E. Till, eds. *Textures of Place: Exploring Humanist Geographies*. Minneapolis: University of Minnesota Press, 2001.

Aguilar, Sara, director. *Activating Cultural Assets: Boyle Heights*. Alliance for California Traditional Arts, 2014.

Aldern, Jared. "Native Sustainment: The North Fork Mono Tribe's Stories," Ph.D. diss., Prescott College, 2010.

Alfred, Taiaiake. *Peace, Power, Righteousness: An Indigenous Manifesto*. New York: Oxford University Press, 2009.

Alliance for California Traditional Arts. "Activating Cultural Assets: Boyle Heights." YouTube video, September 10, 2014. Available at https://www.youtube.com/watch?v=vcZE3xJhbwI.

Allooloo, Siku. "'I Have Waited Forty Years for This. Keep It Going and Don't Stop': An Interview with Siku Allooloo." With Leanne Betasamosake Simpson. In *The Winter We Danced: Voices from the Past, the Future, and the Idle No More Movement*, edited by the Kino-nda-niimi Collective, 193–199. Winnipeg, MB: Arp Books, 2014.

Althusser, Louis. "Ideology and Ideological State Apparatuses." In *Lenin and Philosophy and Other Essays*, 127–187. Translated by Ben Brewster. New York: Monthly Review, 1971.

Alvarez, Robert. *Mangos, Chiles, and Truckers: The Business of Transnationalism.* Minneapolis: University of Minnesota Press, 2005.

American Experience. "James Baldwin on 'The Negro and the American Promise.'" April 5, 2015. Accessed September 26, 2018. Available at https://www.rimaregas .com/2015/04/05/video-james-baldwin-on-the-negro-and-the-american-promise -american-experience-pbs/.

Amnesty International. "On the Streets of America: Human Rights Abuses in Ferguson." October 23, 2014. Accessed January 1, 2015. Available at http://www.amnestyusa .org/research/reports/on-the-streets-of-america-human-rights-abuses-in-ferguson.

Anderson, Benedict. *Imagined Communities; Reflections on the Origins and Spread of Nationalism.* New York: Verso, 2016.

Anderson, J., and P. Applebome. "Exam Cheating on Long Island Hardly a Secret." *New York Times*, December 2, 2011. Accessed September 27, 2018. Available at https://www.nytimes.com/2011/12/02/education/on-long-island-sat-cheating-was -hardly-a-secret.html.

Anderson, Kim. *A Recognition of Being: Reconstructing Native American Womanhood.* Toronto: Second Story, 2000.

Anderson Gallery and Virginia Museum of Fine Arts. *Alfredo Jaar: geography=war.* Richmond: Virginia Commonwealth University Press, 1991.

Arch City Defenders. "Municipal Courts White Paper." Updated November 23, 2014. Accessed October 5, 2018. http://www.archcitydefenders.org/wp-content/uploads /2014/11/ArchCity-Defenders-Municipal-Courts-Whitepaper.pdf.

Arend, Orissa. "A Book Review: Talk That Music Talk." *New Orleans Tribune*, 2016. Accessed February 10, 2017. Available at http://www.theneworleanstribune.com /main/music-for-all-ages/.

Arendt, Hannah. *Eichmann in Jerusalem: A Report on the Banality of Evil.* Revised and enlarged edition. New York: Penguin Books, 1994.

Aristide, Marx V., and Laurie Richardson. "Haiti's Popular Resistance." In *Haiti: Dangerous Crossroads*, edited by North American Congress on Latin America. Boston: South End, 1995.

Armstrong, Nancy. *How Novels Think: The Limits of Individualism from 1719–1900.* New York: Columbia University Press, 2005.

Asimov, Nanette. "Oakland Principal in Cheating Stink Quits." *San Francisco Chronicle*, July 13, 2007. Available at http://articles.sfgate.com/2007-07-13/news /17254315_1_test-scores- cheating-english-and-.

Austin, Joe. *Taking the Train.* New York: Columbia University Press, 2001.

Bacon, David. "Displaced People: NAFTA's Most Important Product." *NACLA Reports* 41, no. 5 (2008): 23–27.

Bambara, Toni Cade. *The Salt Eaters.* New York: Vintage, 1992.

Banet-Weiser, Sarah. *Authentic™: The Politics of Ambivalence in a Brand Culture.* New York: New York University Press, 2012.

Baudrillard, Jean. *Simulacra and Simulation.* Ann Arbor: University of Michigan Press, 1994.

Belafonte, Harry. *My Song: A Memoir of Art, Race and Defiance.* New York: Vintage, 2011.

Bellegarde-Smith, Patrick, and Claudine Michel. "Danbala/Ayida as Cosmic Prism: The Lwa Trope for Understanding Metaphysics in Haitian Vodou and Beyond." *Journal of Africana Religions* 1, no. 4 (2013): 458–487.

Benjamin, Medea. "America Dropped 26,171 Bombs in 2016. What a Bloody End to Obama's Reign." *The Guardian*, January 9, 2017. Accessed March 24, 2017. Available at https://www.theguardian.com/commentisfree/2017/jan/09/america -dropped-26171-bombs-2016-obama-legacy.

Benjamin, Walter. "Theses on the Philosophy of History." *Illuminations: Essays and Reflections*, 253–264. Edited by Hannah Arendt. Translated by Harry Zohn. New York: Schocken Books, 1968.

Bernhard, Blythe. "Life Expectancy in St. Louis Depends Greatly on Geography," *St. Louis Post-Dispatch*, August 3, 2016. Accessed January 12, 2018. Available at http:// www.stltoday.com/lifestyles/health-med-fit/health/life-expectancy-in-st-louis -depends-greatly-on-geography/article_9398e077-27f9-5c51-b43d-1d9891f76a4e .html.

Bhabha, Homi K. "Foreword. Remembering Fanon: Self-Psyche and the Colonial Condition." Foreword to the 1986 Edition. *Black Skin, White Masks*, by Franz Fanon, xii–xxv. London: Pluto Press, 2008.

Blackwell, Angela Glover. "Remarks on the Inauguration of Melvin Oliver as Sixth President of Pitzer College." March 25, 2017. Claremont, CA. Authors' notes.

Bloch, Ernst. *The Principle of Hope.* Cambridge, MA: MIT Press, 1995.

Bock, Scott M. "The Music of Lafayette and Southwest Louisiana." *Living Blues* 42, no. 5 (2011): 10–37.

Bonnett, Alastair. *What Is Geography?* Thousand Oaks, CA: Sage, 2008.

Bourdieu, Pierre. "The Essence of Neoliberalism." Translated by Jeremy J. Shapiro. *Le Monde diplomatique.* December 1998. Available at https://mondediplo.com /1998/12/08bourdieu.

Boyle, Gregory. *Tattoos on the Heart.* New York: Free Press, 2010.

Branch, Taylor. *Parting the Waters: America in the King Years 1954–63.* New York: Simon and Schuster, 1989.

Brown, Karen McCarthy. "Afro-Caribbean Spirituality: A Haitian Case Study." In *Vodou in Haitian Life and Culture: Invisible Powers*, edited by Claudine Michel and Patrick Bellegarde-Smith, 1–26. Basingstoke, U.K.: Palgrave Macmillan, 2006.

Brown, Wendy. *Undoing the Demos: Neoliberalism's Stealth Revolution.* Brooklyn, NY: Zone Books, 2015.

Bueno-Hansen, Pascha. "Feminicido: Making the Most of an 'Empowered Term.'" In *Terrorizing Women: Feminicide in the Américas*, edited by Rosa-Linda Fregoso and Cynthia Bejarano, 290–231. Durham, NC: Duke University Press, 2010.

Burgess, John W. "The Ideal of the American Commonwealth." *Political Science* 10, no. 3 (1895): 404–425.

Butler, Judith. *Notes Toward a Performative Theory of Assembly.* Cambridge: Harvard University Press, 2015.

Byrd, Jodi. *The Transit of Empire.* Minneapolis: University of Minnesota Press, 2011.

Callahan, Manuel. "Rebel Dignity." *Kalfou* 3, no. 2 (2016).

Camp, Jordan, and Christina Heatherton, eds. *Freedom Now! Struggles for the Human Right to Housing in LA and Beyond*. Los Angeles: Freedom Now Press, 2012a.

———. "Introduction: Breaking the Silence." In *Freedom Now! Struggles for the Human Right to Housing in LA Freedom and Beyond*, edited by Jordan T. Camp and Christina Heatherton, 4–7. Los Angeles: Freedom Now Press, 2012b.

———. *Policing the Planet: Why the Policing Crisis Led to Black Lives Matter*. New York: Verso, 2016.

Camp, Stephanie. *Closer to Freedom: Enslaved Women and Everyday Resistance in the Plantation South*. Chapel Hill: University of North Carolina Press, 2014.

Campbell, James. "James Baldwin and the FBI." *Threepenny Review* 77 (1999): 11.

Canadian Artists Statement of Solidarity with Idle No More. "Idle No More: The Winter We Danced." In *The Winter We Danced: Voices from the Past, the Future, and the Idle No More Movement*, edited by the Kino-nda-niimi Collective, 278–274. Winnipeg, MB: Arp Books, 2014.

Canadian Union of Postal Workers. "Letter to Chief Theresa Spence." In *The Winter We Danced: Voices from the Past, the Future, and the Idle No More Movement*, edited by the Kino-nda-niimi Collective, 225–226. Winnipeg, MB: Arp Books, 2014.

Carmichael, Stokely (Kwame Ture). "Toward Black Liberation." *Massachusetts Review* 7, no. 4 (1966): 639–651.

Casey, Edward. *The Fate of Place: A Philosophical History*. Berkeley: University of California Press, 1997.

———. *Getting Back into Place: Toward a Renewed Understanding of the Place World*. Bloomington: Indiana University Press, 1993.

Casey, Edward, and Mary Watkins. *Up against the Wall: Re-Imagining the U.S.-Mexico Border*. Austin: University of Texas Press, 2014.

Center for Collaborative Research for an Equitable California. Accessed March 22, 2017. Available at https://ccrec.ucsc.edu/center.

Césaire, Aimé. *Discourse on Colonialism*. New York: Monthly Review, 2001.

Chávez, Alex E. *Sounds of Crossing: Music, Migration, and the Aural Poetics of Huapango Arribeño*. Durham, NC: Duke University Press, 2017.

Chavez, Leo. *The Latino Threat: Constructing Immigrants, Citizens, and the Nation*. Stanford, CA: Stanford University Press, 2013.

Chun, Jennifer, George Lipsitz, and Young Shin. "Immigrant Women Workers at the Center of Social Change." *Kalfou*, inaugural issue (2010): 127–132.

———. "Immigrant Women Workers at the Center of Social Change: Asian Immigrant Women Advocates." In *Immigrant Women Workers in the Neoliberal Age*, edited by Nilda Flores-Gonzalez, Anna Romina Guevara, Maura Toro-Morn, and Grace Chang, 207–231. Urbana: University of Illinois Press, 2013b.

———. "Intersectionality as a Social Movement Strategy: Asian Immigrant Women Advocates." *Signs: Journal of Women in Culture and Society* 38, no. 4 (2013a): 917–940.

Clarke, Rachel, and Marion Castillo. "Michael Brown Shooting: What Darren Wilson Told the Ferguson Grand Jury." CNN. November 25, 2014. Accessed October 5, 2018. https://www.cnn.com/2014/11/25/justice/ferguson-grand-jury-documents/index.html.

Collins, Laura, and Daniel Bates. "Darren Wilson and the Violent Confrontation with His Wife's Ex-lover." *Daily Mail*, November 27, 2014. Available at http://www.dailymail.co.uk/news/article-2851015/Darren-Wilson-violent-confrontation-wife-s-ex-lover-Court-documents-reveal-volatile-home-life-officer-shot-Michael-Brown-grand-jury-never-told-of.html, accessed January 15, 2018.

Comaroff, Jean, and John L. Comaroff. *Theory from the South: Or, How Euro-America Is Evolving toward Africa*. Boulder, CO: Paradigm, 2012.

Costa Vargas, João. "Always Already Excluded: Brazil's Male Selecao." In *A Companion to Sport*, edited by Ben Carrington and David L. Andrews, 465–480. New York: Wiley-Blackwell, 2013.

Coulthard, Glen Sean. *Red Skin, White Masks*. Minneapolis: University of Minnesota Press, 2014.

Council of UC Faculty Associations, The. *The UC Commission on the Future and the Edley Proposal for a Cyber-Campus: An Interim Report from the Berkeley Faculty Association*. Berkeley: Council of University of California Faculty Associations, 2010. Available at http://www.cucfa.org/news/2010_may18.php.

Crozier, Michael J., Samuel P. Huntington, and Joji Watanuki. *The Crisis of Democracy: Report on the Governability of Democracies to the Trilateral Commission*. New York: New York University Press, 1975.

Cuevas, Marco Polo Hernàndez. *African Mexicans and the Discourse of the Modern Nation*. Lanham, MD: University Press of America, 2004.

Davey, Monica, and Steven Greenhouse. "Angry Demonstrations in Wisconsin as Cuts Loom." *New York Times*, February 16, 2011. Available at http://www.nytimes.com/2011/02/17/us/17wisconsin.html.

Davidoff, Leonore, and Catherine Hall. *Family Fortunes: Men and Women of the English Middle Class, 1780–1850*. London: Routledge, 2003.

Davies, Bronwyn, and Peter Bansel. "Governmentality and Academic Work: Shaping the Hearts and Minds of Academic Workers." *Journal of Curriculum Theorizing* 26, no. 3 (2010): 5–20.

Davies, Bronwyn, and Sue Saltmarsh. "Gender Economies: Literacy and the Gendered Production of Neoliberal Subjectivities." *Gender and Education* 19, no. 1 (2007): 1–20.

DeBerry, Jarvis. "Jerome Smith, Outspoken Freedom Fighter, Once Struggled to Talk: Jarvis DeBerry." Nola.com. *Times Picayune*, February 24, 2014. Accessed February 15, 2107. Available at http://www.nola.com/opinions/index.ssf/2014/02/jerome_smith_outspoken_freedom.html.

Deloria, Philip J. "Broadway and Main: Crossroads, Ghost Roads, and Paths to an American Studies Future." *American Quarterly* 61, no. 1 (2009): 1–25.

Denning, Michael. *The Cultural Front*. New York: Verso, 1996.

Dent, Tom. *Southern Journey: A Return to the Civil Rights Movement*. Athens: University of Georgia Press, 2001.

———. *The Tom Dent Reader*. Edited by Kalamu ya Salaam. New Orleans: University of New Orleans Press, 2018.

Dent, Thomas, and Richard Schechner, eds. *The Free Southern Theatre by the Free Southern Theatre*. Indianapolis: Bobbs-Merrill, 1969.

Ditmars, Hadani. "Palestinians and Canadian Natives Join Hands to Protest Colonization." *Haaretz*, February 1, 2013. Accessed April 21, 2017. Available at http://www

.haaretz.com/israel-news/palestinians-and-canadian-natives-join-hands-to-protest
-colonization.premium-1.500057.

Dryden, Ken. *The Game*. New York: Times Books, 1983.

Dumm, Thomas L. *Democracy and Punishment: Disciplinary Origins of the United States*. Madison: University of Wisconsin Press, 1987.

Edge, John T. "Rapping about Tamales and Deportation." *New York Times*, May 24, 2011.

Eligon, John. "Michael Brown Spent Last Weeks Grappling with Problems and Promise." *New York Times*, August 24, 2014.

Escobar, Arturo. *Encountering Development: The Making and Unmaking of the Third World*. Princeton, NJ: Princeton University Press, 1995.

Eucher, Charles. *Nobody Turn Me Around: A People's History of the 1963 March on Washington*. Boston: Beacon, 2011.

Eze, Emmanuel Chukwudi. "The Color of Reason: The Idea of 'Race' in Kant's Anthropology." In *Postcolonial African Philosophy*, edited by Emmanuel Chukwudi Eze, 103–140. Cambridge, MA: Blackwell, 1997a.

———. "Hume, Race, and Human Nature." *Journal of the History of Ideas* 61 (2000): 691–698.

———, ed. *Postcolonial African Philosophy: A Critical Reader*. Cambridge, MA: Blackwell, 1997b.

Fabian, Johannes. *Time and the Other: Anthropology Makes Its Object*. New York: Columbia University Press, 1983.

Farmer, Paul. *To Repair the World: Paul Farmer Speaks to the Next Generation*. Edited by Jonathan Weigel. Berkeley: University of California Press, 2013.

Feldman, Keith P. *A Shadow over Palestine: The Imperial Life of Race in America*. Minneapolis: University of Minnesota Press, 2015.

Finch, Mark, Susan LeMessurier Quinn, and Ellen Waterman. "Improvisation, Adaptability, and Collaboration: Using AUMI in Community Music Therapy." *Voices* 16, no. 3 (2016): 8–34. Accessed May 3, 2017. Available at https://voices.no/index.php/voices/article/view/834/739.

Fischlin, Daniel, Ajay Heble, and George Lipsitz. *The Fierce Urgency of Now: Improvisation, Rights and the Ethics of Cocreation*. Durham: Duke University Press, 2013.

Fitzhugh, George. *Sociology for the South: or, The Failure of Free Society*. Richmond, VA: A. Morris, 1854.

Foucault, Michel. "Afterword: The Subject and Power." In *Michel Foucault: Beyond Structuralism and Hermeneutics*, edited by Herbert L. Dreyfus and Paul Rabinow, 208–226. Chicago: University of Chicago Press, 1983.

Fregoso, Rosa-Linda. "Mexico's Living Dead." *Kalfou* 3, no. 2 (2016): 185–206.

Fregoso, Rosa-Linda, and Cynthia Bejarano. "Introduction." In *Terrorizing Women: Feminicide in the Américas*, edited by Rosa-Linda Fregoso and Cynthia Bejarano, 1–24. Durham, NC: Duke University Press, 2010b.

———, eds. *Terrorizing Women: Feminicide in the Américas*. Durham, NC: Duke University Press, 2010a.

Friedel, Tracy L. "Understanding the Nature of Indigenous Youth Activism in Canada: Idle No More as a Resumptive Pedagogy." *South Atlantic Quarterly* 114, no. 4 (2015): 878–891.

Fukumura, Yoko, and Martha Matsuoka. "Redefining Security: Okinawan Women's Resistance to U.S. Militarism." In *Women's Activism and Globalization: Linking Local Struggles and Global Politics*, edited by Nancy Naples and Manisha Desai, 239–266. New York: Routledge, 2002.

Fullilove, Mindy Thompson. *Urban Alchemy: Restoring Joy in America's Sorted Out Cities*. New York: New Village, 2013.

Garfinkel, Herbert. "Conditions of Successful Degradation Ceremonies." *American Journal of Sociology* 61, no. 5 (1956): 420–424.

Garrett, Aaron, and Silvia Sebastiani. "David Hume on Race." In *The Oxford Handbook of Philosophy and Race*, edited by Naomi Zack. Oxford Handbooks Online, 2017. DOI: https://doi.org/10.1093/oxfordhb/9780190236953.013.43.

George, François. "Forgetting Lenin." *Telos* no. 18 (1973): 53–88.

Gilio-Whitaker, Dina. "Idle No More and Fourth World Social Movements in the New Millennium." *South Atlantic Quarterly* 114, no. 4 (2015): 866–867.

Gilmore, Ruth Wilson. "Forgotten Places and the Seeds of Grassroots Planning." In *Engaging Contradictions: Theory, Politics and Methods of Activist Scholarship*, edited by Charles R. Hale, 31–61. Berkeley: University of California Press, 2008.

———. *Golden Gulag: Prisons, Surplus, Crisis, and Opposition in Globalizing California*. Berkeley: University of California Press, 2007.

Giroux, Henry A. *Against the Terror of Neoliberalism: Politics beyond the Age of Greed*. New York: Routledge, 2013.

———. "Cultural Studies in Dark Times: Public Pedagogy and the Challenge of Neoliberalism." *Fast Capitalism* 1, no. 2 (2005). Available at http://www.fastcapitalism.com/.

———. "Neoliberalism and the Death of the Social State: Remembering Walter Benjamin's Angel of History." *Social Identities* 17, no. 4 (2011): 587–601.

Goldberg, David Theo. *The Threat of Race: Reflections on Racial Neoliberalism*. Malden, MA: Wiley-Blackwell, 2009.

Goldman, Shifra. *Dimensions of the Americas: Art and Social Change in Latin America and the United States*. Chicago: University of Chicago Press, 1994.

Goldwasser, Katherine. "The Prosecution, the Grand Jury, and the Decision Not to Charge." In *Ferguson's Fault Lines: The Race Quake That Rocked a Nation*, edited by Kimberly Jade Norwood, 37–56. Chicago: American Bar Association, 2016.

González. Martha. "Creating a Mexican-Afro-Cuban-American Beat." *Zocalo Public Square*, December 5, 2014. Accessed June 5, 2017. Available at http://www.zocalopublicsquare.org/2014/12/05/creating-a-mexican-afro-cuban-american-beat/chronicles/who-we-were/.

———. "*Zapateado* Afro-Chicana *Fandango* Style: Self-Reflective Moments in *Zapateado*." In *Dancing Across Borders: Danzas y Bailes Mexicanos*, edited by Olga Nájera-Ramírez, Norma E. Cantú, and Brenda Romero, 359–378. Urbana: University of Illinois Press, 2009.

Gordon, Colin. *Mapping Decline: St. Louis and the Fate of the American City*. Philadelphia: University of Pennsylvania Press, 2008.

Gould, Deborah B. *Moving Politics: Emotion and ACT UP's Fight against AIDS*. Chicago: University of Chicago Press, 2009.

Gould, Stephen Jay. *The Mismeasure of Man*. New York: Norton, 1981.

Gramsci, Antonio. *Selections from Cultural Writings*. Cambridge, MA: Harvard University Press, 1985.

———. *Selections from the Prison Notebooks of Antonio Gramsci*, edited by Quintin Hoare and Geoffrey Nowell Smith. New York: International Publishers, 1989.

Graveline, Fyre Jean. "Idle No More: Enough Is Enough." *Canadian Social Work Review* 29, no. 2 (2012): 293–300.

Green, Percy, Robin D. G. Kelley, George Lipsitz, Tef Poe, and Jamala Rogers. "Generations of Struggle: Panel Discussion on Protest before, during, and after the Ferguson Rebellion." *Kalfou* 3, no. 1 (2016): 7–35.

Greenwood, Davydd J. "Theoretical Research, Applied Research, and Action Research: The Deinstitutionalization of Activist Research." In *Engaging Contradictions: Theory, Politics, and Methods of Activist Scholarship*, edited by Charles R. Hale, 319–340. Berkeley: University of California Press, 2008.

Guera, Joey. "H-Town Rapper Chingo Bling Gets His Shine On." *Houston Chronicle*, August 19, 2007.

Guralnick, Peter. *Dream Boogie: The Triumph of Sam Cooke*. Boston: Back Bay Books, 2005.

Guthman, Edwin O., and Jeffrey Shulman, eds. *Robert Kennedy in His Own Words*. New York: Bantam Dell, 1991.

Gutiérrez, Gustavo. *A Theology of Liberation: History, Politics and Salvation*. Maryknoll, NY: Orbis, 1988.

Habermas, Jürgen. "Ernst Bloch—A Marxist Romantic." *Salmagundi* 10–11 (1969–1970): 311–325.

Hale, Charles R., ed. *Engaging Contradictions: Theory, Politics, and Methods of Activist Scholarship*. Berkeley: University of California Press, 2008a.

———. "Introduction." In *Engaging Contradictions: Theory, Politics, and Methods of Activist Scholarship*, edited by Charles R. Hale, 1–28. Berkeley: University of California Press, 2008b.

Hall, Stuart. "Ethnicity, Culture and the Search for Prestige." Economy of Prestige Conference. Unpublished paper, University of Minnesota, Minneapolis, April 1988.

———. "Gramsci's Relevance for the Study of Race and Ethnicity." *Journal of Communication Inquiry* 10, no. 5 (1986): 5–27.

———. "The Neo-Liberal Revolution." *Cultural Studies* 25, no. 6 (2011): 705–728.

Halpern, Jake. "The Cop." *The New Yorker* 91, no. 23 (August 10 & 17, 2015). Available at https://www.newyorker.com/magazine/2015/08/10/the-cop Accessed October 5.

Hamer, Jennifer F., and Clarence Lang. "Race, Structural Violence, and the Neoliberal University." *Critical Sociology* 41, no. 6 (2015): 897–912.

Harris, Cheryl. "Whiteness as Property." *Harvard Law Review* 106, no. 8 (1993): 1707–1791.

Hart, Rebecca R. *Mi Tierra: Contemporary Artists Explore Place*. Denver, CO: Denver Art Museum, 2017.

Harvey, David. *A Brief History of Neoliberalism*. New York: Oxford University Press, 2005.

———. *The New Imperialism*. Oxford: Oxford University Press, 2003.

Hayden, Tom. "Dismantling the Myth of Bill Bratton's LAPD." *The Nation*, December 6, 2013. Accessed February 20, 2015. Available at http://www.thenation.com/article/177505/dismantling-myth-bill-brattons-lapd#.

Hayhurst, Dirk. *The Bullpen Gospels: Major League Dreams of a Minor League Veteran.* New York: Citadel, 2010.

Hayter, Roger. "'The War in the Woods': Post-Fordist Restructuring, Globalization, and the Contested Remapping of British Columbia's Forest Economy." *Annals of the Association of American Geographers* 93, no. 3 (2003): 706–729.

Heatherton, Christina. "All Eyes on Skid Row." In *Downtown Blues: A Skid Row Reader*, edited by Christina Heatherton, 4–6. Los Angeles: Southern California Library and Los Angeles Community Action Network, 2011.

Heble, Ajay, ed. *Classroom Action: Human Rights, Critical Activism, and Community-Based Education.* Toronto: University of Toronto Press, 2017.

Hegel, Georg Wilhelm Friedrich. *The Philosophy of History.* Translated by J. Sibree. Kitchener, ON: Batovhe Books, 2001.

Hernández, Kelly Lytle. *City of Inmates: Conquest, Rebellion, and the Rise of Human Caging in Los Angeles, 1771–1965.* Chapel Hill: University of North Carolina Press, 2017.

Hiltzik, Michael. "How Scientists Failed the Public in Flint Water Crisis." *Los Angeles Times*, February 8, 2016.

Hirmer, Lisa, and Elizabeth Jackson. "Dispatch: Stopgap Beats + Other Strategies of Being in Public Space." *Studies in Social Justice* 10, no. 1 (2016): 4–5.

Holloway, John. "Dignity's Revolt." In *Zapatista! Reinventing Revolution in Mexico*, edited by John Holloway and Eloina Peláez. London: Pluto Press, 1998.

Hondagneu-Sotelo, Pierette. *Domestica: Immigrant Workers Cleaning and Caring in the Shadows of Affluence.* Berkeley: University of California Press, 2001.

Horne, Lena, and Richard Schickel. *Lena.* Garden City, NY: Doubleday, 1965.

Hughes, Henry. *A Treatise on Sociology: Theoretical and Practical.* Philadelphia: Lippincott, Gramco, 1854.

Hume, David. *Essays: Moral, Political and Literary.* Edited by Eugene Miller. Indianapolis: Liberty Fund, [1742/1777] 1985.

Hunt, Sarah. "More Than a Poster Campaign: Redefining Colonial Violence." In *The Winter We Danced: Voices from the Past, the Future, and the Idle No More Movement*, edited by the Kino-nda-niimi Collective, 190–193. Winnipeg, MB: Arp Books, 2014.

Huntington, Samuel P. "The Bases of Accommodation." *Foreign Affairs* 46 no. 4 (1968): 642–656.

———*The Clash of Civilizations and the Remaking of the World Order.* New York: Simon and Schuster, 1996.

———*Who Are We? The Challenges to America's National Identity.* New York: Simon and Schuster, 2004.

Jay, Dru Oja. "What if Natives Stop Subsidizing Canada?" In *The Winter We Danced: Voices from the Past, the Future, and the Idle No More Movement*, edited by the Kino-nda-niimi Collective, 108–112. Winnipeg, MB: Arp Books, 2014.

John, Sonja. "Idle No More—Indigenous Activism and Feminism." *Theory in Action* 8, no. 4 (2015): 38–54.

Johnson, Walter. *Soul by Soul: Life inside the Antebellum Slave Market*. Cambridge, MA: Harvard University Press, 1999.

———. "What Do We Mean When We Say 'Structural Racism'? A Walk Down West Florissant Avenue, Ferguson, Missouri." *Kalfou* 3, no. 1 (2016): 36–62.

Jones, Clarence B., and Joel Engel. *What Would Martin Say*. New York: HarperCollins, 2009.

Joseph, Miranda. *Against the Romance of Community*. Minneapolis: University of Minnesota Press, 2002.

Kajikawa, Loren. "The Possessive Investment in Classical Music: Confronting Legacies of White Supremacy in U.S. Schools and Departments of Music." In *Seeing Race Again*, edited by Kimberlé Crenshaw, Luke Harris, Daniel HoSang, and George Lipsitz. Berkeley: University of California Press, 2019.

Kant, Immanuel. "Physical Geography." *Race and the Enlightenment: A Reader*, edited by Emmanuel Chukwudi Eze, 58–64. Cambridge, MA: Blackwell, 1997.

Kappo, Tanya. "'Our People Were Glowing': An Interview with Tanya Kappo." In *The Winter We Danced: Voices from the Past, the Future, and the Idle No More Movement*, edited by the Kino-nda-niimi Collective, 67–61. Winnipeg, MB: Arp Books, 2014.

Kelley, Robin D. G. "Beyond Black Lives Matter." *Kalfou* 2, no. 2 (2015): 330–337.

———. "Black Study, Black Struggle." *Boston Review* 42, no. 2 (March 7, 2016). Accessed March 31, 2017. Available at http://bostonreview.net/forum/robin-d-g-kelley-black-study-black-struggle.

———. *Freedom Dreams: The Black Radical Imagination*. Boston: Beacon. 2002.

———. *Race Rebels: Culture, Politics, and the Black Working Class*. New York: Free Press, 1994.

Kelling, George L., and James Q. Wilson. "Broken Windows: The Police and Neighborhood Safety." *The Atlantic* (1982): 29–38.

Kershaw, Geoffrey G. L., Heather Castleden, and Colin P. Laroque. "An Argument for Ethical Physical Geography Research on Indigenous Landscapes in Canada." *The Canadian Geographer/Le Geographe canadien* 58, no. 4 (2014): 393–399.

Keyso, Ruth Ann. *Women of Okinawa: New Voices from a Garrison Island*. Ithaca, NY: Cornell University Press, 2000.

Kiel, Paul, and Annie Waldman. "The Color of Debt: How Collection Suits Squeeze Black Neighborhoods." *ProPublica*. October 8, 2015. Accessed June 12, 2017. Available at https://www.propublica.org/article/debt-collection-lawsuits-squeeze-black-neighborhoods.

King, Martin Luther, Jr. *Strength to Love*. Minneapolis, MN: Fortress, 2010.

———. *A Testament of Hope: The Essential Writings and Speeches of Martin Luther King, Jr.* Edited by James M. Washington. New York: HarperCollins, 1991.

Kino-nda-niimi Collective, The. "Idle No More: The Winter We Danced." In *The Winter We Danced: Voices from the Past, the Future, and the Idle No More Movement*, edited by the Kino-nda-niimi Collective, 32–51. Winnipeg, MB: Arp Books, 2014a.

———. *The Winter We Danced: Voices from the Past, the Future, and the Idle No More Movement*. Winnipeg, MB: Arp Books, 2014b.

Klein, Naomi. *Shock Doctrine: The Rise of Disaster Capitalism*. New York: Metropolitan Books-Henry Holt, 2007.

LaDuke, Winona. *All Our Relations: Native Struggles for Land and Life.* Chicago: Haymarket Books, 2015.

———. "Why First Nations Movement Is Our Best Chance for Clean Land and Water." In *The Winter We Danced: Voices from the Past, the Future, and the Idle No More Movement*, edited by the Kino-nda-niimi Collective, 142–147. Winnipeg, MB: Arp Books, 2014.

Lang, Clarence. *Grassroots at the Gateway: Class Politics and the Black Freedom Struggle in St. Louis.* Ann Arbor: University of Michigan Press, 2009.

Layton, Lynne. "Irrational Exuberance: Neoliberal Subjectivity and the Perversion of Truth." *Subjectivity* 3 (2010): 303–322.

Lee, James Kyung-Jin. *Urban Triage: Race and the Fictions of Multiculturalism.* Minneapolis: University of Minnesota Press, 2004.

Leonnig, Carol, Kimberly Kindy, and Joel Achenbach. "Darren Wilson's First Job Was On a Troubled Police Force Disbanded by Authorities." *Washington Post*, August 23, 2014. Accessed October 5, 2018. Available at https://www.washingtonpost.com/national/darren-wilsons-first-job-was-on-a-troubled-police-force-disbanded-by-authorities/2014/08/23/1ac796f0-2a45-11e4-8593-da634b334390_story.html?utm_term=.8029f923e1c5.

Leval, Susana Torreula. "Recapturing History: The (Un)Official Story in Contemporary Latin American Art." *Art Journal* 51, no. 4 (1992): 69–80.

Leyte, Ximena. "Narratives of Our Land." *Boulder Weekly*, May 25, 2017. Accessed June 7, 2017. Available at http://www.boulderweekly.com/entertainment/arts-culture/narratives-of-our-land/.

Light, Ivan. *Deflecting Immigration.* New York: Russell Sage, 2006.

———. "How Los Angeles Deflected Mexican Immigrants to the American Heartland." *Migration Information Source*, October 9, 2007. Available at http://www.migrationinformation.org/Feature/display.cfm?ID=645.

Lipman, Pauline. *The New Political Economy of Urban Education: Neoliberalism, Race and the Right to the City.* New York: Routledge, 2011.

Lippe-Klein, N., and S. Hendy. "L.A. Teachers Use Privatization Fight to Build Community Power." *Labor Notes*, March 11, 2011. Available at http://labornotes.org/2011/02/la-teachers-use-privatization-fight-build-community-power.

Lipsitz, George. *American Studies in a Moment of Danger.* Minneapolis: University of Minnesota Press, 2001.

———. "Challenging Neoliberal Education at the Grass Roots: Students Who Lead, Not Students Who Leave." *Souls* 17, nos. 3–4 (2015): 303–321.

———. *Dangerous Crossroads: Popular Music, Postmodernism, and the Poetics of Place.* London: Verso, 1994.

———. "Education for Liberation, Not Mainstream Socialization: The Improvisation Pedagogy of Students at the Center in New Orleans." In *Improvisation and Music Education: Beyond the Classroom*, edited by Ajay Heble and Mark Laver, 266–279. London: Routledge, 2016.

———. *How Racism Takes Place.* Philadelphia: Temple University Press, 2011.

———. Interview with Ramiro Gomez, California Ethnic and Multicultural Archives, University of California, Santa Barbara. February 27, 2012.

———. "Learning from New Orleans: The Social Warrant of Hostile Privatism and Competitive Consumer Citizenship." *Cultural Anthropology* 21, no. 3 (2006): 451–468.

———. *The Possessive Investment in Whiteness: How White People Profit from Identity Politics*. Philadelphia: Temple University Press, 2005.

Lipsitz, George, and Russell Rodriguez. "Turning Hegemony on Its Head: The Insurgent Knowledge of Americo Paredes." *Journal of American Folklore* 125, no. 495 (2012): 111–125.

Lomax, John Nova. "Chingo Bling vs. La Migra." *Houston Press*, August 14, 2007.

———. "Money and Masa." *Houston Press*, September 4, 2003.

Lowe, Donald. *History of Bourgeois Perception*. Chicago: University of Chicago Press, 1983.

Lowery, Wesley. "Darren Wilson Told Attorneys He and Other Ferguson Officers Used the N-Word." *Washington Post*, March 14, 2017. Accessed October 5, 2018. Available at https://www.washingtonpost.com/news/post-nation/wp/2017/03/14/court-document-former-officer-darren-wilson-says-ferguson-officers-used-n-word-to-refer-to-african-americans/?utm_term=.e9794abad520.

Lyman, Stanford. "Race Relations as Social Process: Sociology's Resistance to a Civil Rights Orientation." In *Race in America: The Struggle for Equality*, edited by James Jones and Herbert Hill, 370–401. Madison: University of Wisconsin Press, 1993.

Lynd, Alice, and Staughton Lynd. *Stepping Stones*. Lanham, MD: Lexington Books, 2009.

Lynd, Staughton. *Accompanying: Pathways to Social Change*. Oakland: PM Press, 2012.

Mainville, Lori. "We Are Free Human Beings, Part Two." In *The Winter We Danced: Voices from the Past, the Future, and the Idle No More Movement*, edited by the Kino-nda-niimi Collective, 345–347. Winnipeg, MB: Arp Books, 2014.

Malcolm X. "Speech at the Founding Rally of the Organization of Afro-American Unity." In *By Any Means Necessary: Speeches, Interviews, and a Letter by Malcolm X*, edited by George Breitman, 63–64. New York: Pathfinder, 1992.

Mann, Jennifer S. "Police Representative Says DOJ's 'Band of Marauders' Concealed Truth about Ferguson Shooting." *St. Louis Post-Dispatch*, March 28, 2015.

Marcos, Subcommandante. *Conversations with Durito: Stories of the Zapatistas and Neoliberalism*. Brooklyn, NY: Autonomedia, 2005.

Maturana, Humberto, and Francisco Varela. *The Tree of Knowledge: The Biological Roots of Human Understanding*. Boston: Shambhala, 1992.

McClary, Susan. *Feminine Endings: Music, Gender, and Sexuality*. Minneapolis: University of Minnesota Press, 1991.

McGregor, Deborah. "Indigenous Women, Water Justice and *Zaagidowin* (Love)." *Canadian Woman Studies/Les Cahiers de laFemme* 30, nos. 2–3 (2013): 71–78.

McLean, Nancy. *Democracy in Chains: The Deep History of the Radical Right's Stealth Plan for America*. New York: Penguin Books, 2017.

McLean, Sheelah. "Idle No More: Re-storying Canada." In *The Winter We Danced: Voices from the Past, the Future, and the Idle No More Movement*, edited by the Kino-nda-niimi Collective, 92. Winnipeg, MB: Arp Books, 2014.

McNeal, Caitlin. "Fired Ferguson Clerk Says Racist Emails Were Funny." *TPM Livewire*, April 8, 2015. Accessed April 8, 2015. Available at http://talkingpointsmemor.com/livewire/ferguson-official-racist-emails-de.

McSpadden, Lezley. *Tell the Truth and Shame the Devil: The Life, Legacy, and Love of My Son Michael Brown*. New York: Regan Arts, 2016.

Medley, Keith Weldon. *Black Life in Old New Orleans*. Gretna, LA: Pelican Publishing Company, 2014.

Memmi, Albert. *The Colonizer and the Colonized*. Boston: Beacon, 1991.

Metzl, Jonathan M. *The Protest Psychosis: How Schizophrenia Became a Black Disease*. Boston, MA: Beacon Press, 2009.

Meyer, David. *Winter of Discontent: The Nuclear Freeze and American Politics*. New York: Praeger, 1990.

Mignolo, Walter D. *The Darker Side of Western Modernity: Global Futures, Decolonial Options*. Durham, NC: Duke University Press, 2011.

Milkman, Ruth, Ana Luz González, and Victor Narro. *Wage Theft and Workplace Violations in Los Angeles: The Failure of Employment and Labor Law for Low Wage Workers*. Los Angeles: UCLA Labor Center, 2010.

Mills, Charles W. *The Racial Contract*. Ithaca, NY: Cornell University Press, 1997.

———. "White Time: The Chronic Injustice of Ideal Theory." *Du Bois Review* 11, no. 1 (2014): 27–42.

Mirzoeff, Nicholas. "The Murder of Michael Brown: Reading the Ferguson Grand Jury Transcripts." *Social Text* 34, no. 1 (2016): 49–71.

Miyoshi, Masao. "Ivory Tower in Escrow." *boundary 2* 27, no. 1 (2000): 7–50.

Moglen, Seth. *Mourning Modernity: Literary Modernism and the Injuries of American Capitalism*. Stanford, CA: Stanford University Press, 2007.

Montgomery, David. "Protest Artist's Cardboard Cutouts Draw Attention to Immigration Issue." *Washington Post*, February 13, 2013.

Moon, D. Thomas. "Bob Stroger: First Call Bass." *Living Blues* 32, no. 4 (2001): 26–53.

Moreton-Robinson, Aileen. *The White Possessive: Property, Power and Indigenous Sovereignty*. Minneapolis: University of Minnesota Press, 2015.

Morris, Aldon D. *The Scholar Denied: W.E.B. Du Bois and the Birth of Modern Sociology*. Berkeley: University of California Press, 2015.

Morris, Amanda. "Twenty-First-Century Debt Collectors: Idle No More Combats a Five-Hundred-Year-Old-Debt." *WSQ: Women's Studies Quarterly* 42, nos. 1–2 (2014): 242–256.

Moseby, Kevin. "Changing the Color of HIV Prevention: Black Community Activism, U.S. Public Health and the Biopolitics of Race, Gender, Sexuality and Citizenship," Ph.D. diss., Department of Sociology, University of California, San Diego, 2012.

Moten, Fred. *In the Break*. Minneapolis: University of Minnesota Press, 2003.

Muhammad, Khalil Gibran. *The Condemnation of Blackness: Race, Crime and the Making of Modern America*. Cambridge, MA: Harvard University Press, 2010.

Nagel, Joane. *American Indian Ethnic Renewal: Red Power and the Resurgence of Identity and Culture*. New York: Oxford University Press, 1997.

Nason, Dory. "We Hold Our Hands Up: Our Indigenous Women's Love and Resistance." In *The Winter We Danced: Voices from the Past, the Future, and the Idle No More Movement*, edited by the Kino-nda-niimi Collective, 186–190. Winnipeg, MB: Arp Books, 2014.

———. "We Hold Our Hands Up: Our Indigenous Women's Love and Resistance." *Decolonization: Indigeneity, Education and Society* (blog). February 12, 2013. Accessed

January 7, 2018. Available at https://decolonization.wordpress.com/2013/02/12/we-hold-our-hands-up-on-indigenous-womens-love-and-resistance/.

Neighborhood Story Project. *Talk That Music Talk: Passing on Brass Band Music in New Orleans the Traditional Way.* December 11, 2014. Accessed February 10, 2017. Available at http://www.antenna.works/book-release-party-the-neighborhood-story-project-presents-talk-that-music-talk-passing-on-brass-band-music-in-new-orleans-the-traditional-way-excerpt-and-photos/.

Newfield, Christopher. *The Great Mistake: How We Wrecked Public Universities and How We Can Fix Them.* Baltimore: Johns Hopkins University Press, 2017.

————. *Unmaking the Public University: The Forty-Year Assault on the Middle Class.* Cambridge, MA: Harvard University Press, 2008.

Norwood, Kimberly Jade. "From BROWN to Brown: Sixty-Plus Years of Separately Unequal Education." In *Ferguson's Fault Lines: The Race Quake That Rocked a Nation*, edited by Kimberly Jade Norwood, 93–119. Chicago: American Bar Association, 2016.

Oaxacalifornian Reporting Team. *Voices of Indigenous Oaxacan Youth in the Central Valley: Creating Our Sense of Belonging in California.* Santa Cruz, CA: Center for Collaborative Research for an Equitable California, UC Santa Cruz, 2013.

O'Donoghue, F. *The Last Professors: The Corporate University and the Fate of the Humanities.* New York: Fordham University Press, 2008.

Oliver, Melvin L., and Thomas M. Shapiro. *Black Wealth/White Wealth: A New Perspective on Racial Inequality.* New York: Routledge, 2005.

Olivera, Mercedes. "Violencia Feminicida: Violence against Women and Mexico's Structural Crisis." In *Terrorizing Women: Feminicide in the Américas*, edited by Rosa-Linda Fregoso and Cynthia Bejarano. Durham, NC: Duke University Press, 2010.

Otero, Gerardo. "Neoliberal Globalization, NAFTA, and Migration: Mexico's Loss of Food and Labor Sovereignty." *Journal of Poverty* 15, no. 4 (2011): 384–402.

Palmater, Pamela. "Why Are We Idle No More?" In *The Winter We Danced: Voices from the Past, the Future, and the Idle No More Movement*, edited by the Kino-nda-niimi Collective, 37–40. Winnipeg, MB: Arp Books, 2014.

Pasternak, Shiri. "Occupy(ed) Canada: The Political Economy of Indigenous Dispossession." In *The Winter We Danced: Voices from the Past, the Future, and the Idle No More Movement*, edited by the Kino-nda-niimi Collective, 40–44. Winnipeg, MB: Arp Books, 2014.

Patterson, Sunni. "Resilient Love in a Time of Hate." American Studies Association Annual Meeting. November 19, 2016. Denver, CO. Authors' notes.

Payne, Charles. *I've Got the Light of Freedom: The Organizing Tradition and the Mississippi Freedom Struggle.* Berkeley: University of California Press, 2007.

Peck, Jamie. *Constructions of Neoliberal Reason.* New York: Oxford University Press, 2010.

Phillips, Nia, Glenn Adams, and Phia Salter. "Beyond Adaptation: Decolonizing Approaches to Coping with Oppression." *Journal of Social and Political Psychology* 3, no. 1 (2015): 365–387.

Phillips, Susan. "Gangs, Globalization and Critical Security Studies: Teaching Counternarratives to Public Audiences." *Kalfou* 2, no. 2 (2015): 360–368.

————. *Operation Fly Trap: L.A. Gangs, Drugs and the Law.* Chicago: University of Chicago Press, 2012.

———. *Wallbangin': Graffiti and Gangs in L.A.* Chicago: University of Chicago Press, 1999.

Piff, Paul K. "Wealth and the Inflated Self: Class, Entitlement, and Narcissism." *Personality and Social Psychology Bulletin* 40, no. 1 (2014): 34–43.

Polletta, Francesca. *Freedom is an Endless Meeting: Democracy in American Social Movements.* Chicago: University of Chicago Press, 2002.

Premo, Michael, director. *Water Warriors: Nothing Can Live Without Water.* Storyline Films, 2017.

Quijano, Anibal. "Coloniality of Power, Eurocentrism and Latin America." *Nepantla: Views from the South* 1, no. 3 (2000): 533–580.

Ransby, Barbara. *Ella Baker and the Black Freedom Movement: A Radical Democratic Vision.* Chapel Hill: University of North Carolina Press, 2005.

Rawick, George. *Listening to Revolt: Selected Writings.* Chicago: Charles H. Kerr, 2010.

Readings, Bill. *The University in Ruins.* Cambridge, MA: Harvard University Press, 1997.

Recinos, Eva. "Meet Ramiro Gomez, the Artist Making LA's Laborers Hard to Overlook." *Remezcla*, July 24, 2013. Accessed June 7, 2017. Available at http://remezcla.com/culture/ramiro-gomez-profile-beverly-hills-cardboard-cutouts/.

Reddy, Chandan. *Freedom with Violence: Race, Sexuality, and the U.S. State.* Durham, NC: Duke University Press, 2011.

Reiter, Keramet. *23/7: Pelican Bay Prison and the Rise of Long-Term Solitary Confinement.* New Haven, CT: Yale University Press, 2016.

Rios, Jodi. "Flesh in the Street." *Kalfou* 3, no. 1 (2016): 63–78.

Robinson, Cedric J. *Black Movements in America.* New York: Routledge, 1997.

———. *Forgeries of Memory and Meaning: Blacks and Regimes of Race in American Theater and Film before World War II.* Chapel Hill: University of North Carolina Press, 2007.

———. "Manichaeism and Multiculturalism." In *Mapping Multiculturalism,* ed. Avery F. Gordon and Christopher Newfield, 116–124. Minneapolis: University of Minnesota Press, 1996.

———. *The Terms of Order.* Chapel Hill: University of North Carolina Press, 2016.

Rodney, Walter. *How Europe Underdeveloped Africa.* Washington, DC: Howard University Press, 1982.

Rodriguez, Russell. "*Folklórico* in the United States: Cultural Preservation and Disillusion." In *Dancing Across Borders: Danzas y Bailes Mexicanos*, edited by Olga Nájera-Ramírez, Norma E. Cantú, and Brenda M. Romero, 335–358. Urbana: University of Illinois Press, 2009.

———. "Rámon 'Chunky' Sánchez—!Presente!" *Kalfou* 4, no. 1 (2017): 118–122.

Rogers, Jamala. *Ferguson Is America: Roots of Rebellion.* St. Louis, MO: Mira Digital, 2015.

Rogers, Kim Lacy. *Righteous Lives: Narratives of the New Orleans Civil Rights Movement.* New York: New York University Press, 1993.

Roithmayr, Daria. *Racial Cartels.* University of Southern California Law and Economics Working Papers Series, Working Paper 66, 2007.

———. *Reproducing Racism: How Everyday Choices Lock in White Advantage.* New York: New York University Press, 2014.

Rose, Nikolas. *Powers of Freedom: Reframing Political Thought*. Cambridge: Cambridge University Press, 1999.

Rosenfelt, Deborah. *Salt of the Earth*. New York: The Feminist Press at CUNY, 1993.

Rothstein, Richard. *The Color of Law: A Forgotten History of How Our Government Segregated America*. New York: Liveright, 2017.

Sagot, Montserrat, and Ana Carcedo Cabanas. "When Violence against Women Kills: Feminicide in Costa Rica." In *Terrorizing Women: Feminicide in the Américas*, edited by Rosa-Linda Fregoso and Cynthia Bejarano, 138–156. Durham, NC: Duke University Press, 2010.

Said, Edward. *Culture and Imperialism*. New York: Vintage, 1994.

Salaam, Kalamu Ya. *Poetic Visions*. Center for Black Studies Research Video. Presentation at the American Studies Association Annual Meeting, Washington, DC. November 5, 2009.

Sanchez, Omar. "How a Motion-Tracking Software Is Breaking Down Barriers for People with Disabilities." *University Daily Kansan*, March 15, 2017. Accessed May 3, 2017. Available at https://kansan.atavist.com/a-new-instrument-at-the-university-of-kansas-is-breaking-the-social-barriers-against-disability.

Santos, Boaventura de Sousa. "Oppositional Postmodernism and Globalizations." *Law and Social Inquiry* 23, no. 1 (1998): 121–139.

Sassen, S. "Beyond Protests: Students Making the Pieces of a Different Society." *Huffington Post*, May 22, 2010. Available at http://www.huffingtonpost.com/saskia-sassen/beyond-protests-students_b_586138.html.

Schechner, Richard. *Performance Studies: An Introduction*. New York: Routledge, 2013.

Schlesinger, Arthur M., Jr. *Robert Kennedy and His Times*. New York: Mariner Books, 2002.

Schmidt Camacho, Alicia. "Ciudana X: Gender Violence and the Denationalization of Women's Rights in Ciudad Juarez, Mexico." In *Terrorizing Women: Feminicide in the Americas*, edited by Rosa-Linda Fregoso and Cynthia Bejarano, 275–289. Durham, NC: Duke University Press, 2010.

Schneider, Michael. "Vanguard, Vanguard, Who's Got the Vanguard?" *Liberation* 17 (1972).

Scholes, Robert. "Presidential Address 2004: The Humanities in a Posthumanist World." *PMLA* 120, no. 3 (2005): 724–733.

Scott, Dayna Nadine. "Commentary: The Forces That Conspire to Keep Us 'Idle.'" *Canadian Journal of Law and Society/Revue Canadienne Droit et Societe* 28, no. 3 (2013): 425–428.

Segato, Rita. "Territory, Sovereignty, and Crimes of the Second State: The Writing on the Body of Murdered Women." In *Terrorizing Women: Feminicide in the Americas*, edited by Rosa-Linda Fregoso and Cynthia Bejarano, 70–92. Durham, NC: Duke University Press, 2010.

Sennett, Richard. *The Culture of the New Capitalism*. New Haven, CT: Yale University Press, 2006.

Severson, K. "Systematic Cheating Is Found in Atlanta's School System." *New York Times*, July 5, 2011. Available at http://www.nytimes.com/2011/07/06/education/06atlanta.html?pagewanted+.

Shah, Nayan. *Stranger Intimacy: Contesting Race, Sexuality, and the Law in the North American West*. Berkeley: University of California Press, 2011.

Shapiro, Thomas. *Toxic Inequality: How America's Wealth Gap Destroys Mobility, Deepens the Racial Divide, and Threatens Our Future.* New York: Basic Books, 2017.

Siddall, Gillian, and Ellen Waterman, eds. *Negotiated Moments: Improvisation, Sound and Subjectivity.* Durham, NC: Duke University Press, 2016.

Simpson, Audra. "The State Is a Man: Theresa Spence, Loretta Saunders and the Gender of Settler Sovereignty." *Theory and Event* 19, no. 4 (2016): 1–14.

Simpson, Leanne. *Dancing on Our Turtle's Back: Stories of Nishinaabeg Re-Creation, Resurgence, and a New Emergence.* Winnipeg, MB: ARP Books, 2011.

Simpson, Leanne Betasamosake. "Fish Broth and Fasting." In *The Winter We Danced: Voices from the Past, the Future, and the Idle No More Movement*, edited by the Kinonda-niimi Collective, 154–157. Winnipeg, MB: Arp Books, 2014.

———. "Queering Resurgence: Taking on Heteropatriarchy in Indigenous Nation Building." June 1, 2012. Available at https://www.leannesimpson.ca/writings/queering-resurgence-taking-on-heteropatriarchy-in-indigenous-nation-building.

Soble, Jonathan. "Okinawa Murder Case Heightens Outcry over U.S. Military's Presence." *New York Times*, June 4, 2016, available at https://www.nytimes.com/2016/06/05/world/asia/okinawa-murder-case-heightens-outcry-over-us-militarys-presence.html?_r=0, accessed March 24, 2017.

Sommer, Doris. *The Work of Art in the World: Civic Agency and Public Humanities.* Durham, NC: Duke University Press, 2014.

Sommer, Doris, and Pauline Strong. "Theory Follows from Practice: Lessons from the Field." *University of Toronto Quarterly* 85 no. 4 (2016): 67–81.

Speed, Shannon. "Forged in Dialogue: Toward a Critically Engaged Activist Research." In *Engaging Contradictions: Theory, Politics and Methods of Activist Scholarship*, edited by Charles R. Hale, 213–236. Berkeley: University of California Press, 2008.

———. "States of Violence: Indigenous Women Migrants in the Era of Neoliberal Multiculturalism." *Critique of Anthropology* 36, no. 3 (2016): 280–301.

Spelman, Elizabeth V. *Fruits of Sorrow: Framing Our Attention to Suffering.* Boston: Beacon, 1997.

Spitzer, Nick. *American Routes: Songs and Stories from the Road.* Audio CD. High Bridge Audio. Unabridged Edition, 2008.

Steinberg, Stephen. *Race Relations: A Critique.* Stanford, CA: Stanford University Press, 2007.

Stuesse, Angela. *Scratching Out a Living: Latinos, Race and Work in the Deep South.* Berkeley: University of California Press, 2016.

Sze, Julie. *Noxious New York: The Racial Politics of Urban Health and Environmental Justice.* Cambridge, MA: MIT Press, 2007.

Tang, Eric. *Unsettled: Cambodian Refugees in the NYC Hyperghetto.* Philadelphia: Temple University Press, 2015.

Taylor, Diana. "'You Are Here': The DNA of Performance." *TDR: The Drama Review* 46, no. 11 (T 173) (2002): 149–169.

Taylor, Keeanga-Yamahtta. *From #BLACKLIVES MATTER to Black Liberation.* Chicago: Haymarket Books, 2016.

Thomas, Evan. *Robert Kennedy: His Life.* New York: Simon and Schuster, 2002.

Thomas, Hugh. *Rivers of Gold: The Rise of the Spanish Empire, from Columbus to Magellan.* New York: Random House, 2013.

————. *The Slave Trade: The Story of the Atlantic Slave Trade 1440–1870*. New York: Simon and Schuster, 1997.

Thomas-Muller, Clayton. "The Rise of the Native Rights-Based Strategic Framework: Our Last Best Hope to Save Our Water, Air and Earth." In *The Winter We Danced: Voices from the Past, the Future, and the Idle No More Movement*, edited by the Kino-nda-niimi Collective, 365–379. Winnipeg, MB: Arp Books, 2014.

Tomlinson, Barbara. *Feminism and Affect at the Scene of Argument: Beyond the Trope of the Angry Feminist*. Philadelphia: Temple University Press, 2010.

————. *Undermining Intersectionality: The Perils of Powerblind Feminism*. Philadelphia: Temple University Press, 2019.

Tomlinson, Barbara, and George Lipsitz. "Insubordinate Spaces for Intemperate Times: Countering the Pedagogies of Neoliberalism." *Review of Education, Pedagogy, and Cultural Studies* 35 (2013): 3–26.

Tuck, Eve, and K. Wayne Yang. "Decolonization is Not a Metaphor." *Decolonization: Indigeneity, Education and Society* 1, no. 1 (2012): 1–40.

Turner, Dale. "The White Paper and the Idle No More Movement." In *The Winter We Danced: Voices from the Past, the Future, and the Idle No More Movement*, edited by the Kino-nda-niimi Collective, 120–123. Winnipeg: ARP Books, 2014.

Turpel-Lafond, Mary Ellen. "Through Our Eyes—Who Leads?" In *The Winter We Danced: Voices from the Past, the Future, and the Idle No More Movement*, edited by the Kino-nda-niimi Collective, 335–351. Winnipeg, MB: Arp Books, 2014.

United States Department of Justice Civil Rights Division. *Investigation of the Ferguson Police Department*. Washington, DC: Department of Justice, 2015.

Valdes, Francisco, and Sumi Cho. "Critical Race Materialism: Theorizing Justice in the Wake of Global Neoliberalism." *Connecticut Law Review* 43, no. 5 (2011): 1513–1572.

Vargas, João Costa. *Catching Hell in the City of Angels: Life and Meanings of Blackness in South Central Los Angeles*. Minneapolis: University of Minnesota Press, 2006.

Varsanyi, Monica. "Immigration Policing through the Backdoor: City Ordinances, the 'Right to the City,' and the Exclusion of Undocumented Day Laborers." *Urban Geography* 29, no. 1 (2008): 29–52.

Vartanian, Hrag. "The People behind Your Images of Luxury." *Hyperallergic*, December 18, 2013. Available at https://hyperallergic.com/99056/the-people-behind-your-images-of-luxury/.

Veracini, Lorenzo. *Settler Colonialism: A Theoretical Overview*. New York: Palgrave Macmillan, 2010.

Vigil, María López. *Oscar Romero: Memories in Mosaic*. London: Darton, Longman and Todd, 2000.

Vitalis, Robert. *White World Order, Black Power Politics: The Birth of American International Relations*. Ithaca, NY: Cornell University Press, 2015.

Vowell, Chelsea. "Canada, It's Time: We Need to Fix This in Our Generation." In *The Winter We Danced: Voices from the Past, the Future, and the Idle No More Movement*, edited by the Kino-nda-niimi Collective, 129–133. Winnipeg, MB: Arp Books, 2014.

Walia, Harsha. "Decolonizing Together: Moving beyond a Politics of Solidarity toward a Practice of Decolonization." In *The Winter We Danced: Voices from the Past, the Future and the Idle No More Movement*, edited by the Kino-nda-niimi Collective, 44–51. Winnipeg, MB: Arp Books, 2014.

Wallerstein, Immanuel. *After Liberalism*. New York: New Press, 1995.

———. *Open the Social Sciences: Report of the Gulbenkian Commission on the Restructuring of the Social Sciences*. Stanford, CA: Stanford University Press, 1996.

———. "Remembering Andre Gunder Frank while Thinking about the Future." *Monthly Review* 60, no. 2 (2008): 50–61.

Walters, Joanna. "Troops Referred to Ferguson Protesters as 'Enemy Forces,' Emails Show." *Guardian*, April 17, 2015. Accessed October 5, 2018. Available at https://www .theguardian.com/us-news/2015/apr/17/missouri-national-guard-ferguson-protesters -email.

Washburn, Jennifer. *University, Inc.: The Corporate Corruption of Higher Education*. New York: Basic Books, 2006.

Watkins, Mary. *Accompaniment and the Creation of the Commons*. New Haven: Yale University Press, 2019.

Watkins, Mary, and Helene Shulman. *Towards Psychologies of Liberation*. New York: Palgrave Macmillan, 2008.

Weir, Stan. *Singlejack Solidarity*. Minneapolis: University of Minnesota Press, 2004.

Weissman, Deborah M. "Global Economics and Their Progenies: Theorizing Femicide in Context." In *Terrorizing Women: Feminicide in the Américas*, edited by Rosa-Linda Fregoso and Cynthia Bejarano, 225–242. Durham, NC: Duke University Press, 2010.

Weschler, Lawrence. *Domestic Scenes: The Art of Ramiro Gomez*. New York: Abrams, 2016.

Whiteman, Roberta Hill. "Preguntas." In *Philadelphia Flowers: Poems by Roberta Hill Whiteman*, 89–91. Duluth, MN: Holy Cow! Press, 1996.

Wilder, Craig. *Ebony and Ivy: Race, Slavery and the Troubled History of America's Universities*. New York: Bloomsbury, 2013.

Wilkinson, Richard, and Kate Pickett. *The Spirit Level: Why Equity Makes Societies Stronger*. New York: Bloomsbury, 2010.

Williams, Raymond. *The Politics of Modernism*. New York: Verso, 1999.

Wilson, Nina. "Kisikew, Iskwew, The Woman Spirit." In *The Winter We Danced: Voices from the Past, the Future, and the Idle No More Movement*, edited by the Kino-nda-niimi Collective, 102–108. Winnipeg, MB: Arp Books, 2014.

Winerip, M. "Pa. Joins States Facing a School Cheating Scandal." *New York Times*, August 1, 2011. Accessed September 27, 2018. Available at https://www.nytimes.com /2011/08/01/education/01winerip.html.

Wirch, Jenna. "'The Megaphone Girl': An Interview with Jenna Wirch." With Leah Gazan. In *The Winter We Danced: Voices from the Past, the Future, and the Idle No More Movement*, edited by the Kino-nda-niimi Collective, 168–172. Winnipeg, MB: Arp Books, 2014.

Wong, Deborah. *Louder and Faster: Pain, Joy, and the Body Politic in Asian American Taiko*. Berkeley: University of California Press, 2019.

———. *Speak It Louder: Asian Americans Making Music*. New York: Routledge, 2004.

Wood, Lesley J. "Idle No More, Facebook and Diffusion." *Social Movement Studies* 14, no. 5 (2015): 615–621.

Woods, Clyde. "Do You Know What It Means to Miss New Orleans? Katrina, Trap Economics and the Rebirth of the Blues." *American Quarterly* 57, no. 4 (2005): 1005–1018.

———, ed. "In the Wake of Hurricane Katrina: New Paradigms and Social Visions." Special issue, *American Quarterly* 61, no. 3 (2009).

Wotherspoon, Terry, and John Hansen. "The 'Idle No More' Movement: Paradoxes of First Nations Inclusion in the Canadian Context." *Social Inclusion* 1 (2013): 21–36.

Wright, Melissa W. "Paradoxes, Protests, and the Mujeres de Negro of Northern Mexico." In *Terrorizing Women: Feminicide in the Américas*, edited by Rosa-Linda Fregoso and Cynthia Bejarano, 312–330. Durham, NC: Duke University Press, 2010.

Yuen, Eddie, Daniel Burton-Rose, and George Katsiaficas. *Confronting Capitalism.* San Francisco: Soft Skull Press, 2004.

Zavella, Patricia. *"I'm Neither Here Nor There": Mexicans' Quotidian Struggles with Migration and Poverty.* Durham, NC: Duke University Press, 2011.

Zemeño, Sergio. "Desolation: Mexican Campesinos and Agriculture in the 21st Century." *NACLA Report on the Americas* 41, no. 5 (2008): 28–32.

Zimskind, Lyle. "Framed: Ramiro Gomez Jr. Maintains a Different Image of Contemporary Art." *Los Angeles Magazine*, May 2, 2014. Accessed October 6, 2018. Available at https://www.lamag.com/culturefiles/framed-ramiro-gomez-jr-maintains -a-different-image-of-contemporary-art/.

Zuberi, Tukufu. "Critical Race Theory of Society." *Connecticut Law Review* 43, no. 5 (2011): 1573–1591.

Index

Page numbers in *italics* indicate an illustration.

Barbara Tomlinson is a Professor of Feminist Studies at the University of California, Santa Barbara. She is the author of *Undermining Intersectionality: The Perils of Powerblind Feminism*, *Feminism and Affect: Beyond the Trope of the Angry Feminist* (both Temple), and *Authors on Writing: Metaphors and Intellectual Labor*. She received the Academic Senate Distinguished Teaching Award from the University of California, Santa Barbara.

George Lipsitz is a Professor of Black Studies and Sociology at the University of California, Santa Barbara. His previous books include *The Possessive Investment in Whiteness: How White People Profit from Identity Politics, How Racism Takes Place,* and *A Life in the Struggle: Ivory Perry and the Culture of Opposition* (all Temple). Lipsitz serves as Chair of the Boards of Directors of the African American Policy Forum and of the Woodstock Institute and is senior editor of the comparative and relational ethnic studies journal *KALFOU.*

www.ingramcontent.com/pod-product-compliance
Lightning Source LLC
Chambersburg PA
CBHW050808270326
41926CB00026B/4613